Agri-environmental Governance as an Assemblage

In recent decades, the governance of the environment in agri-food systems has emerged as a crucial challenge. A multiplicity of actors have been enrolled in this process, with the private sector and civil society progressively becoming key components in a global context often described as neoliberalization. Agri-environmental governance (AEG) thus gathers a highly complex assemblage of actors and instruments, with multiple interrelations.

This book addresses this complexity, challenging traditional modes of research and explanation in social science and agri-food studies. To do so, it draws on multiple theoretical and methodological insights, applied to case studies from Asia, Europe, Africa, and the Americas. It elaborates an emergent approach to AEG practices as assemblages, looking at the coming-together of multiple actors with diverse trajectories and objectives. The book lays the foundations for an encompassing theoretical framework that transcends pre-existing categories, as well as promoting innovative methodologies, which integrate the role of social actors – including scientists – in the construction of new assemblages. The chapters define, first, the multiplicities and agencies inherent to AEG assemblages. A second set tackles the question of the politics in AEG assemblages, where political hierarchies interweave with economic power and the search for more democratic and participative approaches. Finally, these insights are developed in the form of assemblage practice and methodology. The book challenges social scientists to confront the shortcomings of existing approaches and consider alternative answers to questions about environmental governance of agri-food systems.

Jérémie Forney is Assistant Professor, Anthropology Institute, University of Neuchâtel, Switzerland.

Chris Rosin is Senior Lecturer in the Department of Tourism, Sport and Society, Lincoln University, New Zealand.

Hugh Campbell is Chair in Sociology, Department of Sociology, Gender and Social Work, University of Otago, New Zealand.

Other books in the Earthscan Food and Agriculture Series

Contract Farming and the Development of Smallholder Agricultural Businesses
Improving markets and value chains in Tanzania
Edited by Joseph A. Kuzilwa, Niels Fold, Arne Henningsen and Marianne Nylandsted Larsen

Agribusiness and the Neoliberal Food System in Brazil
Frontiers and Fissures of Agro-neoliberalism
Antonio Augusto Rossotto Ioris

The Meat Crisis (2ed)
Developing more Sustainable and Ethical Production and Consumption
Edited by Joyce D'Silva and John Webster

Resistance to the Neoliberal Agri-Food Regime
A Critical Analysis
Edited by Alessandro Bonanno and Steven A. Wolf

Food Policy in the United States
An Introduction
(Second Edition)
Parke Wilde

The Commons, Plant Breeding and Agricultural Research
Challenges for Food Security and Agrobiodiversity
Edited by Fabien Girard and Christine Frison

Agri-environmental Governance as an Assemblage
Multiplicity, Power, and Transformation
Edited by Jérémie Forney, Chris Rosin, and Hugh Campbell

For further details please visit the series page on the Routledge website: www.routledge.com/books/series/ECEFA/

Agri-environmental Governance as an Assemblage

Multiplicity, Power, and Transformation

Edited by Jérémie Forney, Chris Rosin, and Hugh Campbell

First published 2018
by Routledge
2 Park Square, Milton Park, Abingdon, Oxon OX14 4RN

and by Routledge
711 Third Avenue, New York, NY 10017

Routledge is an imprint of the Taylor & Francis Group, an informa business

© 2018 selection and editorial matter, Jérémie Forney, Chris Rosin and Hugh Campbell; individual chapters, the contributors

The right of Jérémie Forney, Chris Rosin and Hugh Campbell to be identified as the authors of the editorial matter, and of the authors for their individual chapters, has been asserted in accordance with sections 77 and 78 of the Copyright, Designs and Patents Act 1988.

All rights reserved. No part of this book may be reprinted or reproduced or utilised in any form or by any electronic, mechanical, or other means, now known or hereafter invented, including photocopying and recording, or in any information storage or retrieval system, without permission in writing from the publishers.

Trademark notice: Product or corporate names may be trademarks or registered trademarks, and are used only for identification and explanation without intent to infringe.

British Library Cataloguing-in-Publication Data
A catalogue record for this book is available from the British Library

Library of Congress Cataloging-in-Publication Data
Names: Forney, Jérémie, editor. | Rosin, Christopher J. (Christopher John), editor. | Campbell, Hugh, 1964– editor.
Title: Agri-environmental governance as an assemblage : multiplicity, power, and transformation / edited by Jérémie Forney, Chris Rosin and Hugh Campbell.
Description: Abingdon, Oxon ; New York, NY : Routledge, 2018. | Series: Earthscan food and agriculture series | Includes bibliographical references and index.
Identifiers: LCCN 2017050802| ISBN 9781138070738 (hardback) | ISBN 9781315114941 (ebook)
Subjects: LCSH: Agricultural administration. | Environmental management.
Classification: LCC S484 .A37 2018 | DDC 630.68 –dc23
LC record available at https://lccn.loc.gov/2017050802

ISBN: 978-1-138-07073-8 (hbk)
ISBN: 978-1-315-11494-1 (ebk)

Typeset in Goudy
by Wearset Ltd, Boldon, Tyne and Wear

Contents

Notes on contributors — vii

1 Introduction: agri-environmental governance as assemblage — 1
JÉRÉMIE FORNEY, CHRIS ROSIN AND HUGH CAMPBELL

PART I
Assembling ontologies: multiplicities and agencies — 17

2 Assembling payments for ecosystem services in Wales — 19
SOPHIE WYNNE-JONES AND THOMAS VETTER

3 Carolina dreamin': a case for understanding farmers' decision-making and hybrid agri-environmental governance initiatives as complex assemblages — 38
CAELA O'CONNELL AND DEANNA L. OSMOND

4 Killing two (or more) birds with one stone: the case of governance through multifunctionality payments in Japan — 59
HARUHIKO IBA AND KIYOHIKO SAKAMOTO

5 Assembling halloumi: contesting the EU's food quality label policy in the Republic of Cyprus — 76
GISELA WELZ

6 From 'disciplinary societies' to 'societies of control': an historical narrative of agri-environmental governance in Indonesia — 91
ANGGA DWIARTAMA

PART II
The politics of territorialisation 105

7 Assembling value in carbon forestry: practices of assemblage, overflows and counter-performativities in Ugandan carbon forestry 107
ADRIAN NEL

8 Not defined by the numbers: distinction, dissent and democratic possibilities in debating the data 127
KARLY BURCH, KATHARINE LEGUN AND HUGH CAMPBELL

9 Media, decentralization, and assemblage responses to water quality deterioration in Uruguay 145
DIEGO THOMPSON

10 The "dirty dairying" campaign in New Zealand: constructing problems and assembling responses 161
ISMAËL TALL AND HUGH CAMPBELL

11 Beyond soyisation: Donau Soja as assemblage 177
DANA BENTIA AND JÉRÉMIE FORNEY

PART III
Assemblage for building new AEG practices 193

12 The politics of big data: corporate agri-food governance meets "weak" resistance 195
MICHAEL CAROLAN

13 Assemblage and the epistemology of practice: imagining situated water governance 213
RUTH BEILIN

Index 232

Contributors

Ruth Beilin is Professor, Landscape and Environmental Sociology in the School of Ecosystem and Forest Sciences, Faculty of Science at the University of Melbourne, Australia. Ruth has a long-standing commitment to community-based land and water management, public open space, and the design, co-production and re-imagining of sustainable landscapes. Her research includes gender studies, social-ecological risk and resilience, food supply chains and regional agrifood systems, biosecurity, urban and landscape policy and planning, and coastal climate change. Her teaching reflects an interdisciplinary perspective and practice-based learning.

Dana Bentia is postdoctoral researcher at the Anthropology Institute, Neuchâtel University, Switzerland. Her research focuses on the formation of taste and consumption practices, food activism and the Slow Food Movement, food traceability and the links between production and consumption beyond the supply chain in Europe. As a social scientist, she deploys insights from a range of theories (including Actor–Network Theory, Practice Theory, and Complexity) to shed light on food as a transgressive practice that has the capacity to intervene in everyday routines to remind us of the deep social and ecological moorings of our lives.

Karly Burch is a PhD candidate at the University of Otago's Centre for Sustainability, New Zealand. Her PhD research combines sensibilities from material semiotics and institutional ethnography to explore the coordination of everyday eating following Japan's 2011 nuclear disaster. She is particularly interested in the politics of metrics and how they enter and interfere in the everyday lives of people living both near and far from the disaster.

Hugh Campbell is Professor of Sociology at the University of Otago, New Zealand. From 2000–2010 he was the Director of the Centre for the Study of Agriculture, Food and Environment (CSAFE) and had a leading role in a series of research programmes into the farm-level dynamics of agricultural sustainability. His key areas of academic interest are: sustainable agriculture, agri-environmental governance, neoliberalism, and agri-food theory.

Michael Carolan is a Professor of Sociology and Associate Dean for Research and Graduate Affairs in the College of Liberal Arts at Colorado State University, USA. His areas of expertise include food, agricultural, and environmental policy, environmental sociology, and the sociology of food and food systems. He has published over 150 peer reviewed articles and chapters. Some of his more recent books include *Reclaiming Food Security* (2013), *Cheaponomics: The High Cost of Low Prices* (2014), *No One Eats Alone: Food as a Social Enterprise* (2017) and *Fare Share: Food in the Collaborative Economy* (2018, anticipated).

Angga Dwiartama, PhD, is Assistant Professor at the School of Life Sciences and Technology, Institut Teknologi Bandung, Indonesia. His research focuses on understanding the sustainability and resilience of various commodity systems (rice, sugar, coffee, cacao), and also the growth of alternative food movements in Indonesia.

Jérémie Forney is Assistant Professor at the Anthropology Institute of the University of Neuchâtel, Switzerland. His work developed from a focus on family farmers and their adaptation to political and economic changes to a wider approach of the governance of agri-food systems, with a particular focus on environmental issues.

Haruhiko Iba is Associate Professor of Agricultural Economics at Kyoto University, Japan. His principal areas of research and teaching include farm management and farmers' organizations. He has been studying dilemmas in farming organizations through their farming-related activities especially in remote and disadvantaged rural areas.

Katharine Legun is a Lecturer in Sociology at the University of Otago, New Zealand. Her work focuses on the role of non-human agency in shaping institutional economic change. Her research has looked at the increasing ownership of plant variety rights by grower cooperatives in the apple industry, and the ways different kinds of metrics shape the political spirit of environmental governance. Results from the research have appeared in *Economy and Society*, *Geoforum*, and the *Journal of Rural Studies*.

Adrian Nel is a Senior Lecturer in the Discipline of Geography, School of Agricultural, Earth and Environmental Science at the University of Kwazulu-Natal, Pietermaritzburg, South Africa. He has an interest in teaching and research related to Human Geography and Political Ecology. Previously, he held a Visiting Fellowship with the Institute for Development Studies at the University of Sussex, UK and a Research Associate position with the Institute for Development Studies at the National University of Science and Technology (NUST) in Bulawayo, Zimbabwe.

Caela O'Connell is an Assistant Professor of Anthropology at University of Tennessee Knoxville, USA, and is core faculty for the Disasters, Displacement, and Human Rights Program. Caela is an environmental anthropologist whose research considers the complex intersections of agricultural communities, environmental health and climate change, economics, governance, decision-making, crises, and disasters. She has been working with farming communities in the Caribbean and Latin America and the US since 2003. Her disaster work includes documenting cascading crises in the Eastern Caribbean following the destruction wrought by Hurricane Tomas in 2010 and southeastern Texas from Hurricane Harvey in 2017. She has studied environmental conservation (agri-environmental schemes), water quality, and decision-making with US based farmers since 2012 in North Carolina, Missouri, Ohio, and Tennessee farmers.

Deanna L. Osmond is a Professor, Associate Head, and department extension leader in the Crop and Soil Sciences Department at North Carolina State University in Raleigh, USA. Deanna works at the interface of nutrient management, conservation practices, and water quality. As an agronomist and soil scientist she has worked for over 25 years to ensure agricultural productivity while minimising environmental impacts from agriculture. Her work engages both farmers and agency personnel at both the federal and state level.

Chris Rosin is Senior Lecturer in political ecology at Lincoln University, New Zealand. His research focuses on the emergent subjectivities of participants in agri-food commodity chains, with a particular interest in how these are influenced and shaped by the non-human actors that re-territorialise the agri-food assemblages.

Kiyohiko Sakamoto is Special Appointment Associate Professor of Sociology at Kyoto University, Japan. He holds a PhD in sociology from University of Kentucky, USA, with special emphases on roles of science and technology in agri-food sectors and rural development in Americas and Japan. His recent studies center on neoliberal governmentality and its consequences in rural sectors.

Ismaël Tall is a PhD student in Anthropology at the University of Neuchâtel, Switzerland, and is currently hosted at the Centre for Sustainability, University of Otago, New Zealand. His research focuses on agri-environmental governance in the region of Southland, New Zealand.

Diego Thompson is Assistant Professor in the Department of Sociology at Mississippi State University, USA. His research has focused on sustainable development, agri-food systems, migration, governance, and adaptation to environmental changes in rural communities, in the United States and in Latin America.

Thomas Vetter is a PhD candidate at University of Neuchâtel, Switzerland, and is conducting fieldwork in the United Kingdom. His research interest lies in the transformation of agri-food systems and its implications for society, economy, state, and the environment. He is particularly interested in more sustainable forms of food production and consumption and its associated governance frameworks supporting such transitions.

Gisela Welz is Professor and Chair of Cultural Anthropology and European Ethnology, Goethe University Frankfurt/Main, Germany. Many of her recent publications and research projects address the effects of European integration, focusing on the Republic of Cyprus as a case in point. Her most recent monograph, *European Products. Making and Unmaking Heritage in Cyprus* (Berghahn Books 2015), received the PROSE Award as best book in anthropology 2015, presented by the Association of American Publishers' Professional and Scholarly Publishing Division.

Sophie Wynne-Jones is a Lecturer in Human Geography, at the School of Environment, Natural Resources and Geography of Bangor University, UK. Her research is focused on questions of rural land-use change and agri-environmental governance, addressing issues of stakeholder cooperation and knowledge controversies.

1 Introduction

Agri-environmental governance as assemblage

Jérémie Forney, Chris Rosin and Hugh Campbell

Re-framing agri-environmental governance

The environmental impacts of agricultural production have, since the late 1960s, elicited growing social concerns and increasing scholarly attention especially in regards to the ability to regulate practices in efforts to mitigate degradation. Explanations of the social dynamics associated with regulation – from compliance to open contestation – continue to grapple with the complexities of social response, often following emerging theoretical trends in the fields of rural sociology and geography. Early work looked to explain the adoption of more environmentally friendly technologies and methods, examining the processes through which information was communicated and successful practices were transferred between farmers. These perspectives provided insight to the importance of appropriate technologies (in terms of their accessibility to farmers of diverse financial, temporal and cultural characteristics) and well-functioning modes of demonstrating and communicating the benefits of practices, using the individual decision to adopt as the dominant focus of analysis. The subsequent rise of critical political economic analyses highlighted the structural factors that impacted on the capacity to consider, let alone adopt, environmental practice that limited the productive achievements of conventional capitalist agriculture (for an influential critique of adoption invoking structural factors see Vanclay and Lawrence 1994). This focus on the power differentials among the participants of agricultural production and environmental regulation drew necessary attention to the broader social context within which management decisions were made; it did not, however, account for the persistent diversity of environmental practice nor the situations in which outcomes were not determined by expected power dynamics. Increasing attention is now being paid to theoretical approaches that better address the complexities inherent to the navigation of the often divergent pursuits of profitable production and environmental sustainability, both of which involve myriad participants within networks of production and consumption. In this context, the concept of assemblage has recently attracted the attention of social scientists who want to focus on the emergent and overdetermined nature of agri-environmental practices in agriculture.

In this collection, we want to follow the new and explorative vistas that an assemblage approach exposes for the understanding and analysis of the governance of environmental issues in agriculture and agri-food systems. To provide greater coherence to the diverse perspectives enabled by assemblage, we use 'governance' as a conceptual shortcut to encompass a great diversity of practices led by a wide diversity of actors. Governance has gained much currency in a variety of contexts; but, as a result of this broad applicability, it has become polysemic and a highly contested concept necessitating a concrete definition of its usage. Under the umbrella of governance, we include, for instance, a regulatory scheme resulting from a national policy, a certification process led by a big retailer and a participatory initiative developed by an NGO. We further employ agri-environmental governance (AEG) as a broad framing that encompasses the multiple actions, which aim to implement change in the food system and address environmental issues related to agricultural production. Beyond the original intention of any governance action, localised uses, specific networks and practical norms emerge in a process of interaction, translation and reinterpretation that we can call AEG practices (Forney 2016a). Consequently, AEG emerges through repeated interaction between diverse actors constituting an AEG assemblage. The key actors in such assemblages include humans – from policy makers to private certifiers, from supermarket boards to farmers' associations – and, equally relevant and active, non-humans – legal documents, metrological tools, soils, animals amongst others. These non-human actors are central to the agency of the assemblage, and not merely passive recipients of human action (e.g. Lewis et al. 2013; Rosin et al. 2017). Our framing of AEG thus implies an engagement with modes of social theorisation that advocate the integration of non-human actors (or actants) in the understanding of the social, as evident in assemblage thinking (e.g. Bennett 2009), as well as wider elaborations of Actor-Network Theory (e.g. Callon 1986; Latour 2005; Law and Hassard 1999; Whatmore 2013).

While scholarly interest in AEG has been consistent, the theoretical frameworks through which it has been approached have undergone significant change. Governance has been a point of interest for both post-structural scholars and those coming from Marxist and neo-Marxist inflected political economy approaches (see Higgins and Lawrence 2005). An early focus was on the persistence of peasant and other smaller scale producers with more environmentally appropriate practices in agricultural sectors dominated by highly capitalised and more intensive production associated with environmental degradation. This perspective was augmented through the deployment of ideas of governance which provided an analysis of the power relations (from local to global scales) that structured responses to environmental conditions. One particularly influential framework in this tradition has been the association of AEG with the elaboration of neoliberal forms of governance under late-capitalism (e.g. Lockie and Higgins 2007; Guthman 2008; Higgins et al. 2014; Wolf and Bonnano 2014). Governance of agricultural environments, in these analyses, needs to be understood as an extension of wider market-based modes of economic and political management and a departure from *government*. Understanding AEG in terms of this latter alignment with neoliberal models of policy and market-based solutions to environmental challenges has provided the most dominant recent framework for work in this area.

The association between neoliberalism and market-led environmental governance has begun to fracture and re-assemble along a number of different levels and ontological framings. In some of this new work, focus has shifted to the nuances of neoliberal subjectivities and the structural and/or ontological challenge of alternative agriculture systems (e.g. Harris 2009; Rosin and Campbell 2009), or drawing on Foucauldian understandings of governmentality as a necessary companion to the operation of governance (see Agrawal 2005; Haggerty 2007). These approaches emphasise the potential of forms of agency within governance frameworks that had previously been argued to be closed or fixed. Another compelling challenge came from Actor Network Theory and its recent variants: particularly the opening of critical analysis to broader and flatter sets of relations that recognise the active role of non-human participants. This has compelled, we argue, the need for equally open and more flexible ontologies in the analysis and politics of AEG (e.g. Le Heron *et al.* 2016). These ontologies share a focus on addressing the complexities of governing agriculture practices in the context of environmental sustainability.

This book arrives in the midst of this interesting transitional moment in the theoretical framing of AEG. Recognising the value of analyses grounded in the major tropes of neoliberalism and capitalism, it seeks to explain the ways in which new approaches are either augmenting and elaborating older frameworks in new and interesting ways, or creating entirely new ontological framings of AEG that require a distinct break with the past. We suggest that the theoretical devices of assemblage and territorialisation form the key terrain around which this exploration of new openings and closures can take place. Consider a global agri-food network within which convenience nutrition is a principal objective. What does it mean to acknowledge the relations between bacteria digesting nitrates in the soil, someone breakfasting with a high protein cereal bar on the way to work, and a government deciding to support new plantations for palm oil production? Do we readily detect those links that underlie a story of the development of a global industrial agri-food system that is familiar to existing critical ontologies? Are we convinced that such a framework addresses the whole of the story? Are not these three actors – bacteria, protein bar eater and government – situated within broader and more diverse connections? In recognising a broader scope of explanation, we must also beware of the danger of aimlessly following the threads, lacking a defined endpoint and further losing ourselves in the deep entanglements of the relational processes that create our world. What is an appropriate and viable ontological approach to the assembly of elements, actors and unanswered questions that intertwine in the practice of AEG?

The concept of assemblage, and its partner concept territorialisation, provides a coherent framing for the ontological work of the book. Their roots lie in the work of Deleuze and Guattari, notably their theorisation of the individual and the multiple (Deleuze and Guattari 1987), and their emphasis on the relational and heterogeneous nature of the social is central to the modes of explanation used in the book.

Assemblage as a conceptual and theoretical framing has become more important in recent years, notably in the geographical and anthropological literature with some notable collections like Ong and Collier (2005) and the special issue of the journal *Area* in 2011 anchoring a new interest in Deleuze and Guattari in those disciplines. While it has been applied as an approach for better understanding the uneven and emergent nature of neoliberalism (Higgins and Larner 2017), it remains underexplored in the literature on sustainability (Palmer and Owens, 2015) and, by association, AEG. Some significant exceptions can be noted, however, starting with the work of Tania Li (2007) on forest management in Indonesia, which offers a well-structured analytic of assemblage. Interestingly, many applications of an assemblage framing happen in the analysis and critique of governing actions. For example, Sullivan's (2010) work grapples with alliances, alignments and assemblages of discourses, actors and organisations in the emergence and consolidation of payments for ecosystem services. In a later working paper published by The Leverhulme Centre for the Study of Value, Sullivan (2014) develops this assemblage-oriented approach to policy consolidation that draws on Li's work and connects with other analyses of practices of assemblage and policy orchestrations in contemporary policy consolidation around market-based mechanisms. In the same series of Working Papers, Fredriksen develops a theoretical treatment of assemblage thinking in processes of value creation in environmental policy, through an exploration of the idea of distributed agency in assemblages involving human and non-human actors (Fredriksen, 2014). Taking another notable direction, the work done by New Zealand scholars under the banner of biological economies (see special issue of *New Zealand Geographer* 2013, no. 69) uses assemblage to explore the role of research in *doing* assemblages (see Le Heron et al. 2016; Carolan 2016). This draws together a wider set of international perspectives – particularly around the way in which new research ontologies and objects emerge within an assemblage-inflected methodology (Lewis et al. 2013, 2017; Carolan 2016; Dwiartama et al. 2016; Linke 2016). In the specific context of AEG, work in New Zealand (Rosin et al. 2017; Rosin, Campbell and Reid 2017) elaborates the emergent nature of best practice audits under the influence of the metrics being audited. In addition to these contributions that engage explicitly with assemblage, work by other scholars develops very similar approaches, without naming them as such. As an example, Benabou (2014) traces in considerable detail the alignments and alliances of individuals and organisations around the development of international voluntary biodiversity offsets in which payments are made for biodiversity 'services'.

In this book collection, our objective is to document an emergent assemblage approach that engages with entities as comprised of multiple autonomous and heterogeneous elements assembling in an always moving set of relations. We argue that this concept provides a deeply insightful framing through which to examine AEG as an emergent social dynamic. This approach allows our contributors to both incorporate existing critical analysis, as well as open broader sets of relations, in the conceptualisation of social action. This said, our use of an assemblage framing is far from 'territorialised' and still includes a large diversity of positionings that is reflected in the chapters of this collection, notably around the prioritization of actors, agents or processes.

Assembling this collection

This book brings together a group of social scientists who are engaged in the emergent ontologies that intersect with and contribute explanation to the complexities of AEG as a social process. Their contributions elaborate case studies situated in diverse geographical, cultural and social contexts, and draw inspiration from a variety of theoretical backgrounds. Beyond this diversity, there is a shared intention to propose alternative ways of understanding agricultural policies, certification schemes or participative projects, by looking more specifically at their role in the emergent collection of elements, actors and processes – in other words, assemblages – around food production and the environment. Assemblage acts as our key locus of theoretical investigation and elaboration; although, as the following discussion makes clear, the idea of assemblage comprises a variety of intriguing approaches ranging from the reinterpretation of more conventional ideas of community and decision-making to more radical forms of performativity. Despite the variation in approach, all of the contributions capture something of a similar and wider theoretical moment: a general recognition of a 'turn to ontology' in fields of theoretical endeavour that previously relied on discourse, ideology and subjectivity to provide phenomenological purchase on social processes.

As a whole, therefore, the contributors to this collection challenge established framings (ontologies) that use tightly defined categories as a means to simplify real world complexity in order to improve understanding of social process. Whereas categories such as class, power, conventional/alternative, or neoliberal produce clearer images of 'reality' and impose some order to the chaos of everyday life, our intention in organising this book is to expose important absences and biases inherent to this simplification, reduction and exclusion with specific reference to AEG. Categories have constructed too many walls and oppositions that fail to adequately represent and explain both the complexity of the social processes involved and the enactive political projects that might animate them. Our response, in this collection, is to use the theoretical idea of assemblage to illuminate diverse pathways forward in the academic study of AEG. Assemblage has emerged as a common theoretical theme in multiple strands of recent work: some of which is seeking ways to render more elaborate the interaction between neoliberalism and AEG, other strands which see assemblage as comprising an alternative to neoliberalism as a theoretical framing through the introduction of more ANT-inflected ontologies. Finally, there are those that see assemblage as a pathway from a more passive/analytical to an enactive/engaged style of scholarship.

It is this combination of theoretical and methodological/political experimentation that makes assemblage such a useful gateway to new discussions about AEG. This understanding that the current moment is a period of high innovation and change in the scholarship around AEG is born out in the origins of the book collection. In 2014, Jérémie Forney put together a successful proposal to the *Swiss National Science Foundation* and invited Chris Rosin and Hugh Campbell to join a conversation on new approaches to the theorisation of AEG. All three of us were grappling with the transition from 'neoliberal' to new theoretical framings of practice and action in agriculture and food worlds – particularly as influenced by theoretical ideas like assemblage and multiple ontologies being generated in agrifood studies. This small collaboration was clearly taking place alongside other similar clusterings and collaborations of like-minded scholars – particularly in Wales, elsewhere in New Zealand and Australia, and in the United States. As a group, we first gained a glimpse of the wider impetus for theoretical innovation in this space when we proposed a session on new theoretical approaches to AEG at the International Rural Sociology Association (IRSA) conference in Toronto in August 2016. Most of the contributors to this volume responded to the (what we feared might be seen as eccentric and narrow) theoretical language in the call for papers and came to Toronto with a range of new insights and elaborations, derived from diverse study sites including Japan, Africa and South America. By the end of that conference, it was clear that we were experiencing something of a break-out moment in the theorisation of AEG and this book collection was proposed.

The following chapters are indicative of the distinctive pathways that the various authors have taken to arrive at a consideration of assemblage as both ontologically disrupting and re-constituting the framing of AEG. Some have come from traditional consideration of rural economy and rural development and have been long attempting to reconcile economic and environmental pressures in specific spaces. For these chapters, the grounded challenges of environmental governance in particular rural spaces and regions are the foundation for a consideration of the reframing and ontologically disruptive power of assemblage thinking. Others come from the agri-food space and bring a consideration of the dynamics of food production, the practices and subjectivities of farmers and farming, the configuration and disruption of supply chains and consumption dynamics and the governance arrangements that extend through these economic networks. Others come directly from the world of environmental governance initiatives like carbon emissions trading and follow where these initiatives alight in specific rural spaces and are territorialised into rurally embedded assemblages. A final group is more directly interested in the politics of assembling and the turn towards more enactive and performative approaches to environmental governance.

In these ways, our contributors have arrived at assemblage as a transformative re-working and re-framing of the challenges, dynamics and potentials of AEG. As a collection, they point to the emergence of new ontological perspectives oriented around three central contributions. The first exposes the potential within an assemblage framing to articulate the complexity of things, by acknowledging and incorporating the multiplicity and emergence of assemblages. The second contribution highlights the political encounters that are central to this multiplicity. Assemblages are infused with relations of power, which are under persistent pressures of redefinition as their constituent elements engage in the work of de- and re-territorialisation. Finally, the third group extends beyond the analysis and critique of social processes, using assemblage as the foundation for novel ways of *doing* governance.

Assembling ontologies: multiplicities and agencies

As an initial step in moving beyond the usual categories applied to the analysis of AEG, the first set of contributions focuses on the diversity of elements that assemble around the initial focus of the research. In these chapters, assemblage follows the flows of relations and overflows categories that seemed natural and obvious. Moreover, they represent assemblages as emergent, subject to de-territorialisation and re-territorialisation, thus participating in an ontology of multiplicities and future possibilities. Applied to the analysis of governance, these considerations resonate with the question of the actors' agency, both from the side of the 'governing' and the 'governed'. The capacity of human and non-human actants (individuals or groups) to influence the territorialisation of assemblages becomes central.

The first chapter of this collection by Wynne-Jones and Vetter offers an enlightening application of assemblage that demonstrates the value of going beyond the binary categorisations and reduction of complex processes inherent in a unidimensional explanatory theory of neoliberalism. Rejecting readings of hybrid neoliberalism, the authors look at the multiple motivations and logics behind the application of payments for ecosystem services in Wales, and document the diverse reactions to PES and the multidimensional processes of transformation. These processes are influenced by local actors who, not being passive targets of these governance instruments, actively use them to impact wider circulations of PES discourse and the AEG assemblage. Here the question of the agency of individuals in relation to structural constraints is open and reframed within an assemblage perspective.

Addressing the same discussion of 'hybrid' governance instruments, O'Connell and Osmond explore a Water Quality Trading program in the American context of North Carolina, involving the State, private traders, and agricultural stakeholders. The authors apply an assemblage perspective to farmer decision-making in which multiplicity is revealed at the level of individual motivations and constraints. Stepping away from reductionist explanations of farmers' decision-making and agency, this chapter makes an important contribution by reframing their actions as part of a complex human-natural system. Their analysis of the creation of Water Quality Trading Schemes does the important ontological work of disrupting the highly prescriptive and linear logics of traditional models of adoption. Instead, understood as assemblages, these schemes reveal multiple motivations and diverse logics in similar ways to those seen in the Welsh case study.

The multiplicities characterizing assemblage, the fact that an assemblage is made of a multitude of moving relations, reframe the question of the outcomes of AEG instruments and actions. In other words, an assemblage approach more or less directly questions the ability of 'governing' to control the processes that develop in association with its actions of governance. Iba and Sakamoto's chapter illustrates the wide variability of outcomes of a national multifunctional policy. They compare two local communities and the varying 'successes' of the policy applications, relating indirectly the question of AEG to the more general question of rural changes.

The unexpected outcomes of governance action are sometimes related to internal tensions and contradictions within the governance assemblage. Welz's account of the transformations to halloumi cheese production occurring in Cyprus as a result of Protected Denomination of Origin policies emphasises both the interrelations of policy instruments that are artificially segregated into siloes through formal governance processes, as well as the under-recognised negotiations between actors that participate in the definition, or territorialisation of, what 'is' halloumi cheese.

While the previous chapters detail the capacity for assemblage to take seriously the multiplicity and processual character of the social in the present – in a given time and place – Dwiartama's contribution applies a historical gaze to the governance of agriculture in Indonesia. The chapter first helps to reconsider established and orthodox historical categorisations by focusing on dominant modes of governance, then creates a radical reframing by drawing inspiration from discussions of the concepts of discipline and control in Foucault and Deleuze. At the same time, the chapter goes beyond simplifications reducing the social reality to one single logic and emphasises the accumulation of modes of governance in Indonesian history, resulting in a contemporary assemblage of agricultural governance, characterised by its multiplicity and the co-existence of logics.

The politics of territorialisation

Despite being comprised of multiplicities and irreducible possibilities, assemblages are continually in the process of territorialisation, congealing in specific configurations and identities which are immediately contested and destabilised. In this never-ending process of (de-)(re-)territorialisation, elements of the assemblage – human and non-human – play active roles and express agency, as articulated in the first section. Consciously or not, they engage in struggles and attempts to coordinate the assemblage to fit complex objectives. Consequently, an assemblage can be considered as inherently political. Seen as occurring within an assemblage, however, not all such struggles are about hierarchies and direct relations of power. Many, in fact, act very subtly at the level of the territorialisation of the assemblage.

The challenges inherent to coordination of multiple political interests across global to local scales are addressed in Nel's chapter on the emergence of a carbon forestry centred in Uganda, but extending to interests in Europe and beyond. The efforts to territorialise carbon forestry originate in international climate change negotiations, Ugandan government ministries, the offices of environmental NGOs, carbon investors and donor states as well as the communities inhabiting the newly designated forests. While the financial power of investors and the political power of industrialised countries introduce foreign claims on use and access rights, the activities of communities de-territorialise the resulting coordination. Thus, the assemblage approach is a powerful tool for uncovering these kinds of political tensions and power relations.

The chapter by Burch, Legun and Campbell interrogates the role of metrics in the battlefield to territorialise environmental issues and governance solutions. The authors describe the surge of radionuclides in the Japanese food system that unsettled the usual definition of secure food in the aftermath of the Fukushima nuclear accident. Attempts by governmental agencies to settle and frame these overflowing elements were challenged by groups of consumers offering alternative knowledge and metrics. Again, numbers and metrics reveal their powerful capacity in territorialising complex assemblages in order to render them governable. The authors conclude by highlighting the need for more deliberative processes in the constitution of governance instruments.

Further evidence of the multiple sites and political drivers of resource governance is provided in Thompson's chapter. Located in the context of the re-territorialisation initiated by the de-centralisation of state water policies, he analyses media representations of water degradation attributed to agricultural run-off. Media accounts are shown to reaffirm existing territorialisations defined by the distinct interests of agents in areas of high tourist interest compared to those focused on agricultural production.

This section of the book then considers processes of redefinition and requalification – re-territorialisation – of environmental issues. Tall and Campbell document how the 'dirty dairying' campaign in New Zealand created a new ontology of the developing dairy farming industry by associating it with issues of water quality. The lack of attention given to this connection before the campaign reflected the relative 'invisibility' of water quality degradation and its causes. Once this association between the two elements – dairy farming and water – became a visible 'fact', the related assemblage re-territorialised in an unanticipated and irremediable way.

Soybean production offers a similar reconsideration in its association to the future of the food system. Once seen as a solution to several problems of sustainability, it has become, for some, a problem in itself when associated with: unsustainable farming practices, GMOs, monoculture and deforestation. Bentia and Forney explore in their chapter a European project that aims to transform soy assemblages, by re-localising the production within the EU boundaries and changing the agricultural practices and uses around soy. They document an explicit attempt to re-territorialise the soy assemblage around new objectives of sustainability and changing agricultural and food systems.

Assemblage for building new AEG practices

The last section of the book gathers two chapters that make an additional step in the application of assemblage thinking. They use this theoretical framing to move beyond critical research by applying an assemblage approach not only to the study but also to the creation of AEG practices. By doing so, they offer a valuable intervention in debates surrounding the constitution of enactive research.

In his chapter, Carolan unpacks the use of big data in contemporary US farming. Applying a 'weak theory' of assemblage – that is, resisting the urge to sum up categorisations that lock our understanding of the social in monolithic explanations – he confronts radically different narratives on big data related to specific positionalities (conventional farmers, engineers from the big data industry, and farmer 'hackers'). As a result, he emphasises the multiplicity of the assemblage around big data and the related production of multiple possibilities. Moreover, he encourages scholars to move away from overly critical representations of technologies and to look more 'hopefully' for the platforms where data are assembled in ways that produce 'cracks of difference' and open hopeful possibilities.

In the last chapter of this collection, Beilin interrogates the diverse assemblages that characterise water governance in South-Eastern Australia with the intent of providing ontological framings that enable more equitable and environmentally sustainable policy. She identifies three existing assemblages – the environmental flow, the consumptive flow and the indigenous flow – each of which is limited through its relationships with the same settler-colonial ontology. Developing a dialogue between a theorisation of assemblage and the epistemology of practice, Beilin constructs an "imaginary counter narrative" in the form of an assemblage of small-holder agro-ecological settling. In doing so, she generates a vibrant argument for an assemblage approach that provides the "possibility of transformative re-imagining" to answer the urgent need for perspectives with greater capacity to incorporate the complexity of policy formation and the dispersed nature of power and agency within such practices.

Assembling governance and social sciences: theoretical challenges for breaking new ground in research on AEG

The varying depth and breadth with which our contributors engage with the concept of assemblage is best described as an array of experimentations. In every case, the authors construct what is an emergent theorisation of assemblage – never fully defined and bounded, but always seeking to destabilise existing categories and constraints on the multiplicity of actors, power and process. While at one level, these are 'playful' interventions (see Mol 2010), they are also very serious and intentional efforts. Their intention is to introduce new forms of understanding and coordinating the realities of AEG in hopes of enlightening our understandings of the shortcomings of existing governance practices as well as enacting new and more hopeful ones. The chapters offer the opportunity to progress in the theorisation of assemblage, in the context of AEG and beyond, notably on the more specific discussion around agency, processes of territorialisation and the possibility of developing enactive research practices. In concluding, we identify the ontological by-ways along which our authors have developed assemblage as an approach as well as offering our own hopeful expectations of the emergent theorisations of AEG.

The application of assemblage by our contributors further reflects its resonance with other social theorisations, including the centrality of relations and the active role of non-humans (at the core of Actor Network Theory) and the distributed nature of power and agency (central to Foucault). The intervention of the collected chapters contributes to the reworking and mobilisation of the concept in different contexts, opening new possibilities for analysis and interpretation of the social. As an ontological project, the book inserts assemblage within the theorization of AEG with the intention of focusing on the emergent social dynamics inherent to governance. Moreover, assemblage is offered as a means to address the lacunae inherent to oppositional conceptualisations of: multiple and one, fixed and changing, existence and ideas.

As noted above, we trace our application of assemblage to Deleuze and Guattari and their emphasis on the irrepressible desire to assemble, while acknowledging the always changing and contingent coordination of the resulting assemblage. Their proposition provides two insights of direct relevance to our engagement with AEG. First, it offers an alternative conceptualisation of agency as produced by the assemblage; it is collective, distributed and not the proprietary realm of specific agents (human or non-human). This understanding of agency has strong familiarities with that developed in ANT. However, the insertion of desire as a fundamental force in the territorialisation of assemblages emphasises an individual level of agency, which is not fully acknowledged in ANT (Müller 2015). Our position follows that of McFarlane and Anderson (2011: 63), arguing that an assemblage perspective "attends to the agency of wholes and parts, not one or the other". Actors have projects; they try to influence the assemblage; they engage with the assemblage, even if, at the end, the outcomes never fully match these individual plans. This framing informs Li's (2007: 265) operationalisation of assemblage as having a "potential to finesse questions of agency by recognizing the situated subjects who do the work of pulling together disparate elements without attributing to them a master-mind or a totalizing plan". Our contributors also demonstrate the potential, as suggested by McFarlane (2011), for an assemblage perspective to develop better understanding of the unexpected effects of governance tools, and enable the rethinking and reconceptualisation of critique and issues of power in renewed ways. A diminished emphasis on structural drivers is also the product of the second insight, namely that assemblages are emergent and never fully completed or territorialised. This characteristic of assemblages weakens the constraints imposed by structure on social dynamics and facilitates an emphasis on the opportunities for intervention, experimentation and change. At the same time, it also eliminates the possibility of stasis or optimal outcomes as any territorialisation of an assemblage is subject to de- and re-territorialisation as its elements interact and re-arrange.

This tension initiated by the continuous movements of territorialisation and de-territorialisation produces a perpetuum mobile where assemblages are always oriented toward potentialities and possible and desirable futures. Any given assemblage is open to other assemblages because the forces of de-territorialisation constantly expose it to redefinition. The emergent nature of the assemblage is an important aspect in the concept's diverse applications within this volume. For example, Beilin draws on DeLanda's (2006) theorisation of assemblage as the result of a multiplicity of relations that are always renegotiated to position water governance outside totalities and essentialism. Burch et al. use assemblage in a manner more closely aligned to Actor Network Theory to demonstrate the active potential (or agency) of non-humans through their capacity to divert territorialisation efforts.

If assemblages are defined by their ephemeral nature – always caught in the tension between territorialisation and re-territorialisation and oriented toward becoming and potentialities – are they real? In other words, do assemblages really exist or are they social constructs? The question might, at first glance, seem rhetorical; however, the answer has significant consequences for what an assemblage approach fundamentally allows us to do. On one hand, thinking of assemblage as real, as defended notably by DeLanda (2006), potentially recognises the materiality of assemblages that exist beyond the capacity of human 'assembling' or 'assemblying'. Such an approach arguably gives more agency to non-humans, answering, for instance, Bennett's (2009) call for the ontological redistribution of causalities inherent to political ecologies in which non-humans exhibit political capacities and initiate or drive actions with social consequence that are fully outside the 'agency' of human actors. In Bennett's argument, this opens space to reassess the issue of 'responsibility' – and to shift attention away from assigning ultimate blame to the exclusion of recognising the overdetermined nature of events.

On the other hand, other interpretations of assemblage focus on the assembling that is initiated by – or the assemblage that is recognised by – human actors. This approach (most notably found in Li 2007) allows for a demonstration of an admirable awareness of the multiple, emergent and complex actors in assemblages, while still affording 'special' recognition of human efforts to coordinate and structure – i.e. territorialise – assemblages (a practice that generally involves imposing boundaries on what is included within an assemblage). One benefit of this emphasis on the human construction of assemblages is to open up particular styles and strategies of human political action and intention.

This openness and orientation toward the potentialities characterizing assemblages has also encouraged scholars to explore the implications for the research itself. For McFarlane and Anderson, assemblage thinking relates to an "ethos of engagement attuned to the possibilities of socio-spatial formations to be otherwise within various constraints and historical trajectories" (2011: 162). These epistemological and methodological implications of the assemblage perspective are apparent in the contributions by Carolan and Beilin. Their chapters reinforce similar reflections on the possibility of developing enactive research practices (Forney 2016b; Lewis *et al.* 2013). What interests us here is that thinking with assemblage provides a mechanism through which the role of research and academics in territorialization processes can be addressed. This goes beyond a typical reflexive stance. By asserting the participation of research in the construction of social life, an assemblage approach opens spaces to think about the potential and desirability of our engagements with the possibilities as well as our responsibilities as elements of the assemblage.

These discussions emphasise the emergent nature of assemblage as an approach to explanation in the social sciences. They point to alternative understandings of and engagement with AEG in which the assemblage is co-constituted by humans and non-humans and where conceptual and material aspects are considered to make different but equal contributions to the construction of assemblages as both "real" and "constructed". In pursuing this argument, we are aligning with Deleuze and Guatarri when they say that assemblages are both content and expression (1987, 504).

The chapters we have collected in this book leave as many open questions as they provide answers. This is indicative of an emergent theorisation of AEG. Rather than providing a fully structured theory of assemblage, we offer instead the encouragement to engage with assemblage as a tool for expanding not only our understandings of AEG, but also the potentialities through which successful governance and improved environmental practice might be achieved. As indicated by our contributors, such an achievement begins with the de-territorialisation of predominant forms of explanation. Initial steps involve the undermining of categories related to markets, decision-making, multifunctionality and quality designations whereby the agency of less recognised or unacknowledged actors is introduced. Further steps are taken in efforts to articulate the multiplicity of power relations in environmental governance in the form of multi-scalar interests, the role of non-humans, the overdetermination of context, the emergence of environmental awareness and the re-articulation of sustainability. At the same time, assemblage approaches also provide the opportunity to re-territorialise AEG with alternative and enactive modes of research (in the manner of weak assemblying or an epistemology of practice). Thus, this book orients us toward new paths of thinking about and reflecting on the governance of agri-food-systems, while also emancipating our own practice as we promote the experimentation with new practices and policies of governance.

References

Agrawal, Arun. 2005. *Environmentality: Technologies of Government and the Making of Subjects*. Duke University Press: North Carolina.

Benabou, Sarah. 2014. "Making up for lost nature?: A critical review of the international development of voluntary biodiversity offsets". *Environment and Society* 8: 103–123.

Bennett, Jane. 2009. *Vibrant Matter: A Political Ecology of Things*. Chapel Hill, NC: Duke University Press.

Callon, Michel. 1986. "Some elements of a sociology of translation: Domestication of the scallops and the fishermen of St Brieuc Bay. Power, action and belief". *A New Sociology of Knowledge* 32: 196–233.

Carolan, Michael. 2016. *Decentering Biotechnology: Assemblages Built and Assemblages Masked*. Abingdon: Routledge.

DeLanda, Manuel. 2006. *A New Philosophy of Society: Assemblage Theory and Social Complexity*, London: Continuum.

Deleuze, Gilles and Félix Guattari. 1987. *A Thousand Plateaus*. Minneapolis, MN: University of Minnesota Press.

Dwiartama, Angga, Christopher Rosin and Hugh Campbell. 2016. "Understanding agri-food systems as assemblages: Worlds of rice in Indonesia". In *Biological Economies: Experimentation and the Politics of Agrifood Frontiers*, edited by Richard Le Heron, Hugh Campbell, Nick Lewis and Michael S. Carolan. London/New York: Routledge.

Forney, Jérémie. 2016a. "Blind spots in agri-environmental governance: Some reflections and suggestions from Switzerland". *Review of Agricultural, Food and Environmental Studies* 1–13. doi: 10.1007/s41130-016-0017-2.

Forney, Jérémie. 2016b. "Enacting Swiss cheese: About the multiple ontologies of local food". In *Biological Economies: Experimentation and the Politics of Agrifood Frontiers*, edited by Richard Le Heron, Hugh Campbell, Nick Lewis and Michael S. Carolan. London/New York: Routledge.

Fredriksen, Aurora. 2014. *Assembling value(s) What a focus on the distributed agency of assemblages can contribute to the study of value*. LCSV Working Paper Series No. 7. Available: http://thestudyofvalue.org/wp-content/uploads/2014/07/WP7-Fredriksen-Assembling-values.pdf.

Guthman, Julie. 2008. "Neoliberalism and the making of food politics in California". *Geoforum* 39 (3): 1171–1183. doi: http://dx.doi.org/10.1016/j.geoforum.2006.09.002.

Haggerty, Julia Hobson. 2007. "I'm not a greenie but …": Environmentality, eco-populism and governance in New Zealand Experiences from the Southland whitebait fishery. *Journal of Rural Studies* 23 (2): 222–237.

Harris, Edmund. 2009. "Neoliberal subjectivities or a politics of the possible? Reading for difference in alternative food networks". *Area* 41 (1): 55–63. doi: 10.1111/ j.1475-4762.2008.00848.x.

Higgins, Vaughan, Clive Potter, Jacqui Dibden and Chris Cocklin. 2014. "Neoliberalising rural environments". *Journal of Rural Studies* 36 (Supplement C): 386–390. doi: https://doi.org/10.1016/j.jrurstud.2014.10.006.

Higgins, Vaughan and Geoffrey Lawrence (eds). 2005. *Agricultural Governance: Globalization and the New Politics of Regulation*. Routledge: London and New York.

Higgins, Vaughan and Wendy Larner (eds). 2017. *Assembling Neoliberalism: Expertise, Practices, Subjects*. New York: Palgrave Macmillan USA.

Latour, Bruno. 2005. *Reassembling the Social. An Introduction to Actor-Network-Theory*. New York: Oxford University Press.

Law, John and John Hassard. 1999. *Actor Network Theory and After*. Oxford: Blackwell.
Le Heron, Richard, Hugh Campbell, Nick Lewis and Michael S. Carolan (eds). 2016. *Biological Economies: Experimentation and the Politics of Agrifood Frontiers*. London/New York: Routledge.
Lewis, Nick, Richard Le Heron, Hugh Campbell, Matthew Henry, Erena Le Heron, Eric Pawson, Harvey Perkins, Michael Roche and Christopher Rosin. 2013. "Assembling biological economies: Region-shaping initiatives in making and retaining value". *New Zealand Geographer* 69 (3): 180–196. doi: 10.1111/nzg.12031.
Lewis, Nick, Richard Le Heron and Hugh Campbell. 2017. "The mouse that died: Stabilizing economic practices in free trade space". In *Assembling Neoliberalism: Expertise, Practices, Subjects* edited by Vaughan Higgins and Wendy Larner. New York: Palgrave Macmillan USA.
Li, Tania, M. 2007. "Practices of assemblage and community forest management". *Economy and Society* 36 (2): 263–293.
Linke, Janke. 2016. "Re-shaping 'soft gold': Fungal agency and the bioeconomy in the caterpillar fungus market assemblage". In *Biological Economies: Experimentation and the Politics of Agrifood Frontiers*, edited by Richard Le Heron, Hugh Campbell, Nick Lewis and Michael S. Carolan. London/New York: Routledge.
Lockie, Stewart and Higgins, Vaughan. 2007. "Roll-out neoliberalism and hybrid practices of regulation in Australian agri-environmental governance". *Journal of Rural Studies* 23(1): 1–11.
McFarlane, Colin. 2011. "Assemblage and critical urbanism". *City* 15 (2): 204–24. doi: 10.1080/13604813.2011.568715.
McFarlane, Colin, and Ben Anderson. 2011. "Thinking with assemblage". *Area* 43 (2): 162–4. doi: 10.1111/j.1475-4762.2011.01012.x.
Mol, Annemarie. 2010. "Actor-network theory: Sensitive terms and enduring tensions". *Kölner Zeitschrift für Soziologie und Sozialpsychologie*. Sonderheft, 50: 253–269.
Müller, Martin. 2015. "Assemblages and actor-networks: Rethinking socio-material power, politics and space". *Geography Compass* 9 (1): 27–41. doi: 10.1111/gec3.12192.
Ong, Aihwa and Stephen. J. Collier (eds). 2005. *Global Assemblages. Technology, Politics, and Ethics as Anthropological Problems*. Malden MA/Oxford UK: Blackwell.
Palmer, James and Susan Owens. 2015. "Indirect land-use change and biofuels: The contribution of assemblage theory to place-specific environmental governance". *Environmental Science & Policy* 53: 18–26.
Rosin, Christopher and Hugh Campbell. 2009. "Beyond bifurcation. Examining the conventions of organic agriculture in New Zealand". *Journal of Rural Studies* 25 (2009): 35–47.
Rosin, Christopher, Hugh Campbell and John Reid. 2017. "Metrology and sustainability: Using sustainability audits in New Zealand to elaborate the complex politics of measuring". *Journal of Rural Studies* 52: 90–99.
Rosin, Christopher, Katharine Legun, Hugh Campbell and Marion Sautier. 2017. "From compliance to co-production: Emergent forms of agency in sustainable wine production in New Zealand". *Environment and Planning A*. https://doi-org.ezproxy.lincoln.ac.nz/10.1177/0308518X17733747.
Sullivan, Sian, 2010. "'Ecosystem service commodities' – a new imperial ecology? Implications for animist immanent ecologies, with Deleuze and Guattari". *New Formations: A Journal of Culture/Theory/Politics* 69: 111–128.
Sullivan, Sian. 2014. "The natural capital myth; or will accounting save the world? Preliminary thoughts on nature, finance and values". *Leverhulme Centre for the Study of*

Value (LCSV) Working Paper Series No. 3 Available: http://thestudyofvalue.org/wp-content/uploads/2013/11/WP3-Sullivan-2014-Natural-Capital-Myth.pdf.

Vanclay, Frank and Geoff Lawrence. 1994. "Farmer rationality and the adoption of environmentally sound practices; a critique of the assumptions of traditional agricultural extension". *European Journal of Agricultural Education and Extension* 1 (1): 59–90.

Whatmore, Sarah J. 2013. "Earthly powers and affective environments: an ontological politics of flood risk". *Theory, Culture & Society* 30 (7/8): 33–50.

Wolf, Eric R. and Alessandro Bonnano (eds). 2014. *The Neoliberal Regime in the Agri-food Sector: Crisis, Resilience and Restructuring*. Abingdon/New York: Routledge.

Part I
Assembling ontologies
Multiplicities and agencies

2 Assembling payments for ecosystem services in Wales

Sophie Wynne-Jones and Thomas Vetter

Introduction

'Payments for Ecosystem Services' [PES] has become an increasingly dominant globalised policy narrative to describe a range of initiatives aiming to extend the principles of market governance to the management of ecosystem processes and functions (Gomez-Baggethun *et al.* 2010; Sullivan 2013). Despite blueprints setting out the desirability of 'pure' market transactions (Engel *et al.* 2008) PES developments exhibit differing degrees of commodification and marketisation as they have been adapted to tackle a broad suite of environmental challenges (Muradian *et al.* 2013), whilst also accommodating diverse socioeconomic and political issues pertinent to varying contexts (Roth and Dressler 2012). Consequently, critical social scientists identifying such developments as indicative of neoliberalisation, have begun to articulate such mutations and accommodations as forms of 'hybrid neoliberalism' (Higgins *et al.* 2014a). However, the coherence and relevance of this frame has increasingly been questioned (Hodge and Adams 2012; Wolf 2014). In this chapter we evaluate PES developments in Wales (UK) over the last ten years to offer an alternate, assemblage-inspired reading.

Here, agri-environmental governance has provided a forum within which PES has been explored as a new policy instrument. This has involved a shift in the rhetoric and rationale of governance, changing the framing of State-led transactions and leading to calls for non-State finances to supplement and expand previous funding mechanisms (Davies 2013a). This has led to the involvement of a more diverse range of stakeholders including NGOs, development agencies, utilities, industry, and individual farm businesses to provide a matrix of 'pan-Wales' and place specific governance arrangements operating alongside one another.

These shifts in discourse and preferred mechanisms of finance have also been accompanied by a change in the framing of farmers and the expectations placed upon them. Availability of public monies have been withdrawn and refined so that farmers have to be more pro-active in the pursuit of payments, and an expectation of clearer deliverables has accompanied this (Wynne-Jones 2013a, 2014). These changes demonstrate a shift in governing style, with government no longer wanting to be seen to impose and dictate, but rather to incentivise desired behaviours and outcomes. This new relationship is intended to move towards market transactions, where the farmer delivers (ecosystem) goods and services that the consumer will then wish to buy (WG 2009). The State is reframed as that consumer, on behalf of its citizens, but equally an array of additional actors (as noted above) have also stepped forward to develop new arrangements (WG 2016a).

Nevertheless, developments continue to fall short of full marketisation (c.f. Boisvert et al. 2013; Potter and Wolf 2014). In earlier evaluations (Wynne-Jones 2012, 2013a), this has prompted recourse to a frame of hybrid neoliberalism and readings of neoliberal governmentality to understand the otherwise apparently contradictory moves of the State and the new subjectivities nurtured amongst governed populations. This chapter takes a different – assemblage inspired – approach responding to recent critiques of hybridity and neoliberalism as analytical categories, which will be outlined in the next section. We also seek to respond to three key distinctions emerging in our case material that set it apart from earlier discussions.

First, the actors and institutions now involved in Welsh agri-environmental reforms are multiple and come together in increasingly complex forms that may mimic and learn from other arrangements but appear as context – and often place – specific groupings. This is not simply a balancing of public and private, state and market, but much more multifaceted and diffuse (see also Hodge and Adams 2012); raising questions around the levels of control that the State continues to assert and the appropriate scale of governance.

Second, the label of PES is being applied here to an array of notably different projects, serving diverse ends and operating through a range of governance mechanisms; meaning that multiple iterations and incarnations of 'PES' exist alongside each other (see also Potter and Wolf 2014). Sometimes these are operating at different spatial scales (national or place specific), but often act concurrently within the same territorial units (e.g. a catchment, region or farm).

Third, the coherence and ultimate trajectory of what we are witnessing needs to be considered carefully in order to capture the reactive and contingent nature of decision-making throughout. Thinking in terms of policy mobility (McCann and Ward 2012; Prince 2017), to assess the current form of PES in Wales without attention to the continuing negotiations, amendments and unexpected opportunities arising, would be to erase critical political moments. Imagining PES development as having followed a linear and singular trajectory would be an unhelpful simplification. As Nicholas Rose observes:

> Programmes and technologies of government ... are assemblages which may have a rationality, but this is not one of a coherence of origin or singular essence.... To analyse ... is not to seek for a hidden unity beyond this complex diversity.... It is to reveal the historicity and the contingency of the truths that have come to define the limits of our contemporary ways of understanding....
>
> (Rose 1999, 276–277)

This chapter follows Rose's prompt, to read the emergence of PES in Wales as a form of assemblage in order to unravel the complex networks, reconfigurations and antagonisms involved.

Assembling governance

Understanding policy transfer as processes of assemblage allows us to break with totalising narratives in which 'neoliberalism' is universalised and always dominant (McCann and Ward 2012). Assemblage can be understood as both a descriptor of form and the processes that bring such arrangements into being. An assemblage reading allows us to better understand the interplays and coming together of diverse priorities and agencies occurring in place, along with the over-determining and emergent nature of life (Prince 2017). Ontologically, Anderson et al. (2012, 175) argue that assemblage helps us to undo and rethink the categorisation of neoliberalism by attending to "*the processes of composition that produce durable orderings and of the ontic indeterminacy of what might ordinarily be thought of as totalizing practices and processes*".

Whilst assemblage thinking has been popularised in other areas of policy mobility (see Anderson et al. 2012; McCann and Ward 2012; Prince 2017) the literature on agri-environmental governance and PES has remained somewhat constrained by meta-narratives of neoliberalism, in which variation is understood as forms of hybridisation (Higgins et al. 2014a). The PES literature in particular has focused-in on the extent to which schemes adhere to market blueprints as a desired endpoint, although questions regarding the utility of such imaginaries are now being asked given the continued failure to achieve 'pure' markets (Muradian et al. 2013; McElwee et al. 2014).

Notions of institutional blending (Hodge and Adams 2012) have been suggested to replace the imprecision of 'hybridisation'. Specifically, Hodge and Adams argue that:

> ... projects blur the boundaries between state, private owners and civil society. This blurring is increasingly characteristic of some forms of neoliberalisation. Yet that concept is too broad and crude, to capture the subtleties of the changes taking place.
>
> (2012, 476)

> [... there has been] a failure to unpick the different and often contradictory processes that are bundled up ...
>
> (Ibid., 474)

Their efforts to set out a different imaginary are particularly informed by the UK context, where NGOs have taken an increasingly prominent role in new modalities of rural governance. This has happened in conjunction with a broader diversification of stakeholders that resonates with the scenarios we have encountered in Wales. Their conception of institutional blending seeks to offer finer purchase on a *"complex mix of formal legal provisions, separation of property rights, design and provision of external incentives and forms of partnerships between actors"* (ibid., 477), whilst avoiding automatic recourse to the normative inference of neoliberal analytics. It also seeks to describe *"solutions worked out on the ground by a wider range of social actors"* (ibid.) which connects to our concern with the trajectory and intentionality of policy developments.

Unpicking the ways in which PES has been made to work by crafting together different institutional forms and tools, is a theme similarly tackled by Higgins *et al.* (2014b) as a means to advance readings of hybridity (see also Fletcher and Breitling 2012; McElwee 2012; McElwee *et al.* 2014; Potter and Wolf 2014). Higgins *et al.* (2014b) contend that the identification of hybridity is not enough if we don't understand why the different components and adaptations are necessary. Their account of PES development in Queensland Australia offers an assessment of how different governance approaches have succeeded one another and the failures tackled in each re-iteration, showing how different forms and tools meet specific stakeholder needs.

Yet their reading also leaves unresolved questions about the levels of rationality and pre-intention that can be ascribed to the actors concerned, which a more continuous form of ethnographic research engagement could better address. Their narrative, although highly detailed, is somewhat sanitised of the struggle and unexpected emergences that are revealed in assemblage readings of policy transitions. Similarly, we contend that Hodge and Adams' (2012) analysis could be enriched through application of an assemblage lens by enabling a clearer appreciation of how the different institutional forms inter-relate as part of a broader process of negotiation and experimentation to draw out connecting (f)actors, and temporal references, in the production and realignment of the different projects. Overall, we argue that PES scholarship would be enriched by a more explicit focus on the policy *mobilities* involved to augment analyses of the forms taken.

The assemblage literature offers key tools to advance these aspirations, but it is diverse – inspired by theorists including Deleuze, DeLanda, Latour and Foucault (Woods *et al.* 2015). Clarity in the terms of reference and epistemological parameters employed is therefore important. For our analysis we draw on the work of Tania Murray Li (2007), who advances a Foucauldian-inspired approach, to uncover and explore the processes and rationalities of State-craft. Rather than addressing the *resultant* governance formation as a settled or complete entity, Li directs us towards their contingency as *"elements are drawn together at a particular conjuncture only to disperse or realign …"* (2007, 265) and *"the hard work required to draw heterogeneous elements together"* (ibid.). As such, we are encouraged to attend to the diversity of agendas and priorities that could be written-out if we only consider specific moments of stabilisation within the ongoing processes of policy production and reformation. To apply this reading, Li sets out six practices of assemblage (see Table 2.1).

Whilst not intended as a strict method of ordering and explanation, these practices offer a useful heuristic to trace and position the messy policy emergences we

Table 2.1 Practices of assemblage (paraphrased from Li 2007, 265)

Forging alignments	Building alliances and compromises between different governance actors
Rendering technical	Devising mechanisms through which complex issues can be simplified to work within a universal schema, enabling the measurement of outcomes
Authorising knowledge	Endorsing a specific, often technical and elite, body of knowledge that is conducive to the assemblage
Managing failures	Masking fundamental weaknesses through new adjustments, devising compromises
Anti-politics	De-limiting debate about how and what to govern and the effects of particular arrangements
Reassembling	Reworking failures; deploying existing discourses to new ends

are seeking to make sense of. It is an approach that lends itself to the analysis of micro-processes and the diversity of influences, as well as the unexpected and incoherent outcomes that are subsequently smoothed-over. It allows us to see politics and governing as fundamentally disordered and fraught; an ongoing challenge that is too often streamlined in official and academic narratives to produce neat linear trajectories of change and control (Li 2007; Rose 1999). Applying an assemblage reading is, therefore, a means to better understand why and how things change in a particular way; to appreciate the sheer difficulty of arriving at constructive results and the persistent need to re-assemble, but also to attend to the frictions of different contexts, noting what persists under new (dis)guise. As such, we use Li's (2007) methods as a means to understand how multiple – and not necessarily coherent – incarnations of PES have been produced to work alongside each other and how this label continues to be asserted as a form of legitimation to authorise very different assemblages and the aspirations associated.

Case analysis

To demonstrate the processes involved in assembling PES in Wales, we follow a broadly historical sequence in the narrative presented, although transformations in pan-Wales agri-environment schemes are discussed first before moving to consider two place-based initiatives. In reality, these arenas for PES development operated in parallel and have now coalesced somewhat. Discussions of place-based initiatives are limited to two cases, the 'Pumlumon Project' in Mid-Wales and the 'Ecosystem Enterprise Partnership – Ecobank' Project in Pembrokeshire, South Wales (see Figure 2.1).

The discussion here is informed by formal interviews, ethnography and documentary research undertaken over the last ten years. This has included interviews and observations with government staff and actors associated with the projects outlined, along with analysis of policy and project documentation, government scheme application and operational instructions, Ministerial statements and press material.

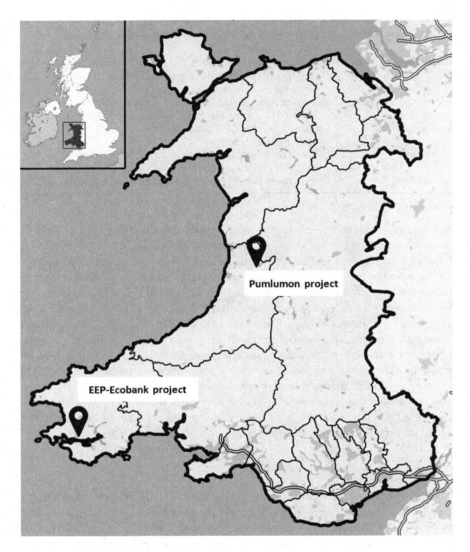

Figure 2.1 Map of Wales showing the two project locations.
Source: adapted from Wikimedia Commons, not to scale.

Transforming agri-environment schemes

Within Wales, interest in 'payments for ecosystem services' first appeared in 2008 as part of reforms to agri-environmental schemes operating under the Common Agricultural Policy [CAP]. Adoption of the PES discourse was in response to critiques about the effectiveness of pre-existing schemes and questions surrounding the continued legitimacy of farm supports more broadly. This was particularly from environmental lobby groups who demanded clearer public benefits from payments to farmers, but also from civil servants concerned about the degree of dependency within the farming sector upon decreasing CAP payments (WG 1[1] interview April 2016). Simultaneously, the Welsh Government [WG] sought to address public and European legislative pressures for widening environmental responsibilities, including concerns around climate and water governance (WG 2009). At this time, the language of 'ecosystem services' was becoming popularised, following the 2005 Millennium Ecosystem Assessment and the potential of a more 'results based' model of agri-environmental payments was being explored (see Burton and Schwarz 2013).

Despite a step-change in rationale, the resulting scheme, known as 'Glastir', was not markedly different from its predecessors. Whilst the language had changed to authorise the terminology of 'ecosystem services', the broad mechanisms and basis of payments had not (Wynne-Jones 2013a). Rather than a radical rupture from previous approaches, a more gradual process of *forging alignments* between diverging interest groups was evident. Opposing pressures for substantive reform, Ministerial favouring of farming interests ensured that an entry-level scheme was available to a broad cross-section of farmers, countering concerns that targeting environmental outcomes would be done at the expense of maintaining socio-economic benefits across the sector (WG 2 pers. comm. May 2016). Traversing the growing divide between farming and environmental interests, support for reframing farmers as more entrepreneurial and self-regulating subjects was aligned with desires for increased accountability in public spending. However, not all aspects of this compromise suited the different actors, with farming representatives wanting more autonomy but expressing concerns about the risks of more variable and contingent payment methods (Farmers' Union interview October 2010). Environmentalists and civil servants, by contrast, had previously sought to intervene in farmers' control over land management rather than granting more self-direction, but they did want to make environmental payments more conditional.

These areas of overlap formed a space for *alignment* through which reforms could proceed. In the very act of constructing new terms of debate around the delivery of ecosystem services, diverse conflicts were being *rendered technical* and disassociated with previous argumentation. Another key method for rationalising diverging opinions was through the production of targeting maps, where different priorities could be accounted for in GIS layers. These were produced through a public consultation resulting in 130 maps, which were subsequently refined to provide the data and strategy for an 'advanced' level scheme superseding the earlier 'entry level' model.[2] Despite the process of open consultation, critics contend that the maps authorise particular sets of knowledge while inevitably excluding others who do not have the capacity to relay information in the necessary format (Farmer 1 interview April 2016).

Defusing the ongoing dissensus that continued to emerge through these developments was not easy and instances of *failure* continued to have to be *managed*. Sometimes these were overtly political (as we outline below) and sometimes more arbitrary in their nature. For example, whilst all parties expressed enthusiasm for a more responsive output-based approach to paying for ecosystem services, this was curtailed by European Commission regulations on the basis of payments that tied costing to the income foregone by not undertaking production activities (Wynne-Jones et al. 2013). In light of this impasse, civil servants suggested that there was little expectation of 'proper PES schemes' emerging through the vehicle of CAP payments (WG 1 interview August 2011; WG 2 pers. comm. October 2013). Instead, agri-environment payments were envisaged to work alongside other measures that could incorporate private finance and were not subject to the same regulatory restrictions. Hence new avenues have been *reassembled*, responding to the barriers and opportunities emerging.

Taking this forward, announcements were made that private money was being sought to supplement government funding (Davies 2013a). Critically, this was also presented as a means to counter shortfalls in public-finance, which were increasingly being emphasised as EU budgets tightened:

> The Welsh Government is considering all possible funding streams for developing a more sustainable and robust land management. At a time of budgetary constraint WG is keen to explore the possibilities of attracting private funding to buy ecosystems services provided by land from the landowners.
>
> (WG 2013a, 1)

Here it is evident that a desire to prepare farmers for a future of decreasing public monies was becoming a dominant factor in these ongoing reforms, reinforcing earlier discourses of accountability in public spending and the changing role of farmers: *"Going forward, we know we need less reliance on subsidy payments and more focus on business and profitability"* (Davies 2013b).

In terms of continued efforts towards *alignment*, and the *anti-politics* evident within actions to *reassemble*, what is notable here is the marrying of an impetus to cut public spending, which has an immediate detrimental impact upon the farming sector, with positive rhetoric around how this will ultimately improve and sustain their businesses. For example: *"One of the drivers for PES is to broaden the incomes for farms … to make them more resilient"* (WG 2 interview March 2016).

However, despite efforts to sweeten the message and evidence of genuine sympathies from some civil servants, much of the rhetoric advanced did not appeal to farmers. In particular, farmers contested the perceived over-emphasis upon environmental concerns and insufficient coherence with their cultural identification as food producers (Wynne-Jones 2013b; Farmer 1 interview April 2016); highlighting persisting contradictions underlying the *failures* witnessed. Consequently, many rejected the government scheme reinforcing a need to *reassemble*.[3]

To do this WG offered seed-funding to support PES pilot-projects, first through the 'Nature Fund' (WG 2013b) and subsequently through the Sustainable

Management Scheme (SMS), which is now a formal component of the 2014–2020 Rural Development Programme. This has enabled them to reach-out to a variety of non-state actors prioritising: *"… action to further develop the interest in payment for ecosystem services … increase[ing] the potential for alternative incomes …"* (Davies 2013c).

Public statements[4] reveal a clear emphasis on collaboration and learning from 'bottom-up' approaches, with acknowledgement that the necessary knowledge and stimulus for successful arrangements is not always forthcoming from government staff. This de-centring of expertise is similarly affirmed in the scoring criteria for SMS applications which require strong local embeddedness and tailoring (WG 2016b). However, this is not seen to simply equate with a devolvement of government control, as central resources have been allocated to cover the staffing and administration costs to catalogue and facilitate emerging projects, including the introduction of a PES practitioners group in 2015.[5]

Neither should these developments be viewed simply as a victory for farming interests, as the removal of government funding for the 'entry level' Glastir scheme from 2017 has meant the withdrawal of widespread benefits in favour of more environmentally focused targeting.[6] In addition, the process for application to the 'advanced' scheme now involves further levels of expertise and competition, which some interviewees felt placed it beyond the reach of 'normal' farmers (Farmer 1 interview April 2016). Applicants to the SMS have made similar accusations, demonstrating ongoing struggles over the agreed purpose of these funds (Farmer 2 interview January 2017).

Considering the longer term, WG 2 outlined a vision of a 'mosaic approach' whereby bottom-up collaborations can draw in diverse (non-public) finances to address both local (e.g. water quality) and international (e.g. carbon sequestration) concerns, but with a continued need for State funding to *"fill in the gaps"* (WG 2 interview March 2016). Moreover, in recent public presentations WG representatives outline that *"private sector funding is not viewed as a golden bullet"*[4] reflecting growing awareness of the challenges associated with drawing in private interests and ensuring sufficient levels of revenue from such sources.

Collaborations resulting from the Nature Fund and SMS have been diverse, often articulating strongly place-based aspirations (WG 2016a). These exhibit similarities in the approach and framings used, but multiple articulations of PES are being produced, and in many instances applied to scenarios which do not exhibit clear criteria for such nomenclature (c.f. Boisvert *et al.* 2013). Yet, the reference continues to be popularised as an authorising label as we go on to examine in the following section.

The Pumlumon Project

The Pumlumon Project was one of the first PES schemes in Wales, beginning in 2006, led by Montgomeryshire Wildlife Trust [MWT], with an aspiration to *"enhance the natural capital of the project area to allow production of traditional farm produce coupled with new ecosystem services that will provide the local community with a sustainable economic future*" (MWT 2008, 5). As such, it aimed to provide a new avenue for rural development in the remote and chronically marginalised upland area of Mid-Wales. Here, the assemblage-work of *forging alignments* between the conservation and farming sector was evident at the outset.

Echoing wider discourses at play in the Glastir policy forums, PES was framed as a better mechanism for incentivising farmers, granting them the autonomy to deliver outcomes applying their local knowledge rather than following prescriptions (MWT interview September 2007). This seemed to reflect a genuine empathy, in marked contrast with the position of other conservationists and civil servants at the time who were using PES as an implicitly *technical* move to depoliticise persisting conflicts around the future of farming and upland land-use (Wynne-Jones 2012).

The payment mechanisms used were variable, drawing on charitable funding to pay for interventions on their own reserves as well as working with private landowners. In addition, they sought government funds wherever appropriate (e.g. Glastir). As such, MWT took a coordinating and brokering role, approaching farmers to pitch a range of desirable options and undertaking the administrative work of attracting funding – suggesting frictions in the reshaping of farmers as more proactive subjects (c.f. Higgins *et al.* 2014b). Private investment was also sought to offer freedom from the increasing insecurity and bureaucracy associated with public and third sector funding.

Securing funding involved *authorising knowledge* to legitimise the ecosystem service approach, which required the application of new scientific and policy expertise to name, delimit and measure desirable functions and outputs that could be captured within the project area. Links with wider policy programmes, including UK-wide 'PES Pilots' and the 'Ecosystem Knowledge Network',[7] were highlighted to provide official labels through which the project could be identified and benchmarked to reassure interested stakeholders. Similarly, connections to emerging platforms for carbon credit markets, including the Peatland Code,[8] were developed to show the credibility and comparability of the work they were undertaking.[9]

Quantitative measurement was key in these processes of authorisation, in terms of determining the area of land under management, amounts of work undertaken, outputs delivered (e.g. carbon sequestered) and cost effectiveness ('return on investment'). Equally, comparison to the approach of schemes elsewhere was made to provide confidence in a 'tried and tested' concept despite asserting a distinctly local orientation (MWT no date).

Despite much recognition of the project, work to-date has wholly been funded through charitable and public sector sources (MWT 2014, 18–19), and direct market payments have not been realised. To elaborate, investment from insurance brokers was sought to connect upland land-use with the mitigation of downstream flooding (MWT no date, 8–9). However, discussions with the Association of British Insurers in 2011 revealed a lack of confidence in the efficacy of such proposals; reflecting the complexity of catchment hydrology and the difficulties controlling and isolating specific functions.

Water companies were also approached to explore payments for water quality. This was championed due to the perceived simplicity of attaching a value to upstream land management, as the cost-avoided of downstream treatment. These mechanisms have been granted support by the regulatory body OFWAT, who have permitted a levy to be placed on water bills to fund catchment management. Nonetheless, Dwr Cymru (Welsh Water) have been unwilling to participate in the upland regions of Mid-Wales because water here is cleaner than in other areas where companies have entered into partnerships, and so there is no demand as yet (WG 2 pers. comm. October 2013).

Consequently, whilst the Pumlumon Project had attracted £2.3 million of funding by 2014, concerns have been raised about the future sustainability of their financing mechanisms. Future priorities therefore include linkages to 'offsetting' markets; monies from 'corporate social responsibility'; and lobbying for an 'ecosystem service premium' on utilities and insurance payments (MWT 2014, 4–6). Yet, it is equally acknowledged that *"the challenge may be one of re-directing and re-naming sources of existing funding, rather than of creating entirely new and additional sources of funding"* (ibid., 4) – pre-empting some of the Welsh Government's more recent statements, which acknowledge a more multi-stakeholder and multi-layered approach and perhaps indicating a new strategy in their efforts to *reassemble* the project going forwards.

Despite the sense that WG have now embraced a more plural vision, discussions with WG's lead for PES in 2013 demonstrated a shift in their attentions as they realised that drawing funding into such remote upland locations was continuing to prove challenging. As a result new assemblages started to gather interest elsewhere (pers. comm. October 2013).

Ecosystem Enterprise Partnership – Ecobank [EEP-Ecobank]

We witnessed a realignment of WG's PES agenda with lowland farming interests and the more developed coastal region of Pembrokeshire in South-West Wales where opportunities for private sector investment looked more promising. Here diffuse pollution from intensifying dairy production was threatening water quality (in contrast to the scenario above) and limiting development due to the lack of compliance with the EU's Water Framework Directive and targets for the Pembrokeshire Marine Special Area of Conservation. Local waterways were *"considered as 'full' with no headroom … for additional [nutrient or sediment] loading"* (EEP-Ecobank 2015, 30). Consequently, proposed developments causing further nutrient discharge were being vetoed by the statutory environmental body Natural Resources Wales [NRW].

Tackling these issues, regulatory approaches were seen to be ideologically unattractive but also ineffective at lowering pollutant levels even if they could stop further increases. Equally, these issues were poorly targeted in the design of agri-environment schemes (up until Glastir) (PCF interview May 2016). To address the persisting problem this posed, the EPP-Ecobank was initiated by WG and NRW in 2015, inspired by the success story of *First Milk*, a farmer cooperative operating in the area. *First Milk* secured a permit for a new effluent plant in 2014, by committing to offset the additional nutrient load through nutrient management plans on some of their supplying farms.[10] NRW staff were then inspired to scale up the approach (PCF interview May 2016). Supported by WG's Nature Fund, a community interest company *Pembrokeshire Coastal Forum [PCF]* sought to assemble:

> a partnership framework between land managers, industry, commerce, government and third sector working collaboratively to develop and pilot an Ecobank – a nutrient offsetting scheme for the Milford Haven and Cleddau catchment.
>
> (EEP-Ecobank no date)

This attracted considerable interest from a large number of stakeholders, including private sector actors (see Box 2.1), explaining WG's initial excitement about the project.

Box 2.1 EEP-Ecobank Stakeholders

Milford Haven energy port
RWE energy company
Dwr Cymru
Welsh Government
Natural Resources Wales
Pembrokeshire Coast National Park Authority
Pembrokeshire County Council
Pembrokeshire Local Action Network for Enterprise and Development [PLANED]

Framing a potential solution to an intractable problem in the terms of PES had an important *authorising* effect. Competing interests were being *rendered technical*, and accordingly de-politicised by their negotiation through a market forum. Nevertheless, multiple potentially conflicting priorities are evident amongst the partner grouping and worrying exclusions became apparent. Notably, not a single farmer representative was directly involved, even though agriculture accounts for about 95% of the local nitrate loading (EEP-Ecobank 2015: 47) and the *First Milk* exemplar was wholly dependent upon farmer participation. Farmers were only indirectly represented through *PLANED*. This was justified on the grounds of practicability due to the tight time schedule during the early stages of project inception (PCF interview May 2016).

In order to *render technical* pollution rights, possible nutrient trading structures were explored through a feasibility study (undertaken by external consultants) which reviewed a range of other ecosystem banking initiatives, including reverse auctions and brokering arrangements (EEP-Ecobank 2015). Interestingly, the consultants concluded that regulatory efforts could help to address the nutrient problem, even though a PES approach was prioritised by stakeholders:

> Whilst an innovative approach, utilising the market wherever possible, demonstrates leadership ... more traditional methods of reducing loading may actually be the best approach.... The EEP should not be averse to combining approaches wherever possible.
> (EEP-Ecobank 2015, 91)

Similarly, it is notable that the initial approach of nutrient management planning, used by *First Milk*, is equally relevant within a regulatory framework. Consequently, some commentators have argued that the PES label is being forced in such arrangements and does not accurately reflect the relations and incentives in place – a point that was not disputed by WG representatives[11] – but the allure and *authorising* qualities of this nomenclature explain its awkward application.

The feasibility study also highlighted a need for 'scientific robustness' behind management interventions, prompting reference to lists from UK Government scientists to ensure the credibility and measurability of techniques adopted. But some difficulties have been encountered here, in terms of how measures relate to meaningful action. Specifically, excess nitrates have been singled out as the key pollutants to be addressed, whereas concerns around phosphates and sediment have been put on hold, purportedly due to the more complicated nature of measuring and monitoring them (WG 2 interview March 2016; PCF interview May 2016). Yet, recent scientific studies have placed such rationales in question, showing potential complications with nitrates also (Van Meter *et al.* 2016). Tensions are exposed here surrounding the level of precision and forms of authority required to achieve acceptable forms of commodification (Robertson 2012). Outputs have to be clear enough to provide confidence to investors and appease regulatory interests, but there is also pressure to arrive at 'practical solutions' on which all partners can agree. Hence a compromise is met between advancing levels of technicality to ensure accuracy and the adequate levels of information required to move forward. For the Ecobank it is not yet clear where this balance lies.

These potential *failures* continue to be *managed* in ongoing discussions and data gathering that are now being orchestrated in a follow-on project phase funded through the SMS. Further failures yet to be resolved are also apparent in the lack of financial contributions from other stakeholders beyond government, despite early assumptions that the Ecobank was more attractive to private interests. This prompted the Ecobank coordinators to pitch the project idea to the European Investment Bank in Luxembourg to obtain seed funding to pay for a brokering organisation and trial trading (WG 2 interview March 2016).

The scope for the government itself to contribute is limited due to overall budget constraints and the restrictions on double funding.[12] Nevertheless, WG is clearly willing to assist wherever it can; further confirming their eagerness to remain in a steering position while at the same time devolving governance responsibilities. Moreover, this case demonstrates that government involvement continues to be required to establish trust in potential PES markets and to attract financial and institutional buy-in.

Discussion and conclusions

From the empirical analysis, we see that PES is now evident as a mosaic of arrangements – including different actors, mechanisms and modes of relation. These operate over different scales, sometimes to govern discrete areas of territory (i.e. multiple modalities within one space including a farm or 'project' area), sometimes addressing different geographical units (i.e. differences in what the national Glastir schemes seek to govern and the objectives of a 'local' e.g. catchment-based project). They also incorporate different scalar connections, linking place-based actions to national or international concerns (e.g. biodiversity and carbon), as well as including more direct actor to actor relationships (e.g. water companies and farmers). There is no unified objective in terms of the preferred approach and scalar focus, but a greater acceptance that different initiatives can achieve diverse ends. This differs from earlier readings where we see more uniform transitions to implement mechanisms across a national or regional territory (Higgins et al. 2014b; McElwee 2012; Wynne-Jones 2013a).

Appropriate mechanisms are worked out in place, depending on the opportunities and problems in question. PES is not advanced as a pre-formed and fixed template, but provides a container to explore possibilities. Whilst there is a sense of striving towards 'properly functioning markets', with a favouring of private capital, there is also space and freedom to explore workable (i.e. acceptable and adequate) methods whatever they involve (Robertson 2012). Critically, these all sit together under the umbrella term of PES despite the diversity in their form (Boisvert et al. 2013). PES is powerful in its authorising capacity (Rodríguez-de-Francisco and Boelens 2015) but does not necessitate specific transformations or indeed homogeneity.

Linked to this, we see that PES is not just about ecosystem services. It is used to address a range of different concerns, offering a new opening and stage on which to negotiate longstanding issues (Potter and Wolf 2014; Wolf 2014). These include: environmental degradation (to serve local, national and global objectives); conflicts over land-use; managing public spending cuts; reducing subsidy dependence within farming; chronic rural development needs; and obstacles to future economic growth. Consequently, a variety of actors have become involved, working opportunistically to use PES as a vehicle to advance their own causes (c.f. Van Hecken et al. 2015). This has necessitated considered efforts to align diverse rationales to serve similar ends. Observing the oscillations and reformulation involved, it is impossible to frame PES as a coherent and strategic vision heading towards an optimal endpoint. PES is not simply a global agenda that has been 'parachuted in' or 'rolled-out'.

Aligning with Van Hecken et al.'s (2015) call for a 'power-sensitive and socially-informed analysis of PES', we have considered how these different interests are served, noting what is squeezed out and elided through the failures and reassembling undergone.

> Understanding how PES is shaped, resisted, reworked and adapted locally essentially boils down to analysing who is able to frame the problems and set the rules, how they do so and to what end, and why it is possible for them to do so.
>
> (Ibid., 123)

PES empowers, aligns and depoliticises, but not always successfully and not evenly. We have seen clear gains amongst environmental NGOs and civil society organisations, due to their specialised environmental knowledge, tools of measure and networking capacities. But this also creates new dependencies where farmers are beholden to brokers and 'experts' to legitimise their actions and connect to sources of financial capital. The aspiration for PES to provide greater autonomy for farmers has not yet been realised. Moreover, we have witnessed a narrowing of the criteria determining which farmers can participate (e.g. on a target map, or possessing appropriate social connections). This suggests that past deference to the farming unions in policy making forums (Wynne-Jones 2013a) has successively been destabilised through the discrete politics of technical foreclosure.

Tensions of geographical marginalisation are equally important to note, given the difficulties witnessed in supporting PES in 'deep rural' locales, despite the proliferation of energies directed at this cause. To be clear, rural spaces and actors are not simply receiving and being remoulded by PES, it is being used and initiated by them and they in turn are affecting the wider circulations of PES discourse (Wynne-Jones 2012; c.f. Woods *et al.* 2015). However, longstanding issues of marginalisation have not been fully remediated. Identifying and *isolating* potential buyers is as fraught as the commodification processes required to alienate desirable goods for sale. This is precisely why we have 'adequate' hybrid measures, incorporating proxies and proxy buyers, and should not be read to indicate that we need better or more complete commodification. Rather, the critical parameter is reaching enough political will and trust for action (Robertson 2012; Potter and Wolf 2014). Comparative work using the assemblage approach allows us to better see this; to acknowledge the accommodations in place and how different actors are able to set the rules determining these.

Equally, by attending to moments of failure, we contend that an assemblage approach enables us to bear witness to tensions and fractures (i.e. the changes of tactic and reactions to rejections), which could easily be elided losing much of the explanatory insight into why PES is meeting with difficulties. Moreover, even when successful dialogue is achieved, full alignment of agendas is not so seamless – threatening to undermine coalitions and stabilisations into the future. In particular, the aspiration to reshape farmers as more independent and responsive subjects has managed to combine disparate interests up to a point. But the politics of subsidy reform has persisted as a trenchant issue (even – and perhaps more so – in the face of Brexit), which cannot simply be removed by an exercise of recoding.

Addressing questions of politics and power, we also need to consider the implications for our understanding of the State. Whilst the emerging mosaic of PES can appear chaotic, government has still set the terms of engagement. The SMS is used to create a wider forum, which suggests opportunity and openness, but still delimits. This is a masterful work of consensus building and anti-politics; demands for greater local responsiveness and appropriateness are delivered whilst also ensuring engagement and co-operation from and between actors. The State having failed to directly manage these tensions previously has stepped back whilst appearing to concede the need for other actors' skills and knowledge.

Whilst there is more room for manoeuvre in terms of deciding which ecosystem services will be governed, where, and precise modalities to be employed, a set framework is still laid out with scoring on the basis of prescribed criteria (WG 2016b). This is a fascinating step in the crafting of governmentality given the inherent demand for innovation (c.f. Bulkeley and Broto 2013), the ability to set one's own mode of self-government, and the data harvesting inherent (through requisite monitoring by scheme applicants). As with other recent moves in the advance of PES (such as the Glastir maps and PES practitioner group) WG seeks to gain control and oversight whilst giving power. Although it would be naive not to acknowledge the pressures of budget cuts within this move, recent discussions also assert the additional costs of developing such locally adapted mechanisms (WG1 pers. comm. March 2017). Hence, we suggest that this strategy responds as much to the complexity of problems now in hand, leading to a need for greater co-production.

Through this chapter we have sought to enrich existing evaluations of PES, by attending to the temporalities and mobilities that produce geographical difference. We have also sought to show the hard work and compromise involved, which takes us away from damning judgement of PES as a neoliberal project towards a more cautious engagement, which highlights questions of justice and exclusion, but also acknowledges the sincere ambitions many actors have and the frictions they encounter. Whilst our reading indicates much promise in the assemblage approach, it is clear that it can be refined and extended by both a more expanded focus (to follow connections to wider PES assemblages) and a more in-depth one than has been possible in the space of this chapter. It is also important to acknowledge our own roles as academics, not only in terms of the power of 'PES science', but more broadly in a range of articulations where we authorise and accentuate the proliferation of PES as a unified category. Otherwise, there is a danger that the depth and sophistication of the assemblage reading remains detached from more everyday expressions which can reproduce simplistic framings and prevents productive learning within the ongoing assemblages that we work with.

Notes

1 WG1 and 2 refer to interviews with civil servants with responsibilities for agri-environment governance and PES development (job titles changed over time).
2 The maps currently informing the targeting of the Glastir Advanced Scheme can be found here: http://gov.wales/topics/environmentcountryside/farmingandcountryside/farming/schemes/glastir/glastir-advanced/2016-glastir-score-maps/?lang=en.
3 See www.walesonline.co.uk/news/wales-news/glastir-millions-pounds-could-returned-2025293.
4 Specifically presentations by WG's Head of Agricultural Strategy and Policy Unit at a 'Future of Farming in the Uplands' event (14.03.2017).
5 See http://gov.wales/topics/environmentcountryside/consmanagement/payments-for-ecosystems-projects/?lang=en.
6 See www.walesonline.co.uk/business/farming/farmers-unions-accuse-welsh-government-10879528.
7 http://ecosystemsknowledge.net/resources/programmes/pes-pilots/pumlumon.
8 www.iucn-uk-peatlandprogramme.org/projects/pumlumon-project.
9 See www.iucn-uk-peatlandprogramme.org/sites/www.iucn-uk-peatlandprogramme.org/files/Pum_brochure.pdf.
10 This did not involve financial compensations, simply the technical exercise of demonstrating nutrient savings.
11 This was raised in a PES workshop on 30.04.2015: www3.imperial.ac.uk/newsandeventspggrp/imperialcollege/lifesciences/grandchallengesinecosystemsandtheenvironment/eventssummary/event_9-4-2015-14-45-14.
12 WG could not fund farmers to address nutrient management through Glastir and pay them again through other RDP measures.

References

Anderson, Ben, Matthew Kearnes, Colin McFarlane, and Dan Swanton. 2012. "On assemblages and geography". *Dialogues in Human Geography* 2 (2): 171–189.
Boisvert, Valérie, Philippe Méral, and Géraldine Froger. 2013. "Market-based instruments for ecosystem services: institutional innovation or renovation?" *Society & Natural Resources* 26 (10): 1122–1136.
Bulkeley, Harriet, and Vanesa C. Broto, V. 2013. "Governing by experiment? Global cities and the governing of climate change". *Transactions of the Institute of British Geographers* 38: 361–375.
Burton, Rob J. F., and Gerald Schwarz. 2013. "Result-oriented agri-environment schemes in Europe and their potential for promoting behavioural change". *Land Use Policy* 30 (1): 628–641.
Davies, Alun. 2013a. *Written Statement: Glastir Update*. Cabinet Statements. Accessed 10 October 2014. http://wales.gov.uk/about/cabinet/cabinetstatements/2013/glastir/?lang=en.
Davies, Alun. 2013b. *Statement from WG's Annual Farming Conference 23rd May 2013*. Reported through WG's online news article "Industry and government plan for a healthy future for farming in Wales". Accessed 6 November 2013. http://wales.gov.uk/newsroom/environmentandcountryside/2013/130523plan/?lang=en.
Davies, Alun. 2013c. *Written Statement: Welsh Government Nature Fund*. Cabinet Statements. Accessed 21 October 2014. http://wales.gov.uk/about/cabinet/cabinetstatements/2014/naturefund/?lang=en.
EEP-Ecobank [Ecosystem Enterprise Partnership – Ecobank]. 2015. *Developing a Delivery Framework for a Market Based Nutrient Offsetting Scheme for the Milford Haven and Cleddau Catchments*. Final Report 2015. Manchester: Cascade Consulting.

EEP-Ecobank. No date. *Ecosysytem Enterprise Partnership – A Nature Fund Project*. Accessed 7 April 2017. www.eepecobank.co.uk/about/.

Engel, Stefanie, Stefano Pagiola, and Sven Wunder. 2008. "Designing payments for ecosystem services in theory and practise: an overview of the issues". *Ecological Economics* 62 (4): 663–674.

Fletcher, Robert, and Jan Breitling. 2012. "Market mechanisms or subsidy in disguise? Governing payment for environmental services in Costa Rica". *Geoforum* 43: 402–411.

Gomez-Baggethun, Erik, Rudolf de Groot, Pedro L. Lomas, and Carlos Montes. 2010. "The history of ecosystem services in economic theory and practise". *Ecological Economics* 69 (6): 1209–1218.

Higgins, Vaughan, Clive Potter, Jacqui Dibden, and Chris Cocklin. 2014a. "Neoliberalising rural environments". *Journal of Rural Studies* 36: 386–390.

Higgins, Vaughan, Jacqui Dibden, Clive Potter, Katie Moon, and Chris Cocklin. 2014b. "Payments for ecosystem services, neoliberalisation, and the hybrid governance of land management in Australia". *Journal of Rural Studies* 36: 463–474.

Hodge, Ian D., and William M. Adams. 2012. "Neoliberalisation, rural land trusts and institutional blending". *Geoforum* 43 (3): 472–482.

Li, Tania M. 2007. "Practices of assemblage and community forest management". *Economy and Society* 36 (2): 263–293.

McCann, Eugene, and Kevin Ward. 2012. "Policy assemblages, mobilities and mutations: toward a multidisciplinary conversation". *Political Studies Review* 10 (3): 325–332.

McElwee, Pamela D. 2012. "Payments for environmental services as neoliberal market-based forest conservation in Vietnam: panacea or problem?" *Geoforum* 43 (3): 412–426.

McElwee, Pamela, Tuyen Nghiem, Hue Le, Huong Vu, and Nghi Tran. 2014. "Payments for environmental services and contested neoliberalisation in developing countries: A case study from Vietnam". *Journal of Rural Studies* 36: 423–440.

Millennium Ecosystem Assessment. 2005. *Living Beyond Our Means: Natural Assets and Human Well Being*. London: Island Press.

Muradian, Roldan, Murat Arsel, Lorenzo Pellegrini, Fikret Adaman, Bernardo Aguilar, Bina Agarwal, Esteve Corbera, D. Ezzine de Blas, J. Farley, G. Froger, and E. Garcia-Frapolli, 2013. "Payments for ecosystem services and the fatal attraction of win-win solutions". *Conservation Letters* 6 (4): 274–279.

MWT [Montgomeryshire Wildlife Trust]. no date. "Invest in the Pumlumon Project" Brochure for Green Investors www.montwt.co.uk/what-we-do/living-landscapes/pumlumon-project.

MWT. 2007. Pumlumon Living Landscape Project. Montgomeryshire Wildlife Trust. Welshpool.

MWT. 2008. Pumlumon Landscape Scale Conservation Project, Farm Plan Pilot. Montgomeryshire Wildlife Trust. Welshpool.

MWT. 2014 Defra PES Pilot Evaluation of the Pumlumon Project Alison Millward Associates.

Potter, Clive A. and Steven A. Wolf. 2014. "Payments for ecosystem services in relation to US and UK agri-environmental policy: disruptive neoliberal innovation or hybrid policy adaptation?" *Agriculture and Human Values* 31 (3): 397–408.

Prince, Russell. 2017. "Local or global policy? Thinking about policy mobility with assemblage and topology." *Area* 49 (3): 335–341.

Robertson, Morgan. 2012. "Measurement and alienation: making a world of ecosystem services". *Transactions of the Institute of British Geographers* 37 (3): 386–401.

Rodríguez de Francisco, Jean C., and Rutgerd Boelens. 2015. "Payment for environmental services: mobilising an epistemic community to construct dominant policy". *Environmental Politics* 24 (3): 481–500.

Rose, Nikolas. 1999. *Powers of Freedom: Reframing Political Thought*. Cambridge: Cambridge University Press.

Roth, Robin J., and Wolfram Dressler. 2012. "Market-oriented conservation governance: the particularities of place". *Geoforum* 43 (3): 363–366.

Sullivan, Sian. 2013. "Banking nature? The spectacular financialisation of environmental conservation". *Antipode* 45 (1): 198–217.

Van Hecken, Gert, Johan Bastiaensen, and Catherine Windey. 2015. "Towards a power-sensitive and socially-informed analysis of payments for ecosystem services (PES): addressing the gaps in the current debate". *Ecological Economics* 120: 117–125.

Van Meter, Kimberly J., Nandita B. Basu, Jessica J. Veenstra, and Lee C. Burras. 2016. "The nitrogen legacy: emerging evidence of nitrogen accumulation in anthropocentric landscapes". *Environmental Research Letters* 11 (3), article number 035014.

WG [Welsh Government]. 2009. Glastir Press Release. 5 May 5. Cardiff: Rural-Affairs.

WG. 2013a. *Overview of Payments for Ecosystems (PES) Projects and Initiatives across Wales*. Internal Paper produced by the Land, Nature, Forestry and Marine Division, August 2013.

WG. 2013b. *Application form for the Welsh Government Ecosystem Resilience and Diversity Fund 2012/13*. Accessed 21 October 2014: http://naturalresourceswales.gov.uk/apply-and-buy/grants/resilient-ecosystems-fund/?lang=en.

WG. 2016a. *Welsh Government Rural Communities – Rural Development Programme 2014–2020: Sustainable Management Scheme Collaborative Projects*. Accessed 6 April 2017. http://gov.wales/docs/drah/publications/160809-sustainable-management-scheme-collaborative-projects-en.pdf.

WG. 2016b *Sustainable Management Scheme – Expression of Interest – Criteria and Application Form*. Welsh Government.

Wolf, Steven A. 2014. "US Agri-Environmental Policy: Neoliberalization of Nature Meets Old Public Management". In *The Neoliberal Regime in the Agri-Food Sector: Crisis, Resilience, and Restructuring*, edited by Steven A. Wolf and Alessandro Bonanno, 191–208. Abingdon: Routledge.

Woods, Michael, Jesse Heley, Laura Jones, Anthonia Onyeahialam, and Marcus Welsh. 2015. "Assemblage, Place, Power and Globalization". Paper presented at the Annual Meeting of the Association of American Geographers, Chicago, April 21–25.

Wynne-Jones, Sophie. 2012. "Negotiating neoliberalism: conservationists' role in the development of payments for ecosystem services". *Geoforum* 43 (6): 1035–1044.

Wynne-Jones, Sophie. 2013a. "Connecting payments for ecosystem services and agri-environmental regulation: an analysis of the Welsh Glastir Scheme". *Journal of Rural Studies* 31: 77–86.

Wynne-Jones, Sophie. 2013b. "Ecosystem service delivery in Wales: evaluating farmers' engagement and willingness to participate". *Journal of Environmental Policy & Planning*, 15 (4): 493–511.

Wynne-Jones, Sophie, Gerald Schwarz, and Rob J. F. Burton. 2013. "Payment-by-results agri-environmental support for grasslands in Europe: lessons learnt for future agri-environmental support in Wales". In *Proceedings of the European Grasslands Federation Conference*.

Wynne-Jones, Sophie. 2014. "Reading for difference' with payments for ecosystem services in Wales". *Critical Policy Studies* 8 (2): 148–164.

3 Carolina dreamin'
A case for understanding farmers' decision-making and hybrid agri-environmental governance initiatives as complex assemblages

Caela O'Connell and Deanna L. Osmond

Introduction

The proverbial 'pot of gold' at the end of the rainbow for agricultural conservation initiatives and agri-environmental governance (AEG) lies in understanding farmer behavior. This chapter considers a growing tension within AEG of water quality in the United States: despite decades of study, farmers' decision-making around the adoption of farm practices, technology adoption, and environmental conservation (Baumgart-Getz et al. 2012; Daberkow and McBride 2003; Belknap and Saupe 1988) is still not well understood (Stone 2016). While the last four decades have brought progress thanks to a diverse body of research into the subject, ultimately the literature is inconsistent in identifying any causal relationships and generally remains "inconclusive" regarding key factors important to farmer decision-making and drivers of adoption (Prokopy et al. 2008:308). Yet, the stakes for understanding farmer choices remain high because the adoption of conservation practices is vital to reducing environmental pollution in waterways and improving sustainability for rural communities (Lyle 2015; Baumgart-Getz et al. 2012).

In the southeastern United States, a nationally popular policy mechanism to improve water quality through market-based Water Quality Trading schemes (similar to carbon trading in design) has come to fruition. This policy mechanism involves a hybridized public mandate that establishes Water Quality Trading (WQT) markets for private trading. State legislators assumed that WQT markets would be successful because farmers in this region have high levels of participation in other AEG programs; however, through our research we found that 74% of farmers rejected the program based on moral logics and calculations of risk (O'Connell et al. 2017). How did the State get farmers' reactions to the WQT so wrong? This chapter takes on this question and the underlying assumptions about farmer decision-making as an opportunity to better understand participation and outcomes for AEG. Our aim is to re-frame the engagements of the state, rural communities, and farmers as complex assemblages. Instead of continuing the trend within adoption literature of seeking to identify dominant factors that drive participation in AEG, we argue that understanding decision-making should be analyzed as part of a complex human-natural system that is productively conceptualized as an assemblage. We find value in this reframing because improving AEG outcomes involves accepting that such outcomes are inherently connected to the broader social, environmental, political, temporal, and material contexts that impact farmers' decision-making.

Accordingly, in this chapter we present an assemblage of actants involved in farmers' broad participation in two other AEG programs (conservation tillage and exclusion fencing) and their rejection of the State's Water Quality Trading (WQT) markets, by connecting implementation outcomes for these markets to the wider social, economic, and regional contexts that inform farmers' decision-making in the watershed. Instead of identifying particular factors driving adoption, our data indicate that there are multiple pathways to adoption shaped by a variety of actors, and that the degree of importance for specific actors, changes with time and in each distinct situation. By viewing farmer decision-making as complex assemblages, we propose that incongruities are to be expected and gains in water quality will come from diversifying outreach and implementation programs from the beginning to increase the number of early adopters and hasten the overall pace of adoption and diffusion of conservation practices over farmers' social networks. In assessing farmer decision-making as assemblages, we also move decision-making away from being framed as an apolitical process where individuals follow a hierarchy of predictable factors, albeit an opaque one, and into a more fluid framing that recognizes the very process of assembling as a vital and vibrant part of the equation.

Conceptual framework

Decision-making and conservation practice adoption in agricultural communities

The literature on farmer decision-making and adoption of conservation practices is vast and interdisciplinary, with decades of case studies and a series of synthesis studies on how and why farmers adopt (or decline) conservation practices (Lyle 2015; Baumgart-Getz et al. 2012; Pannell et al. 2006). Researchers have found indications of increasing support and acceptance for conservation measures among agricultural landholders (Arbuckle 2013); however, there are also incongruities between what farmers say, know, and practice. These incongruities are evident in that many individuals see themselves as good stewards of their land and identify as caretakers of the environment (Reimer et al. 2012), yet their management choices and actions do not always align with these beliefs (McGuire et al. 2013). Comito et al. have described this juncture among Iowan farmers as one of contradictory "moral imperatives" where farmers' beliefs and goals for stewardship and business were not aligned, and in many cases led to conflicting outcomes (2013:289).

Recent studies, which have tried to make sense of documented incongruities in farmer behavior, have shown that while agronomic and economic utility of the conservation practices remain important elements for decision-making, adoption choices also very much depend on a farmer's social networks and personal beliefs (Stone 2016; Hoag et al. 2012; Sligo and Massey 2007; Fairweather and Campbell 2003). In addition, geography, and place-based or community factors are also known to influence farmer participation in conservation programs (Reimer et al. 2013; Anderson and McFarlane 2011). Syntheses from the literature on adoption and decision-making have noted that "disciplinary fragmentation" (Pannell et al. 2006:1408) and complex "emergent properties" among geographic place, farmer typologies, and social networks (Lyle 2015:44) affect adoption. To explain variation and incongruities in farmer decision-making theories such as Rogers' adoption-diffusion theory (1962), Theory of Planned Behavior (Ajzen 1991), Value-Belief-Norms (Price and Leviston 2014), and Multifunctionality (Valdivia et al. 2012) have all been used, with varying degrees of success. Most recently, Stone has suggested that inattention to processes of didactic learning have also contributed to these shortcomings (2016). However, the focus on seeking causal patterns in the discord of farmers' behavior has yielded limited improvements for conservation practice adoption. Instead of continuing to try to make sense out of incongruities when 30-plus years of data suggest that differences in behavior are to be expected, we suggest embracing the complexity of decision-making. Our perspective takes as its premise that the "complex human-natural system," of which Reimer et al. (2014) write, is an inherently discordant and intricate system, and efforts to explain predictable order out of that complexity are misguided. In essence, we suggest it is not especially useful to rank certain factors as *drivers* of decision-making, because all the research shows us that the importance of such factors varies from place to place and changes over time and miss the complex human-natural system altogether. Instead we propose that efforts need to shift towards better understanding the *process* of decision-making and ultimately, how to effectively engage with it.

Farmer decision-making as complex assemblages

To address these incongruities, we draw upon work with complex assemblages to understand farmers' choices as a process made within a large constellation of factors, practices and relationships (Anderson and McFarlane 2011; Bennett 2005; Law and Mol 2002). We will show with our case study that the individuals and instruments that comprise decision-making constellations are multifaceted, influenced by local situations, history, personal beliefs, environment, time, utility, and social change. Moreover, framing these processes as assemblages allows for the recognition that importance or measure of influence is not fixed, but shifts within contexts of each decision, the people involved in the situation, the perceived risks and benefits that the farmer associates with that decision, and can change over time. Finally, these decisions are made in exchange with the material world; soils, water, weather, plants, animals, pests, and diseases are all part of these decision-making assemblages, recognizing that farmers' interactions and choices take place *with* them, and not alongside them as would be expected in a modernist ontological construction of nature and culture (Goodman 1999). With all of these moving pieces, the maddening task of understanding farmer behavior across a field, much less accounting for regional and cultural specificity of a given community or territory (Escobar 2008; Holland and Lave 2009) comes into full focus. Individually, these issues have been observed before (Arbuckle 2013; Comito et al. 2012; Sligo and Massey 2007). What we are suggesting here is a shift in ontological focus – from searching for factors that can be ranked in importance, to seeing all factors as interrelated. Thus, we are advocating for investing efforts in understanding the decision-making process as an assemblage of factors within a set of relationships (social and material) that are informed by the ways in which any given assemblage comes to be, such as history and current events, or what Carolan calls the "assemblying process" (2013:177). In the context of decision-making, the farmer serves as a nexus to a great number of interrelated factors with linked and separate relationships (Figure 3.1). However, even with this conceptual map of factors identified by farmers in Jordan Lake watershed, the lines and relationships are not so simple. Instead, factors affect one another because of, and independent of the farmer, leading to a much messier map that can be rather difficult to read or make sense of (Figure 3.2).

Why look at these decisions this way? In trying to identify driving factors for decision-making, the focus has been on ranking what is important. This approach has led to the "inconclusive" state of the literature that Prokopy et al. note (2008), while assemblages provide a framework to view factors as non-hierarchical way to conceive of decision-making scenarios. Viewing social change and related decision-making as assemblages has been shown to be productive for thinking about the challenges to climate change adaptation because it brings perceived risk from climate events into conversation with such factors as "conscious choice … socio-economic conditions and changing patterns of land use" (Head 2010:237). In their introduction to the special issue on assemblages in geography, Anderson and McFarlane highlight commonality among work using the concept stemming from the fact that one thing "the term enables us to think and do" (2011:124), is to understand *components* of an assemblage as "sociomaterial practices that are diffuse, tangled, and contingent" that are *spatial* and *provisional* and therefore able to be organized and scattered over time (2011:125).

Conceiving of human choice and behavior within individual and group practices through a series of decisions about the present and future within an assemblage framework, allows for embracing the complexity and messiness of decision-making. Decision-making is personal and relational, in that individuals define themselves and are aware that they are defined by their actions in relation to others and those with whom they perceive shared commonality (Escobar 2008; Holland and Lave 2009). Both personal and collective identities impact the range

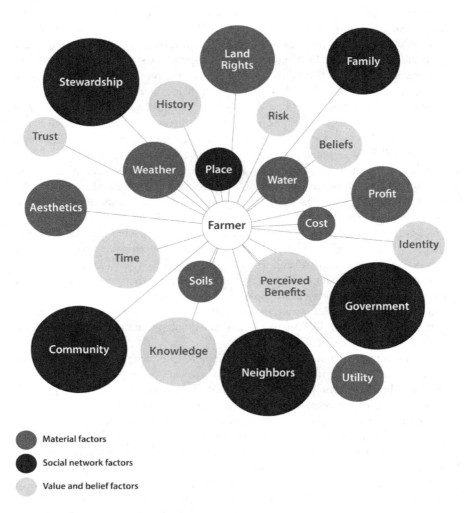

Figure 3.1 Assemblage of farmer decision-making in Jordan Lake, North Carolina.

of farming activities and decision-making from production practices and market decisions to community engagement, political action, and identities of "good farming" (McGuire et al. 2013). On an intimate level, farmers' gender identifications have been shown to relate to the farming practices they use (Campbell et al. 2006; Trauger 2004). Others have noted cases in which farmers take economically irrational actions in order to protect personal identifications with historically and locally situated understandings of morality (Dudley 2000; Barlett 1993). Finally, social commitments to specific values or group identities, through place, community, or other social ties influence everyday choices surrounding livelihood practices and modes of production (Escobar 2008; Minkoff-Zern 2012).

Farmers' decision-making and hybrid AEG 43

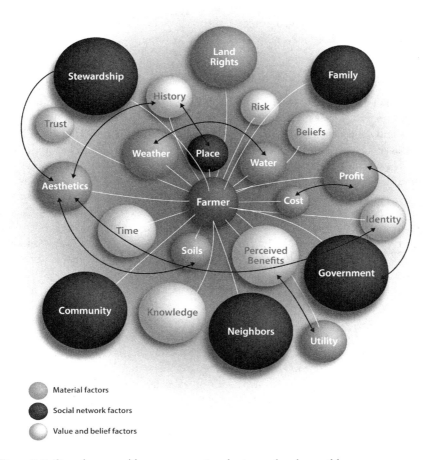

Figure 3.2 Complex assemblages representing the interrelatedness of factors.

Ultimately, people make the choices they do because of shifting sets of reasons that are both rational and irrational, based on habit, experience, and preference leading to incremental shifts in on-farm adoption (Lambert et al. 2014). For our purposes, we are working to address why individual and group behavior sometimes changes, and sometimes does not, despite similar priorities, in relation to the adoption of conservation practices. For example, what might help us to *expect* that one farmer could know about conservation tillage for 15 years and then suddenly adopt the practice, while a neighbor with similar demographics was an early adopter? Recent work in this area has linked understanding human innovation and adoption of new practices (Fløysand and Jakobsen 2011) to complex systems thinking and social elements of life. By framing choices and patterns of farmers' decision-making as guided by an assemblage of factors such as identity, profit, risk, family, place, stewardship, beliefs, and more, we begin to see that assemblage – and any decisions that a farmer makes – as dissimilar on an individual level despite possible externally perceived commonalities, because the context and priorities will align differently (Cleaver 2004).

Research site, population, and methods

Jordan Lake watershed (Figure 3.3) is an interesting place to examine contemporary pressures on conservation and agriculture with its steadily growing urban and suburban land use (from 11–21% between 1992 and 2011) and long-term agricultural land use that mirrors national rates at 22% (National Land Cover Data 2016). The watershed, which covers seven counties in central North Carolina and provides 245 billion gallons of drinking water per day for the region, has a mixed land-use with 19.6% urban/suburban, 54.6% forested and 23.3% agricultural. Jordan Lake is a large (13,940 acres), shallow (14 deep), human-made lake, and is classified as both hyper-eutrophic and nutrient sensitive (NC DEQ, 2017) meaning it is nutrient-rich and at risk for algal blooms and other water pollution issues. Initiatives to improve water quality and reduce point and non-point source pollution have been implemented in agricultural and urban communities within the watershed, yet good water quality remains an issue of importance (Berke et al. 2013).

Our work focused on the watersheds' farmers, ranchers and hobby farmers (collectively referred to as 'farmers' moving forward) in a diversity of agricultural operations including dairy, cow/calf, row-crop, vegetable, equine, poultry, organic, and hobby farms. Our recruitment utilized mail, email, and snowball sampling (Baker et al. 2014) to capture responses from cross-section of the agricultural population, including age, gender, geography as well as targeting niche

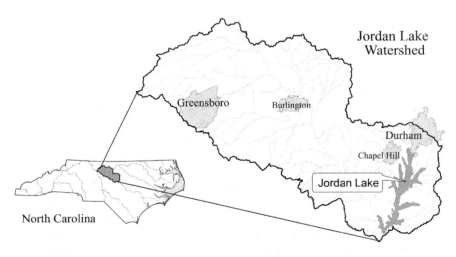

Figure 3.3 Map of Jordan Lake watershed, North Carolina.

agricultural producers (e.g., organic and local-market produce farmers). To document farmers' decision-making and the reasoning behind their decisions related to AEG schemes, policy, and conservation management outcomes, we implemented semi-structured interviews (Bernard 2011). In total, 90 interviews were completed with farmers across the seven counties between July 2012 and March 2013.

Farming and water quality trading in a North Carolina watershed

Our interviews paint a picture of a region with a deep history in farming undergoing changes in agricultural production and community composition (Table 3.1). A vast majority of farmers have lived in their communities for most or all of their lives. This ageing population described witnessing changes in their local communities such as urbanization of the watershed; the sharp decline of dairy and tobacco industries; the rise of pasture, grain crops, poultry, and niche market/hobby farms; and increased agricultural land being sold for development. A hold out dairy farmer described transitions in his county

> Well this is the southern end of [omitted] County. It is largely rural. It used to be a dairy farming community. There used to be within a mile of my house and the store, there used to be 5 Grade A dairies in that little area right there. Now there's me.... Now most everybody has changed into crop production or beef cattle in some form or another.

Most farms were mid-sized operations (100 to 500 acres) with experienced and educated farmers operating at a profit. Agriculture is fulltime work for most interviewed, though many farmers have also diversified their incomes to include additional income from off-farm work such as a second job, investments, or a spouses' job to support household finances and access health insurance (Table 3.1).

Farmers were asked, "What are you presently doing on your farm/ranch (if anything) that you consider conservation practices?" Their responses identified nine practices with varying frequency (Table 3.2). The two most reported practices were conservation tillage, (using limited, or no-till planting techniques to protect soil) and exclusion fencing (to keep livestock out of waterways). In describing how and why they had adopted these practices, farmers discussed family, advice from peers, time, perceived benefits, costs, and profit as central to their decision-making processes. However, the exact importance that each category held for individuals shifted relative to conservation practice, time, and life experience, highlighting the problem of ranking priorities in farmers' decision-making. In our analysis networks (Figure 3.1) we grouped these dynamics into three categories: (1) beliefs and values; (2) materials; and (3) social networks. Figure 3.2 illustrates the multi-dimensional and shifting nature of these assemblages. In the following sections, we demonstrate how farmers' unique assemblages played a role in their decision-making process and their perspectives on the

Table 3.1 Demographics of farmers interviewed in the Jordan Lake watershed

Variables	n	Mean	Standard deviation	Minimum	Maximum
Age in years	90	56.6	11.60	35.0	75.0
Years in community	90	46.6	17.48	5.0	75.0
Hectares (acres) farmed	89	152.6 (377.0)	137.4 (339.4)	0.8 (2.0)	728.4 (1800.0)
Hectares (acres) owned	89	89.6 (221.3)	97.4 (240.6)	0.0 (0.0)	728.4 (1800.0)
Education completed*	89	3.1	1.05	1.0	5.0
Farmer type**	90	1.3	0.63	1.0	3.0
Agriculture income***	89	0.8	0.37	0.0	1.0
Rank of agricultural income****	89	1.2	0.62	0.0	2.0

Notes

* Education completed: 1 = less than high school; 2 = high school; 3 = two-year degree; 4 = four-year degree; 5 = more than a four-year degree.
** Farmer type: 1 = full-time farmer; 2 = part-time farmer; 3 = lifestyle farmer.
*** Agricultural income: 0 = farm is not a major source of income; 1 = farm is a major source of income.
**** Rank of agricultural income: 0 = farm income is neither the primary or secondary source income; 1 = farm income is the primary source of income; 2 = farm income is a secondary source of income.

Table 3.2 Conservation practices identified by informants, number of individuals referencing a practice and number of times the practice was referenced

Conservation practices used on the farm	Number of individuals discussing practice	Number of times practice is mentioned in interviews
No till farming	62*	370
Exclusion fencing	57**	312
Waterways	45	144
Crop rotation	32	54
Terraces	21***	37
Strip cropping	16	29
Field borders	12	22
Filter strips	11	17
Nutrient management	7	17

Notes
* 93.5% of farmers in this study with crops were using this, a much higher than national rates of 35%.
** Of these, 50 use this practice.
*** Many farmers no longer use this practice.

adoption of the two most used conservation practices (conservation tillage, and exclusion fencing) the new WQT program being implemented in the watershed.

Conservation tillage and social assemblages

Conservation tillage, where farmers plant crops directly into the soil with minimal or zero tilling, was the most adopted practice by farmers. Notably, 92.5% of farmers producing crops reported using conservation tillage in North Carolina in contrast to the national average of 35.5% for American cropland (Horowitz et al. 2010). As farmers talked about the situations in which they implemented conservation tillage, their answers demonstrated that it has become both commonplace and commonsense in their region. North Carolina's 40-year promotion of the practice was evident when farmers easily identified the 1970s as the point they became aware of or even started adopting the practice. Most farmers also readily listed several benefits from conservation tillage. One long-time practitioner of conservation tillage reflected:

INTERVIEWER: *"How long have you been doing no-till?"*
FARMER: *"Honey, I don't know. There is no telling."*
INTERVIEWER: *"A good while?"*
FARMER: *"Probably since there was no-till."*
INTERVIEWER: *"What made you want to try them?"*
FARMER: *"I don't know, we try everything that somebody else don't do. When we first did it, people thought it was impossible. I will say that it probably was in the late '70s maybe. I'm not sure. Whenever no-till started, we didn't do a lot, but*

> we did 10 or 20 acres. I don't know exactly when. People think that you have to work the ground. I know people that farm who think that you must work the ground some time. We have the land that is been no-till for 30 years and probably makes better crops now than it did then. You are building a mulch layer and to go work it–. I know one guy who thinks he must work it every two or three years or so. He is probably undoing what he has done up to that point. I don't know if anybody else agrees, but this is what I think. You may agree or you may not agree. I think that point he is probably destroying what he has built in trying to do that and then he is going to start all over. In two or three years he is going to do it again, so he ain't never gonna get there."

This farmers' reflection on his early implementation of no-till demonstrates his reliance on his own beliefs about soil protection and disregard for social conventions in farm management. His choices were unpopular at the time, but have since become commonplace in his community.

Another farmer proudly proclaimed,

> Well, about everything we do is. We no-till 100%. We have been for 20 years. We haven't stuck ah, we haven't tilled ground in 20 years. We have waterways, terraces, field borders, the whole 9 yards. It's our soil, I don't want to lose any of it.

Collectively, farmers assembled a short list of reasons explaining their adoption of conservation tillage including savings in fuel, labor, time, and overall expenses. "*It may sound funny, but the reason I started with no-till, was time.*" one informant explained. This list echoes other research noting how the given reasons for adopting the practice can be categorized as possessing a perceived benefit of utility for the farmer and agricultural land (Amsalu and de Graaff 2006).

Though farmers shared a collective set of traits they perceived as benefits of conservation tillage, throughout their interviews they also described the influence of other people and the ways that the concept of conservation tillage was introduced. As highlighted by the farmer above who tried "*... everything that somebody else don't do. When we first did it, people thought it was impossible,*" social relations (whether positive or negative) were not as frequently part of farmers' narratives about adoption but seemed to be just as important for adoption outcomes. The early adopters we interviewed demonstrated that perceived benefits, legitimacy, and personal knowledge were produced and shared through the farmers' social networks. Farmers narrated their adoptions of conservation tillage as a process in which they learned from a variety of sources, including observation of other farmers, through education, and in conversation with others about successes and advantages of implementation. While there were common references to these processes of learning, the weight of particular influencing factors varied from person to person and changed with time, exhibiting Carolan's "assemblying process" (2013:177). For some, this process involved consultation with a trusted friend or colleague, others simply joined a growing trend, and a few others were looking to take an early calculated risk that might pay off before their peers. For each individual, their priorities differed, but the outcome was the same; they decided to adopt conservation tillage. Viewing these adoptions as an assemblage identifies the overall importance of the beliefs, conditions, and materials involved without fixing them through ranking. As the farmers above illustrate, multiple pathways can lead to adoption and the primacy of particular factors within their decision-making assemblage shift over time (Lambert et al. 2014).

Exclusion fencing

Exclusion fencing was the second most adopted practice, with 55% of farmers reporting that they used it. In North Carolina, Soil and Water Conservation Districts began offering assistance for exclusion fencing in the mid-1990s, making this conservation practice "younger" than conservation tillage. Farmers' reasons for adopting or rejecting exclusion fencing were far more diverse than those about conservation tillage. Overall our data indicate less agreement among participants over any perceived benefits of this practice. Among the many reasons given, participants listed new fencing, healthier livestock, cleaner pastures, and more reliable drinking water access as perceived benefits. Farmers were more reliant on their own experiences and the opinions of people in their social networks to guide their choices. When discussing their decisions to use or reject exclusion fencing they described the influence of people in their social networks 80% of the time, and 91% referenced their beliefs and experience regarding the environment, being good neighbors, and the aesthetic of farms.

Participants' environmental beliefs were significant in their decision-making relative to exclusion fencing adoption irrespective of whether or not they ultimately decided to implement the practice. Many early adopters of this practice described fencing their creeks and streams because they believed it to be the "good thing to do." As one farmer explains, "It's a good thing to do as far as conservation issues. It protects the water quality and keeps the water to where it's.... You know, it's good for the cattle and good for what goes back in." The farmer's explanation demonstrated that the choice was influenced based on environmental beliefs, as well as benefits for the cattle. A poultry and beef farmer described his motivations for exclusion fencing and recalls the negative reactions of his neighbor:

FARMER: *"I wasn't the first by any means, but I was one of the early ones to get in and do a lot of the fencing of cows out of the water."*
INTERVIEWER: *"When did you do that?"*
FARMER: *"Must've been back in the mid-1990s-late '90s is when I really started that. One of the first in this area, because I remember one farmer telling me after I had fenced one of my creeks out, he said, 'Man, you're making it hard on the rest of us farmers' he didn't want to get his cows out of there. Now his cows are out of*

> there and he loves it. They have fresh water to drink and different things. So, I am a pretty strong advocate of good management techniques and proper soil management."

The exchanges this farmer shared and the evolution of his neighbor's opinion, who transitioned from feeling resentful of the fencing practice to eventually adopting and being satisfied with the benefits, was vital to understanding the decision-making process of some farmers. Personal beliefs were enough motivation for the poultry and beef farmer to adopt a new practice early despite the limited perceived benefits from the practice, potential economic loss, and resistance and resentment in his community.

The same influence that personal beliefs had in encouraging adoption also served as a barrier; with some farmers using the exact same language, of being "a good farmer" or being perceived as a good farmer, to describe their reasons for disliking or rejecting exclusion fencing. Nearly 25% of participants who did not adopt the practice described the aesthetic of the vegetation and trees that grow up between the waterways and the fencing to be visually undesirable, even though the buffer strips between the streams and fencing are known to be highly beneficial to water quality (Mayer et al. 2007). These farmers described the result as "unkempt," "poor stewardship," and generally "an eyesore." One longtime farmer reflected on his aversion saying:

> I guess a lot of it is my management style too – I'm a stickler for neatness. So, some of our conservation things don't look very neat. That kind of bothers me to a degree. Like the buffer strip that they wanted us to put along the fence. Well, if we put that buffer strip along the fence then we couldn't maintain the fence. So, that just didn't fit in the line with what I considered keeping the farm neat and in order. Looking tidy.

The aesthetics of fenced riparian buffers were also a source of displeasure for some landholders who did adopt the practice. These farmers were dissatisfied with their implementation specifically due to the conflict between the landscape aesthetic of fenced riparian buffers and the prevailing aesthetic for a well-maintained farm. After participating in an exclusion fencing program for a small portion of his farm, one young farmer was irked that, "... *when we fenced the creek out, it grows up in there and looks nasty, and the trees fall over."* He regretted implementing the practice and did not plan to use exclusion fencing in future land-management. These responses are deeply linked to participants' sense of self – farmers have a longstanding tradition of using the agricultural landscape as a visual indication of farm health and status (Coughenour and Chamala 2000). Or, as one farmer neatly stated, *"Well, it's just, you grow up with the idea that everything be kind of clean."*

Farmers' beliefs about government, regulations, and pending regulations also influenced their decision to both adopt or reject exclusion fencing. Many of the participants who brought up regulation in their discussion about exclusion fencing were preemptively adopting the practice to avoid being forced to as this farmer explained with a chuckle, "*I think that eventually it's going to be required. I'm just trying to get ahead of it. So, somebody won't come by and tell me that I have to do it.*" The objection of individuals like this farmer come from the balance of power, not the actual practice, as another landholder illustrates,

> *I didn't want the government involved telling me what to do.... When you start controlling and telling me where I can put my cows on what piece of land. They want you to fence out my land but you don't want to reimburse me for the loss of the use of the land.*

In these examples, the motivation for adoption or rejection of the practice were more about the individuals' beliefs about governance and autonomy than farm management.

Because outcomes from farmers' beliefs about regulation, aesthetics, and perceived benefits varied widely and result in both adoption and rejection of exclusion fencing, factors were once again not predictive of adoption. Instead, they offer a look at a diverse assemblage of conditions, concerns, and circumstances that led to early adoption for some, and resolute rejection for others. The marginal role of perceived benefits, such as time/money/labor, of exclusion fencing is noteworthy. In comparison to conservation tillage, the choice to implement fencing has far less consensus or common-sense status among farmers. This could be a difference driven by a different practice, or may be a product of the 'youngness' of the practice, and a limited socially cohesive outlook about its effects. Collectively these fencing decisions support our argument that ranking factors is often unhelpful, and that there are multiple pathways to adoption that will shift over time and with social exposure for a given practice.

Water quality trading

When it came to participation in North Carolina's newest AEG scheme of water quality trading (WQT), farmers interviewed were tepid toward the program, with only 10% expressing both interest and eligibility for participating in trading. The high rates of participation in other AEG programs promoting conservation tillage and exclusion fencing had fueled assumptions that farmers' reception for another water quality program would be positive. These assumptions highlight the flaw in ranking externally perceived commonalities as driving factors, they can give the sense of shared decision-making priorities, that simply do not exist. Such was the case in our analysis; when we examined adoption trends for conservation tillage and exclusion fencing as complex decision-making assemblages, the importance of farmers' decision criteria varied significantly, with individuals relying quite heavily on personal beliefs in the absence of widespread agreement on the utility of practices. This in turn helped to explain the reticence of farmers for the new program, they were not rejecting water quality improvements, reflecting personal beliefs and regional experiences, they were rejecting the political and financial frame of the program.

From a financial standpoint, the North Carolina WQT program was markedly different than previous AEG programs Jordan Lake farmers had encountered, in large part because of its hybrid nature. The payments offered to farmers were from private buyers through the market, with unfixed prices, while their agreement would be a permanent one with the State (for a detailed analysis of the program and farmers' assessment of risk see O'Connell et al. 2017). Farmers rejected this design, offering a range of reasons including tax burdens, environmental culpability and regulatory negligence, and deep tensions around land use. Farmers' decision-making assemblages for WQT were situated in a series of social, material, and belief-based reasoning with strongly held personal beliefs about the role of governance, private developers (the primary WQT market buyers), and views on stewardship and farm management.

In interview after interview, farmers indicated that the end goals of the program mattered, and that their personal analysis of its financial merits as well as ethics influenced their decisions. Where analysis had expected farmers to be willing to accept partial payments for the practice as they had with publicly funded programs, farmers often estimated their price to be much higher, with a few even asking for 30 times the cost of implementation. The reaction to the program was a volatile combination of much greater risk assessments (and more accurate) by farmers than the policy writers, along with a personal rejection to the program that we have described as *moral logics* (O'Connell et al. 2017). As one farming couple explained:

MAN: "I would be willing to talk to whoever is involved in this. I expect our standards are higher than theirs and they are just trying to buy themselves out of a bad situation. We would talk to them. If we can help, we would, but in regard to diminishing the value of our property or interfering with the operation or giving someone else control."
WOMAN: That wouldn't happen.

They added little later in the discussion,

MAN: "I guess we are also saying that we are also not very motivated by the financial incentive."
WOMAN: "We're going to do what's right."
MAN: "And the real estate people control enough."

This conversation clearly parses the program design from the practices, with the couple being willing to help in relation to water quality, but being unmotivated financially to give developers a way to "buy themselves out of a bad situation". Their reasoning is also a product of the *process* of assembling, in which older fights and experiences over regional land and water issues coalesced into their current decision-making assemblage. Efforts to fix water quality problems in

Jordan Lake long-predate the lake itself and are political and relational issues for farmers. Farmers emphasized this point as they objected to the WQT program, mentioning regional polluters including furniture and fabric mills that dumped smell byproducts and dyes in the rivers and covered area farms with layers of black dye over their lifetime. These industries went unchecked by regulation for decades, even as farming regulations grew. One farmer explained his mistrust for WQT as a solution by telling a story from about serious pollution that affected area residents for years from a commercial denim mill's spent dye that went unchecked while he earned a visit from a federal regulator over a single event of non-point source pollution from his own farm:

> I know you have to have regulations. It's not an open shut book on everything.... They [the mill] were running three tractor trailer loads [of the dye] around the clock.... This stuff would cover the ground. They would irrigate this stuff and it would – the wind would blow it up into the trees and it would turn black as they could be. I mean, black, nasty.... When the federal guy came here and said "You're in direct violation of state laws on this stuff and we can shut you down today or fine you $10,000 a day." It didn't make me feel too good hear when down the road they were pouring more in one hour than I could in all year ... But this dye would stay on trees for six months.... Let me tell you, I was kind of hot.... In that instance, I don't feel like it was fair because this thing had been going on down here – and somebody knew it [local officials], that it was going on. Our cows were not endangering anybody. We have a long buffer between here and where it goes into any kind of reservoir.

In this particular case, this farmer was able to show the dye pollution on his farm to the federal regulator and the mill was actually shut down. However, he made a distinction in this outsider enforcing laws, and local officials turning a blind eye. Accounts of spills and leakage from septic systems and wastewater treatment plants were commonly referenced along with new development, power plant spills and a host of other regional problems. Another farmer summarized his take on the situation neatly,

> I've always been thinking about – even in the '50s and '60s my daddy used to say to leave a row of trees between the fields in the rivers. It keeps soil from washing into the river. He used to get real upset when different colored dyes would come down the river from the mills in Saxpawhaw and Burlington. You'd see big fish floating down. I've always been aware of water quality. Plus, I drink water that comes out of the ground and I want it maintained.

The accounts of connecting commercial and municipal pollution to regional water quality were ubiquitous in the interviews, and made farmers wary of trading with private commercial interests to assume responsibility for water pollution they believed to be primarily from other, often unfairly regulated, sources. The State had ignored the local context of farmers' longtime residence and related memories of industry, municipal, and new development pollution in the waterways, especially Jordan Lake.

Conclusion

By conceptualizing farmers' decision-making as complex assemblages, we ontologically frame them in a way that values and anticipates their decisions to be multi-faceted, influenced by local context, history, personal beliefs, and the temporality of social change (Anderson and McFarlane 2011). Our research also shows that irrespective of benefits and economic gain or loss, practices may or may not be adopted due to influences from social networks and personal beliefs about farm aesthetics and regulation. This approach provides an answer to the trends identified in the literature, especially the incongruities and fragmentation relative to understanding producers' decision-making and the adoption of conservation practices (Arbuckle 2013; Ahnström et al. 2009). This means that there is no singular prescriptive conclusion to promoting adoption in AEG programs; instead, multiple pathways lead to adoption and social networks are at times elemental in delivering, promoting, and inhibiting new ideas and information.

By viewing the assemblage of factors involved in farmers' decision-making, we argue that trying to isolate key factors to improve adoption is like aiming for a target that is not only moving, but also changing in shape and nature. This relationship is evident in the disagreement between studies of farmer adoption as identified through synthesis studies (Lyle 2015; Prager and Posthumus 2010), and in our own work. Assemblage thinking allows these patterns of adoption and non-adoption to be viewed as the social processes of decision-making, and not an equation to be solved. Moreover, this approach brings the political experiences of farmers into the decision-making equation as the act of assembling is illuminated and shows why farmers and their landscapes are so much more than receptacles waiting for direction, but actors and actants with their own agendas. For our WQT case, this involved understanding their strong reactions to the neoliberal hybridity of the program design. The farmers found the privatized financing of the WQT program at odds with local moral logics and a slap in face given their memories of inequality in local regulatory enforcement and pollution sources among farmers, industry, and municipalities. In other cases, it will allow for bringing into the view the changing nature of farmer networks including new technologies and online communities as well as what Stone calls "didactic learning" addressing the reality that farmers both consult with and are inundated by unsolicited information and influences by dealers, commercial interests, and NGOs each with unique and often conflicting agendas (2016).

We conclude with reflecting on if and how this data and approach might address methods for working more effectively with landowners and farmers.

While the individual factors involved in adoption may be diverse and changing, the larger patterns have not (Lyle 2015; Prokopy et al. 2008; Pannell et al. 2006). In Jordan Lake watershed, differences among farmers' descriptions of conservation tillage versus exclusion fencing adoption supports the concept that there is a pattern to adoption. The differences also emphasize that there is no prescriptive fix. To shift this pattern and increase adoption rates and improve time-to-adoption, we must pursue multiple pathways to adoption from the beginning of implementation. We suggest that working directly with farmers from the beginning will help bring attention to the myriad of local social and environmental conditions and relationships along with promoting greater diversity in implementation through multiple sustained program strategies (incentives, outreach, education, social network promotion) at the outset, which will potentially yield a wider pool of farmers to adopt earlier. Simply stated, if the data are telling us that there are many reasons that people choose to adopt, and that larger numbers of adopters lead to wider transitions, than a credible conclusion is to broaden understanding of the assemblage to begin with as well as the types of outreach, education, and incentives. We recognize that this is not a simple task to accomplish with personnel, budgetary, and time constraints on government agencies, the results, however, could yield substantially improved water quality outcomes in a shorter timeframe. Moving the discussion from sorting through incongruities in factors that influence adoption, to viewing conservation practice implementation as part of a complex and continually changing process that requires a diversified approach could assemble a more productive and rewarding outcome for farmers, agricultural professionals, and environmental health.

Acknowledgments

The authors would like to thank the farmers in Jordan Lake watershed for their time and the extension agents and SWC personnel for assistance with recruitment. We are also grateful to the volume editors and reviewers for thoughtful feedback and abundant patience, and finally Bill Westermeyer (Highpoint University) for research assistance. This work could not have been completed without vital funding by USDA-NIFA (# 2011–05151).

References

Ahnström, Johan, Jenny Höckert, Hanna L. Bergeå, Charles A. Francis. 2009. Farmers and Nature Conservation: What Is Known about Attitudes, Context Factors and Actions Affecting Conservation? *Renewable Agriculture and Food Systems* 24, no 1: 38–47.

Ajzen, Icek. 1991. The Theory of Planned Behavior. *Organizational Behavior and Human Decision Processes* 50, no 2: 179–211.

Amsalu, Aklilu and Jan de Graaff. 2006. Farmers' Views of Soil Erosion Problems and Their Conservation Knowledge at Beressa Watershed, Central Highlands of Ethiopia. *Agriculture and Human Values* 23, no 1: 99–108.

Anderson, Ben and Colin McFarlane. 2011. Assemblage and Geography. *Area* 43, no 2: 124–7.
Arbuckle, J. Gordon. 2013. Farmer Support for Extending Conservation Compliance Beyond Soil Erosion: Evidence from Iowa. *Journal of Soil and Water Conservation* 68, no 2: 99–109.
Baker, Rachel, Anna Bartczak, Susan Chilton and Hugh Metcalf. 2014. Did People "Buy" What was "Sold"? A Qualitative Evaluation of a Contingent Valuation Survey Information Set for Gains in Life Expectancy. *Journal of Environmental Management* 133: 94–103.
Barlett, Peggy F. 1993. *American Dreams, Rural Realities: Family Farms in Crisis*. Chapel Hill: University of North Carolina Press.
Baumgart-Getz, Adam, Linda S. Prokopy and Kristen Floress. 2012. Why Farmers Adopt Best Management Practice in The United States: A Meta-Analysis of the Adoption Literature. *Journal of Environmental Management* 96, no 1: 17–25.
Belknap, John and William E. Saupe. 1988. Farm Family Resources and the Adoption of No-Plow Tillage in Southwestern Wisconsin. *North Central Journal of Agricultural Economics*, no 1: 13–23.
Bennett, Jane. 2005. The Agency of Assemblages and the North American Blackout. *Public Culture* 17, no 3: 445–65.
Berke, Philip, Danielle Spurlock, George Hess, and Larry Band. 2013. Local Comprehensive Plan Quality and Regional Ecosystem Protection: The Case of the Jordan Lake Watershed, North Carolina, USA. *Land Use Policy* 31: 450–9.
Bernard, H. Russell. 2011. *Research Methods in Anthropology: Qualitative and Quantitative Approaches*. 5th ed. Lanham, MD: AltaMira.
Campbell, Hugh, Michael M. Bell and Margaret Finney. 2006. *Country Boys: Masculinity and Rural Life*. University Park, PA: Pennsylvania State University Press.
Carolan, Michael. 2013. Doing and Enacting Economies of Value: Thinking Through the Assemblage. *New Zealand Geographer*, 69, no 3: 176–9.
Cleaver, Frances. 2004. The Social Embeddedness of Agency and Decision-Making. In *Participation: From Tyranny to Transformation?: Exploring New Approaches to Participation in Development*, edited S. Hickey and G. Mohan, London: Zed Books Ltd. 271–7.
Comito, Jaquline, Jon Wolseth and Lois W. Morton. 2012. Tillage Practices, The Language of Blame, and Responsibility for Water Quality Impacts in Row Crop Agriculture. *Human Ecology Review* 19, no 2: 146–58.
Comito, Jacqueline, Jon Wolseth, and Lois Morton Stewards. 2013. Businessmen, and Heroes?: Role Conflict and Contradiction Among Row-Crop Farmers in an Age of Environmental Uncertainty. *Human Organization* 72, no 4: 283–92.
Coughenour, C. Milton. And Shankariha Chamala. 2000. *Conservation Tillage and Cropping Innovation: Constructing the New Culture of Agriculture*. Ames: Iowa State University Press.
Daberkow, Stan G. and William D. McBride. 2003. Farm and Operator Characteristics Affecting the Awareness and Adoption of Precision Agriculture Technologies in the US. *Precision Agriculture* 4, no 2: 163–77.
Dudley, Katheryn M. 2000. *Debt and Dispossession: Farm Loss in America's Heartland*. Chicago, IL: University of Chicago Press.
Escobar, Arturo. 2008. *Territories of Difference: Place, Movements, Life, Redes*. Durham: Duke University Press.
Fairweather, John and Hugh Campbell. 2003. Environmental Beliefs and Farm Practices of New Zealand Farmers: Contrasting Pathways to Sustainability. *Agriculture and Human Values* 20, no 3: 287–300.

Fløysand, Arnt and Stig-Erik. Jakobsen. 2011. The Complexity of Innovation: A Relational Turn. *Progress in Human Geography* 35, no 3: 328–44.

Goodman, David. 1999. Agro-Food Studies in the 'Age of Ecology': Nature, Corporeality, Bio-Politics. *Sociologia Ruralis* 39, no 1: 17–38.

Head, Leslie. 2010. Cultural Ecology: Adaptation – Retrofitting a Concept? *Progress in Human Geography* 34, no 2: 234–42.

Hoag, Dana, A. E. Luloff and Deanna Osmond. 2012. Socio-Economic Analysis from the NIFA-CEAP Projects. In *How to Build Better Agricultural Conservation Programs to Protect Water Quality: The NIFA-CEAP Experience*, edited Osmond, Deanna, Meals, Donald, Hoag, Dana and Arabi, Madzak. Ankeny, Iowa: Soil and Water Conservation Society.

Holland, Dorothy and Jean Lave. 2009. Social Practice Theory and the Historical Production of Persons. *Actio: An International Journal of Human Activity Theory* no 2: 1–15.

Horowitz, John K., Robert M. Ebel and Kohei Ueda. 2010. *"No-Till"; Farming is a Growing Practice* (No. 96636). United States Department of Agriculture, Economic Research Service.

Lambert, Dayton M., Christopher D. Clark, N. Busko, Forbes R. Walker, A. Layton and Shawn Hawkins. 2014. A Study of Cattle Producer Preferences for Best Management Practices in an East Tennessee Watershed. *Journal of Soil and Water Conservation* 69, no 1: 41–53.

Law, John and Annemarie Mol. 2002. *Complexities: Social Studies of Knowledge Practices*. Durham: Duke University Press.

Lyle, Greg. 2015. Understanding the Nested, Multi-Scale, Spatial and Hierarchical Nature of Future Climate Change Adaptation Decision Making in Agricultural Regions: A Narrative Literature Review. *Journal of Rural Studies* 37: 38–49.

Mayer, Paul M., Steven K. Reynolds, Jr., Marshall D. McCutchen and Timothy J. Canfield. 2007. Meta-Analysis of Nitrogen Removal in Riparian Buffers. *Journal of Environmental Quality* 36, no 4: 1172–80.

McGuire, Jean, Lois Morton and Alicia. Cast. 2013. Reconstructing the Good Farmer Identity: Shifts in Farmer Identities and Farm Management Practices to Improve Water Quality. *Agriculture and Human Values* 30, no 1: 57–69.

Minkoff-Zern, Laura-Anne. 2012. Pushing the Boundaries of Indigeneity and Agricultural Knowledge: Oaxacan Immigrant Gardening in California. *Agriculture and Human Values* 29, no 3: 381–92.

NC Division of Environmental Quality. Jordan Lake Nutrient Strategy. https://deq.nc.gov/about/divisions/water-resources/water-planning/nonpoint-source-planning/jordan-lake-nutrient (accessed 12.14.2017).

National Land Cover Data. 2016. www.mrlc.gov/nlcd11_stat.php (accessed 6.20.2016).

O'Connell, Caela, Marzieh Motallebi, Deanna L. Osmond, and Dana L. K. Hoag. 2017. Trading on Risk: The Moral Logics and Economic Reasoning of North Carolina Farmers in Water Quality Trading Markets. *Economic Anthropology* 4, no 2: 225–38.

Pannell, David J., Graham R. Marshall, Neil Barr, Allan Curtis, Frank Vanclay and Roger Wilkinson. 2006. Understanding and Promoting Adoption of Conservation Practices by Rural Landholders. *Australian Journal of Experimental Agriculture* 46, no 11: 1407–24.

Prager, Katrin and Helena Posthumus. 2010. Socio-Economic Factors Influencing Farmers' Adoption of Soil Conservation Practices in Europe. In *Human Dimensions of Soil and Water Conservation: A Global Perspective*, edited T. Napier, New York: Nova Science. 203–23.

Price, J.C. and Z. Leviston. 2014. Predicting Pro-environmental Agricultural Practices: The social, Psychological and Contextual Influences on Land Management. *Journal of Rural Studies* 34: 65–78.

Prokopy, Linda S., Kristen Floress, Denise Klotthor-Weinkauf and Adam Baumgart-Getz. 2008. Determinants of Agricultural Best Management Practice Adoption: Evidence from the Literature. *Journal of Soil and Water Conservation* 63, no 5: 300–11.

Reimer, Adam, Aaron Thompson and Linda Prokopy. 2012. The Multi-Dimensional Nature of Environmental Attitudes among Farmers in Indiana: Implications for Conservation Adoption. *Agriculture and Human Values* 29, no 1: 29–40.

Reimer, Adam, Ben M. Gramig and Linda S. Prokopy. 2013. Farmers and Conservation Programs: Explaining Differences in Environmental Quality Incentives Program Applications between States. *Journal of Soil and Water Conservation* 68, no 2: 110–19.

Reimer, Adam, Aaron. Thompson, Linda S. Prokopy, J. Gordon Arbuckle, Lois W. Morton, Ken Genskow, Douglas Jackson-Smith, Gary Lynne, Laura McCann and Pete Nowak. 2014. People, Place, Behavior, and Context: A Research Agenda for Expanding our Understanding of What Motivates Farmers' Conservation Behaviors. *Journal of Soil and Water Conservation* 69, no 2: 57A.

Rogers, Everett M. 1962. *Diffusion of Innovations*. New York, Free Press of Glencoe.

Sligo, F.X. and Claire Massey. 2007. Risk, Trust and Knowledge Networks in Farmers' Learning. *Journal of Rural Studies* 23, no 2: 170–82.

Stone, Glenn. 2016. Towards a General Theory of Agricultural Knowledge Production: Environmental, Social, and Didactic Learning. *Culture, Agriculture, Food and Environment* 38, no 1: 5–17.

Trauger, Amy. 2004. 'Because they can do the work': Women Farmers in Sustainable Agriculture in Pennsylvania, USA. *Gender, Place & Culture* 11, no 2: 289–307.

Valdivia, Corinne, Carla Barbieri and Michael A. Gold. 2012. Between Forestry and Farming: Policy and Environmental Implications of the Barriers to Agroforestry Adoption. *Canadian Journal of Agricultural Economics/Revue Canadienne Agroeconomie* 60, no 2: 155–75.

4 Killing two (or more) birds with one stone

The case of governance through multifunctionality payments in Japan

Haruhiko Iba and Kiyohiko Sakamoto

Introduction

The Agricultural Multifunctionality Payment (AMFP) is a fiscal programme introduced by the Japanese Ministry of Agriculture, Forestry and Fishery (MAFF) to support and render material agricultural multifunctionalities in rural areas. Funds are distributed to specific rural communities that are committed to preserving their agricultural assets, such as farmland, irrigation systems, and farm roads, which not only are foundational for the co-production of agricultural products, but also support a myriad of other goods and services that are not usually evaluated within the existing market system. As a programme based on voluntary participation, AMFP invites communities to organize themselves to identify and conserve their assets and, if necessary, solve any problems that may have arisen. To this end, MAFF provides a menu of activities that participating communities can choose from and combine *à la carte* according to their diverse needs in varying conditions. Participation in the AMFP programme enables communities to mobilize diverse actors – beyond the conventional administrative hierarchy, such as MAFF, its regional offices and local governments – instead involving local neighbourhood organizations and other rural organizations such as agricultural cooperatives and land improvement district organisations to meet their needs.

Agri-environmental governance (AEG) in Japan can thus be characterized as an interesting flexible hybrid – an assemblage of diverse measures and actors across varying geographic scales. Notably, this mode of governance encourages the participation of local communities, promoting autonomous organizations and self-disciplined actions. While this supports civic and democratic values, it also encourages entrepreneurial activities to survive and adapt within the world of market competition. Arguably, values like these are indicative of the proliferation of neoliberalisation in agri-food systems in rural communities – both within Japan and around the world – as documented by existing literature (e.g. Higgins *et al.* 2014a, 2014b; Iba and Sakamoto 2013; Lockie and Higgins 2007). These scholarly works, however, demonstrate that neoliberalism could be better understood, not as a universal or hegemonic force infusing market rules everywhere, but as being composed of hybrid practices of rationalities and political techniques that foster self-disciplined entrepreneurial capabilities. Neoliberalisation, in this book collection, is being theorized as an assemblage. It is enacted in hybrid institutions and through complex processes – generated within locally specific socio-material conditions – and can stimulate varying, uneven, and at times contradictory consequences across different localities.

Reflecting on the hybrid nature of AEG in the neoliberalising context of rural Japan, the ways in which the AMFP is enacted, and its outcomes and consequences in different localities, are by no means even and uncontested. On one hand, the flexible hybrid practices of AMFP can theoretically enable the mobilization of resources. On the other hand, AMFP's flexibility may loosen control over participating communities, and may result in uneven, unexpected or undesirable outcomes, if not failure to materialize any of the desired multifunctional practices at all.

This chapter analyses the cases of two communities that have adopted AMFP: *Kanaya* and *Higashisaka* in *Shiga* prefecture, located in central-west Japan. As a consequence of participating in AMFP, these two rural communities implemented the programme in ways and through processes resulting in two highly contrasting orientations. Members of the *Kanaya* community opted to strengthen their agricultural activities through directly involving the community members in order to promote and encourage multifunctionalities, as they recognized the resulting improvements that would happen in their rural environment. In the *Higashisaka* community, however, only a fraction of community members have come to actively engage in AMFP activities, leading the majority of younger generation to engage in off-farming activities outside the community. Drawing on the concept of hybrid assemblage (Higgins *et al.* 2014a, 2014b; Higgins and Lockie 2002; Lockie and Higgins 2007), our examination of the cases will illuminate how AFMP adopted by the two rural communities in *Shiga*, intertwined with their specific socio-material conditions, resulted in divergent outcomes and contradictory consequences.

In what follows, we first briefly introduce our conceptual framework – hybrid assemblage – within the broader context of neoliberalisation as the dominant mode of governmentality over the AEG in rural Japan. Then, an overview of the AMFP programme will be presented. This is followed by case studies delineating how *Kanaya* and *Higashisaka* communities adopted and executed AMFP activities, and what consequences were brought to the two communities through participation in the programme. The Discussion section will explore how the two communities ended up with contrasting orientations in actions toward AFMP programmes and farming activities in the communities. We will conclude the chapter with a summary of our analysis, along with a reflection on roles of research endeavours, such as this, in problematizing AEG as a form of assemblage practice in the context of neoliberalisation.

Hybrid assemblage, neoliberal governance in Japan's rural sectors

Our comparative analysis of the two rural communities is informed by the notion of the hybrid assemblage of governance (Higgins and Lockie 2002; Lockie and Higgins 2007). This concept can be situated in broader theoretical dialogues across the social sciences – geography in particular – on the relevance of assemblage thinking to issues of policy, economy and non-human agents. Drawing on diverse theoretical origins – including Deleuze and Guatarri (1988) and Actor–Network Theory (ANT) (Latour 2005; Müller 2015) – assemblage thinking refers to practices bringing together heterogeneous entities of different categories, including human or non-human, into a spatial formation that has temporal stability and ad-hoc structural properties (Anderson and McFarlane 2011; McFarlane and Anderson 2011). It directs our attention to the conditions and collaborations of multiplicity, instability, relationality and materiality of discrete elements that, at times, stabilize and come together as a temporal unity (Anderson et al. 2012a, 2012b).

With its applicability to a broad spectrum of social phenomena, assemblage thinking is used in a variety of research contexts. For example, it resonates with works on neoliberal governmentality inspired by Michel Foucault (Dean 2010; Foucault 1991; Li 2007a; Rose 1999) although, as Li (2007b) points out, governmentality scholars might have given slightly less attention to *how* governmentality is enabled through assembling practices. In neoliberal governmentality, or the mentality to govern what these theorists term the "conduct of conduct", human behaviours are always controlled vis-à-vis efficiency, through a variety of political techniques that foster an individual orientation and subjectivity of self-discipline, self-responsibility and entrepreneurial capability in order to survive market competition (Dean 2010).

Neoliberal governmentality is also accompanied by an increasing *multiplicity* of actors involved in governance. While neoliberalism generates a rationality that seems primarily to limit the role of central government, it, in fact, reworks governance such that some authorities are decentralized and diffused "up" to international organizations (e.g. World Trade Organization (WTO)), "down" (e.g. local governments, non-profit and non-governmental organizations) or transferred into modes of governance by private and for-profit entities. Hence, neoliberal governmentality implicitly is premised upon multiplicity and forces recognition of a diversity of actors involved in decision-making and actions steering AEG. Therefore, when considering the consequences of neoliberalisation, not only conventional political-administrative actors (e.g. national and local governments), but also private and quasi-private entities (e.g. for-profit and non-profit corporations) are becoming increasingly relevant.

Informed by governmentality literature, Higgins and Lockie (2002) and Lockie and Higgins (2007) put forward the term "hybrid assemblage" to highlight how diverse political techniques are combined with competing and contradictory rationalities, thereby enabling a degree of hybridity in neoliberal AEG practices. Among the many avenues available for employing assemblage thinking in our research, we draw specifically on this idea of hybrid assemblage because of its greater attention to mixed rationalities and contradictory consequences of assemblage practices, without surrendering the relevance of neoliberal governmentality in rural contexts. For instance, AEG programmes combining different regulatory schemes (e.g. standards, direct involvement by government, or civic participation) cause farmers to face tensions between the entrepreneurial pursuit of profit and the responsibility to protect social and environmental values in their communities (Higgins and Lockie 2002; Lockie and Higgins 2007).

In Japan, neoliberal governmentality has come to significantly affect the entire governmental spectrum of society as well as the rural sectors that are the focus of this chapter. Since the 1980s, the government has been advancing neoliberal reforms, including budget cuts, privatization of governmental agencies, deregulation, and the promotion of market-oriented economies (Hirashima 2004). This trend was accelerated in the early 2000s when the Shinichiro Koizumi administration adopted a highly neoliberal posture, insisting that administrative authority be removed from the "stubborn" central bureaucracy and handed to private actors and local entities (city, town, village, or community). During Koizumi's administration, deregulation, fiscal slashdown and organizational streamlining in the public sector were accompanied with the devolution of state authorities to private and local sectors.

Admittedly, neoliberalisation has been gradually penetrating into Japan's agri-food and rural sectors for a considerable period of time. Increasing marketization of agri-food rural sectors, with such examples as trade liberalization for agricultural products, abolishing of governmental control over the supply of rice, and the promotion of entrepreneurial cooperate farms, all exemplify a long-term project of neoliberal transformation. Vocabularies infused with neoliberal values, such as "entrepreneurship" and "self-responsibility", have become norms for farm business managers (Tachikawa and Sakamoto 2017).

Consistent with these wider political projects promoting neoliberal rationalities, complex, hybrid modes of governance have been assembled in rural sectors. Growing market competition has placed economic pressures on farm operators, especially small-scale rice farms, to reduce production costs and run farm business more efficiently. In response, since the 1980s, small-scale family farms have begun to organize community farming enterprises (CFE). A CFE is a community organization in which its members engage in farming, either part-time or full-time, consolidating their labour and machinery by having a small number of core farmers take care of the majority of farming operations, whereby saving on operational costs. In 2016, a survey by MAFF (2016) identified 15,134 CFEs, which cultivated 12% of total farmland in Japan, with a 50% increase compared with the 10,063 CFEs operating in 2005. Today, CFEs are expected not only to be efficient and competitive farming entities, but also to play additional roles in sustaining rural social lives, including the cleaning-up of their communities using their machinery and human resources (Iba and Sakamoto 2013). Combining diverse resources and embracing competing rationalities, CFEs are vital actors in contemporary rural Japan and clearly operate as hybrid assemblages.

Another policy domain where hybrid neoliberal forms have grown is the payment of subsidies to support agricultural multifunctionalities. Though contested in trade negotiations at WTO, multifunctional payment programmes have become a legitimate trade policy measure to protect Japan's uncompetitive farming sector and were successfully incorporated in the country's rural policies by the 2000s (Sakamoto, Choi, and Burmeister 2007). The concept was contested in Free Trade negotiations because it was deemed to be a protectionist and anti-neoliberal concept to justify continuing subsidies to uncompetitive farming sectors in countries advocating multifunctionality, such as the European Union and Japan, thereby acting as an illegitimate barrier to trade liberalization.

Yet, it could hardly be said that actual policies supporting multifunctionalities were simply incompatible with neoliberalism. This is because technical language was devised within WTO negotiations so that policies supporting multifunctionalities were argued to be "detached" from agricultural production per se, allowing the ongoing claim that such "detached" payments would not distort free trade (OECD 2001; Potter and Tilzey 2007). While they may not accord with the spirit of neoliberal rationalities, they were rendered compliant through technical negotiation which opened an opportunity for action in Japan. Accordingly, MAFF introduced the Direct Payment to Mountainous Areas (DPMA) and the Programme for Improvement of Farmlands, Water, and Environment (PIFWE) as subsidy programmes to promote multifunctionalities, especially in less-competitive farming areas. Notably, PIFWE is the predecessor of AMFP, which will be discussed in detail in the following section.

Although the multifunctionalities concept was considered to be a form of negotiated resistance to neoliberalisation, in fact the way in which the above policies were implemented exhibits hybrid practices and still incorporates elements of neoliberal governmentality. These programmes combine national fiscal expenditures with, though varying in degree, participation of rural residents in planning, executing, and monitoring of activities to conserve local farming resources. A variety of organizations and institutions, such as neighbourhood groups, farmer groups, and national and local governments, could be involved in these programmes to work together. Normative values amenable to neoliberalism, such as entrepreneurship, self-help, self-discipline, and civic participation, are called for in order to carry out programme activities effectively and efficiently. More details of the AMFP programme will be presented in the next section.

The AMFP programme

The current AMFP programme was instigated in 2014, following antecedent programmes that had been in effect since 2007. As mentioned, AMFP and the preceding programmes were created with the intention to *materialize* – that is, to be realized materially – the multifunctionalities of agriculture, meaning the effort to acknowledge and evaluate the goods and services that are generated through agricultural activities, yet are treated as externalities by the presiding market system. This is done by providing rural communities with a subsidy for their activities to maintain agricultural activities and local natural resources. Members of rural communities that accept this subsidy are required to work collectively; for instance, to weed and clear mud from irrigation canals, maintain farm roads, create biotopes for wildlife, and to maintain the general aesthetics and functionalities of the landscape.

Groups of farmers and non-farming members within the communities are eligible to participate in AMFP programmes. The rationale for involving non-farming community members in the programme is because they too are beneficiaries of the multifunctional outcomes of agriculture, even though they may not be directly engaged in farming itself. Ultimately, the programme is expected to help depopulating and aging farming communities as a whole to conserve and sustain their local agricultural activities. As a subsidy programme supported by state tax money, the programme is based on the premise that the multifunctional outcomes of agriculture are universally beneficial, and that the aging and depopulated rural communities throughout Japan are in need of extra support to sustain their daily activities, which, in turn, generates multifunctional value.

The amount of subsidies MAFF pays to communities varies from 120 to 9,200 yen per ten ares (0.1 hectares) of farmland. The rate is determined according to the type of land (i.e. paddy, dryland, or grassland) and on the planned activities (e.g. weeding, dredging of irrigation canals and ponds, beautification of landscape, or maintenance of communal farming facilities). Participating communities choose from a "menu" of activities that are relevant to their local circumstances. Some activities are designed to encourage community members to exercise their entrepreneurship and ingenuity to enhance effective conservation of, and/or efficient utilization of their local agricultural resources. For example, a community group that is engaged in the conservation of farmland may collaborate with an agri-food entrepreneur to produce a locally unique product, or create a social welfare programme to provide support to those with disabilities.

The programme is largely voluntary, with only interested and willing communities expected to participate. As a voluntary commitment, local communities are expected to plan, train, execute and conduct follow up checks. In cases where the labour is not outsourced, and work is implemented by the community members themselves, additional subsidies are provided. As of 2016, AMFP has been adopted by farming communities across Japan, covering approximately 54% of the country's total farmland (Rural Development Bureau, MAFF 2017).

The mechanisms of AMEP as a voluntary programme seem to operate with a similar logic and rationale to Payments for Ecosystem (or Environmental) Services (PES). As documented by various scholars (Fletcher and Breitling 2012; Higgins et al. 2014b; McElwee 2012; McElwee et al. 2014), PES can refer to any type of payment to rural people who conserve or properly utilize natural resources that generate ecological services. Operating according to market-based mechanisms, PES are compatible with neoliberalising rationalities and have enjoyed growing popularity across the world. Nonetheless, PES's "market-based" approaches by no means connote sole application of a pure market mechanism. Rather this neoliberalising approach is assembled through hybridized use of more moderate "market-like" mechanisms and rules, such as voluntary participation, competitive application and entrepreneurship, alongside public sector initiatives.

While not promoting market-based approaches as explicitly as PES, the AMFP operates through hybrid practices using a variety of political and material resources, including human and non-human actors. Through assembling, multifunctionalities are expected to materialize. In other words, AMFP mobilizes material resources to preserve agricultural resources properly so that multifunctional values are materially realized.

Neither does the programme operate on a single logic. Even though it is a single programme, AMFP boasts its manifold goals; including maintenance of resources to secure multifunctionality and economic efficiency in agricultural production. A governmental document (MAFF 2014, 1) makes this clear:

> [AMFP] supports community activities to maintain and uplift agricultural and rural multifunctionalities, thereby promoting the sound preservation of regional agricultural resources. Furthermore, it is expected that while agricultural and rural multifunctionalities are sustained and realized properly, farmland use is consolidated around a core group of farmers so as to promote operational efficiency.
>
> (Translation by the authors)

Embracing multiple rationalities, AMFP, as a hybrid assemblage, intends to achieve multiple goals or to "kill two (or more) birds with one stone." Nonetheless, it is uncertain whether multiple goals are always achievable in varying socio-material and geographic settings. Hence our intention is to investigate, as demonstrated in the next section, how the adoption of AMFP in two different communities has been implemented and what consequences were brought about.

Case studies

Our case study compares two farming communities, *Kanaya* and *Higashisaka*, in *Shiga* prefecture, in central-west Japan. Both communities have relatively similar socio-economic conditions, including job opportunities and levels of infrastructural development, and have been implementing AMFP since 2014. Their levels of commitment to AMFP and what they have achieved through their participation, however, have been distinctly different. Members of the *Kanaya* community came to recognize the multifunctional values of their farming assets and devoted their energy to enhancing their own participation in agricultural activities through AFMP. By contrast, in *Higashisaka*, only specific segments of the community members, such as seniors and housewives, have come to engage in AMFP activities, without involving the majority of younger generation. Their contrasting commitment levels and opposite visions of how to sustain farming assets and rural lives drew our attention and made us question what factors and conditions influenced the different responses. To address this concern, and drawing on the hybrid assemblage perspectives outlined above, we formulated the following two questions:

> Q1. What inspired the divergent commitment levels and orientations of interests between the two communities?

> Q2. How is hybrid assemblage as a mode of governance reflected in AMFP and in the respective outcomes in the two communities?

Before tackling these questions, let us first provide a brief background of the two communities.

The Kanaya community: an overview of social conditions

The first community, *Kanaya*, is a farming community located in the eastern part of *Shiga* prefecture. Its population is 370 distributed among 117 households, of which 57 are farmland owners and three are newcomers in the community. Of the farmland owners in *Kanaya*, 24 are actively cultivating their land, while the rest, 23 households, are not cultivating. All of the farming-households derive their income from both farming activities as well as other off-farm jobs.

Of the farmland owner households, 51 gathered to establish a CFE, named "Farm *Kanaya*", in order to collectively improve efficiency in maintaining their 45.5 hectares of farmland. Currently, Farm *Kanaya* manages half of the cultivable farmland in *Kanaya*, and has successfully managed to save on farming expenses while reducing labour time. Furthermore, Farm *Kanaya* was able to diversify the variety of agricultural products and develop their own businesses to market their products, which led to improve profits. Their entrepreneurship, shown in their establishment of their own businesses, is highly significant given how many farmers in Japan opt to simply maintain their complete reliance on Japan Agricultural Cooperatives (JAs) for their sales, rather than trying to establish new market channels on their own.

On a more historical note, it is important to mention two significant shifts that occurred within the farming community during the 1980s. First is the modernization of farming through the improvement of irrigation systems and the expansion of farm tracts through consolidation, which set the stage for improved mechanization. This helped *Kanaya* farmers to decrease labour cost and time on the farm, allowing resources (time and money in this case) to be invested in other off-farm activities. Second, however, the time and money saved through streamlining agriculture, in turn, weakened the community's interests in and attachment to farming. This, then, led to new concerns, such as the lack of farm successors. In other words, increasing efficiency in the short term can lead to the erosion of farm viability over the long term. This is a common irony found throughout Japan.

History of activities for conservation of agricultural resources in Kanaya

The community of *Kanaya*, in the meanwhile, had been engaged in collective actions supporting environmental conservation initiatives since the early 1980s. These initiatives had led the community to consciously work toward maintaining their agricultural resources, such as their irrigation canals and ponds, as a way to beautify and improve the agricultural landscape and adjacent residential areas.

Given its history, *Kanaya* willingly decided to adopt AMFP and organized a special committee for conservation and protection called the "*Mamoru Kai*". While there were already several community associations, the *Mamoru Kai* was put in charge of coordinating and implementing activities required for AMFP. Activities included conservation of agricultural resources, beautification of landscape, preservation of biodiversity in and around residential areas and farmlands, and adoption of environmentally-friendly farming techniques. Steering the activities within the *Mamoru kai* were five core resident members. Significantly, they were also employees of the *Shiga* prefectural government, which made them quick to learn about and act on AMFP when it was first launched by the national government. Having public servants well versed in rural policies as core members was vital for the implementation of AMFP activities. Today, the *Mamoru Kai* receives 1.9 million yen annually as their AMFP subsidy from the government to perform activities toward conserving agricultural resources.

Changes brought by the AMFP to Kanaya

Since its introduction, there have been changes that can be attributed to the AMFP programme in *Kanaya*. As mentioned above, farming households in *Kanaya* had become less enthusiastic about agriculture; but today, they show keen interest in their surrounding environment and are committed to activities that lead to its conservation. This growing enthusiasm seems to owe much to the leadership of the *Mamoru Kai*, which has continually organized public events to involve community members in actions for environmental conservation in *Kanaya*. Yet at the same time, residents' interests seem to have become more outward oriented, seeking opportunities outside of the community.

The combinations of outcomes are multi-fold: with two simultaneous directions for change that appear to be directed in opposite directions. An explanation may be attributable in both situations to the consequences of having some of the burdens of farm labour alleviated, which then might have helped the residents broaden their perspectives on rural life in a way that prompted them to re-evaluate the value of living in *Kanaya*. In essence, participating in AMFP might lead the residents to engage in a balance where they redirect their interests both inward (i.e. activities to conserve local agriculture) and outward (i.e. broader life experiences, whether it be for employment or personal life). It can be argued that it is this balance that served to avoid a drastic change that may have forced a discontinuation of farming in the community all together.

Higashisaka: an overview of social conditions

Higashisaka is another farming community located in the southern regions of Shiga prefecture, approximately one hour by a car from Kanaya. Higashisaka has been developed as a commuter town, for those working in Kyoto city, and is thus more urbanized compared with Kanaya. For this reason, the majority of its residents commute and work outside the community.

The population of Higashisaka is 154 distributed within 50 households, of which 22 are farmland owners (accounting for 44% of all households in Higashisaka). Of the farmland owners, 20 are still cultivating, while two have stopped farming activities. All the farming-households earn their income from farming activities as well as from other jobs. The total area of farmland in Higashisaka amounts to 17.5 hectares, only one third of that in Kanaya. The average acreage for each farming household is 0.8 hectares, which is less than half the size in Kanaya.

The Higashisaka community established a cooperative for machinery-sharing among farmers to promote increased efficiency in farming. In addition, almost all the cooperative members, however, also hire a local resident as a contractor to operate the machinery on the field. This arrangement has been considered largely successful, as almost all the farmers are unable to allot sufficient time and money to their farming activities. As with the case of Kanaya, this modernization and rationalization of farming has resulted in a substantial shift in life style for the Higashisaka residents, leading farming household members to become interested in employment opportunities outside the community.

History of activities for conservation of agricultural resources in Higashisaka

Higashisaka launched their own community environmental conservation initiative and established a committee, called the "ECO Committee", in 2007 when PIFWE, the predecessor of AMFP, was introduced. The ECO Committee collaborates with other community associations and groups within Higashisaka and has been led by one leader. They learned about AMFP from the city office and have mainly been engaged with the beautification of residential areas and the conservation of agricultural resources. The ECO Committee has been receiving 0.6 million yen annually, as a government subsidy via AMFP. As a public expenditure, the subsidy is meant to encourage Higashisaka residents to take part in AMFP activities in the community.

Changes brought by AMFP to Higashisaka

Historically, *Higashisaka* has also seen a shift in its farming operations through the streamlining of labour and costs associated with farming. As with the case in *Kanaya*, the residents of *Higashisaka* became increasingly inclined to invest more time on activities outside the community: for both employment as well as leisure. However, compared with *Kanaya*, the *Higashisaka* community members seemed less interested in conserving their local environment. Seniors and housewives who tend to stay always in the community are relatively active in AMFP activities. The younger community members, however, are hardly attracted to AMFP activities and continue to engage in off-farm jobs and spend leisure time outside the community.

Furthermore, the ECO Committee leader expressed anxiety over the negative impact of the AMFP scheme. His concern stemmed from previous experiences with government subsidies, such as PIFWE. Before PIFWE and AMFP, community members volunteered to participate in conservation activities, despite the lack of monetary compensation. In recent years, however, especially after AMFP was fully enacted, community members seem reluctant to devote their time to community conservation activities, particularly if there is no monetary reward. This represents a dilemma facing rural communities – while a subsidy can initially boost the community's commitment, it may gradually make the community members overly dependent on the subsidy alone.

Discussion

As summarized in Table 4.1, the two communities examined in this study show similarities in their demographic and general farming conditions. Both communities are typical Japanese farming hamlets located near suburban areas, which consist of three types of household: part time farming households, former farming households (who own most of the farmland), and households that do not own farmland nor are engaged in farming. Farmland surrounding the residential areas generates not only revenue through agricultural production, but also positive externalities that improve the environment around each community.

In addition, *Kanaya* and *Higashisaka* have already established highly efficient farming systems thanks to land improvement (farmland consolidation) programmes initiated in 1981 and 1985, respectively (Figure 4.1), as well as through efforts to set up collective farming entities, namely, a CFE in *Kanaya* and a machinery cooperative in *Higashisaka*. These physical and organizational infrastructures have enabled the two communities to successfully reduce both cost and labour for farming so that members can devote their time to other non-farm-related activities. As a result, members of both communities, especially the younger generations, have increased their time spent outside the community.

Despite the commonalities between the two communities, however, the introduction of AMFP has resulted in divergent outcomes. In *Kanaya*, the programme

Table 4.1 Community and farming profiles of *Kanaya* and *Higashisaka*

		Kanaya	Higashisaka
Demographic and farming conditions	# of households	117	50
	Population	370	114
	# of farmland owners (%)	57 (49%)	22 (44%)
	Farmland areas (ha)	45.5	17.5
Efficiency for farming	Physical condition	1981: Farmland consolidation	1985: Farmland consolidation
	Farming entities	One CFE managing 19.8 hectares. 24 independent farm-households	One cooperative for sharing maintenance and operational cost of machines. A few other groups are organized for cooperation
Introduction of AMFP	Introduction	2007	2007
	Previous experience with conservation programmes	1982: New irrigation system constructed. 1989: Environment beautification	None
	Organization and management	Highly organized, streamlined, and efficient	Highly organized, streamlined, and efficient
	Who runs AMFP mainly?	Five core members	President of the committee
	Environmental preservation activity	Developing new activities	Sticking to basic activities
Changes	Community interests	Interested in issues both outside and inside of the community	More interested in issues outside of the community
	Interest in farm business	Less interested in the farm businesses – increasingly facing multiple competing choices	Less interested in the farm businesses – increasingly facing multiple competing choices

Figure 4.1 Paddies in *Higashisaka*, arranged orderly by a land improvement project in the 1980s. (Photo by the author Iba).

was able to encourage the community members to become interested in issues both inside and outside the community. Meanwhile in *Higashisaka*, community members' interests toward agri-environmental concerns decreased.

Such differences between the two communities can be attributed to a combination of socio-economic and material factors. The constellation of factors played out differently as pulling or pushing forces, resulting in divergent interests and consequences.

At a practical level, the difference between the two communities might be attributable to different levels of intensity or frequency with which community members witnessed and experienced AMFP activities in the community. In *Higashisaka*, AMFP activities are directed by one person, and have been initiated less frequently compared with *Kanaya*. The active organizational network in *Kanaya* was a key factor in enabling many public events. The *Mamoru Kai*, with its five skilled core members, was able to work with diverse community associations to mobilize community members to participate in events. In *Higashisaka*, AMFP activities may have narrowed community members' perceptions of the values of farming, limiting their concerns to their immediate surroundings, such as their own living conditions.

At a broader level, the reorganization of farmlands and improvements to the irrigation system allowed farmers to save both labour costs and time dedicated

Figure 4.2 Flowers along a canal running through the residential area in *Kanaya*. They were decorated in beautification activities subsidized by AMFP. (Photo by the author Iba).

to farming in both communities. The physical setting of communal farming facilities, however, may have also played a role in allowing community members to have greater opportunities for emotional and material interactions with the local environment. Specifically, in *Kanaya*, irrigation canals in the community ran through the residential areas, which allowed for community members, especially women and non-farmers, to develop a sense of care and responsibility toward agricultural resources and the wider environment that was sustaining it (Figure 4.2).

In *Higashisaka*, however, irrigation canals were constructed relatively away from the residential areas. This suggests that chances for community members in *Higashisaka* to encounter agricultural activities, both visually and through direct engagement, would have been fewer compared with *Kanaya*, further weakening their connection to agricultural resources and the environment.

Conclusion

Prior to our analysis of the two communities, we raised two questions as follows:

> Q1. What inspired the divergent commitment levels and orientations of interests between the two communities?

Q2. How is hybrid assemblage as a mode of governance reflected in AMFP and in what resulted in the two respective communities?

In response to the first question, we point to the commonalities and differences between the two communities. On one hand, the past land improvement projects equally enabled the farmers of both communities to devote time to non-farming activities. On the other hand, between *Kanaya* and *Higashisaka*, there were remarkable differences as to the organizational structures of the groups steering AMFP activities, as well as the physical settings of and emotional distances from agricultural resources. We argue that although the members of both communities were involved in AMFP activities, the complex intertwining of these locally specific factors and conditions resulted in the different levels of enthusiasm and engagement with AMFP and contrasting views on rural lives between community members in the two localities.

In response to the second question, AMFP as a hybrid assemblage involved a variety of actors from the national and local government, local community members and their neighbourhood groups. It also embraced multiple rationalities and purposes, such as the efficient operation of farming, building the self-organizing capability of the community members, along with conserving agricultural resources and securing agricultural multifunctionalities. While some of these elements seem to resonate well with neoliberal values, the outcomes were clearly assembled in a more hybrid way as processes of neoliberalisation were enacted and modified. This shows, as discussed above, the multiplicity and intertwining of these assemblages in complex interactions with the locally-specific socio-material conditions.

Given the responses to the questions, what lessons can we derive from these cases? We suggest that theoretically framing AMFP as a hybrid assemblage can allow us to recognize how such assemblages have the potential to engender uneven consequences across different localities. Recognizing this uneven commitments demonstrates how these processes yield uneven, or worse, unsatisfactory materialities of multifunctional agricultural practices across the country. This observation reveals an interesting contradictory quality to the key premise of AMFP that multifunctionalities broadly benefit the entire nation. In a world where neoliberal rationalities permeate AEG programmes, calls for voluntary participation are the desired norm for obtaining successful outcomes of programmes using public expenditure – whether AMFP or other PES projects. However, a question should be raised as to who are capable of participating and who are eligible to enjoy the benefits from participation. This question becomes especially pertinent when we recall that the communities we studied were equipped with different levels of resourcefulness, past experiences and socio-material conditions.

A final lesson we can elicit from the cases relates to the reflexive roles of researchers, like us, who *assemble* stories delineating processes and consequences of practices of AEG. Using "assemblage thinking" emphasizes that the unity of assembled elements is temporal and ephemeral, hence it always has the potential to re-assemble in different ways. This premise also applies to our practices as researchers. While we have delineated and explicated some positive and not-so-positive outcomes of AMFP in two communities, assemblage thinking suggests we should always seek other possibilities and potentials to illuminate unexplored and unpredicted outcomes of assembling.

References

Anderson, Ben and Colin McFarlane. 2011. "Assemblage and Geography". *Area* 43 (2): 124–127. doi:10.1111/j.1475-4762.2011.01004.x.

Anderson, Ben, Matthew Kearnes, Colin McFarlane, and Dan Swanton. 2012a. "On Assemblages and Geography". *Dialogues in Human Geography* 2 (2): 171–189. doi: 10.1177/2043820612449261.

Anderson, Ben, Matthew Kearnes, Colin McFarlane, and Dan Swanton. 2012b. "Materialism and the Politics of Assemblage". *Dialogues in Human Geography* 2 (2): 212–215. doi: 10.1177/2043820612449298.

Dean, Mitchell. 2010. *Governmentality: Power and Rule in Modern Society*, 2nd ed. Los Angles; London: Sage Publication.

Deleuze, Gilles and Félix Guatarri. 1988. *A Thousand Plateaus: Capitalism and Schizophrenia*. London: Athlone.

Fletcher, Robert and Jan Breitling. 2012. "Market Mechanism or Subsidy in Disguise? Governing Payment for Environmental Services in Costa Rica". *Geoforum* 43 (3): 402–411. doi: 10.1016/j.geoforum.2011.11.008.

Foucault, Michel. 1991. "Governmentality". In *The Foucault Effect: Studies in Governmentality*, edited by G. Burchell, C. Gordon and P. Miller, 87–104. Chicago: University of Chicago Press.

Higgins, Vaughan and Stewart Lockie. 2002. "Re-Discovering the Social: Neo-Liberalism and Hybrid Practices of Governing in Rural Natural Resource Management". *Journal of Rural Studies* 18 (4): 419–428. doi: 10.1016/S0743-0167(02)00034-7.

Higgins, Vaughan, Clive Potter, Jacqui Dibden, and Chris Cocklin. 2014a. "Neoliberalising Rural Environments". *Journal of Rural Studies* 36: 386–390. doi: 10.1016/j.jrurstud.2014.10.003.

Higgins, Vaughan, Jacqui Dibden, Clive Potter, Katie Moon and Chris Cocklin. 2014b. "Payments for Ecosystem Services, Neoliberalisation, and the Hybrid Governance of Land Management in Australia". *Journal of Rural Studies* 36: 463–74. doi:10.1016/j.jrurstud.2014.10.003.

Hirashima, Kenji. 2004. "Regime Shift in Japan? Two Decades of Neoliberal Reforms". *Swiss Political Science Review* 10 (3): 31–54. doi: 10.1002/j.1662-6370.2004.tb00031.x.

Iba, Haruhiko and Kiyohiko Sakamoto. 2013 "Beyond Farming: Cases of Revitalization of Rural Communities through Social Service Provision by Community Farming Enterprise". In *The Neoliberal Regime in the Agri-Food Sector: Crisis, Resilience and Restructuring*, edited by Steven Wolf and Alessandro Bonanno, 129–149. New York: Routledge.

Latour, Bruno. 2005. *Reassembling the Social*. Oxford: Oxford University Press.

Li, Tania Murray. 2007a. "Governmentality". *Anthropologica* 49 (2): 275–281.

Li, Tania Murray. 2007b. "Practices of Assemblage and Community Forest Management". *Economy and Society* 36 (2): 263–293. doi: 10.1080/03085140701254308.

Lockie, Stewart and Vaughan Higgins. 2007. "Roll-Out Neoliberalism and Hybrid Practices of Regulation in Australian Agri-Environmental Governance". *Journal of Rural Studies* 23 (1): 1–11.

MAFF (Ministry of Agriculture, Forestry and Fishery). 2014. *Tamenteki kinou shiharai koufukin jissi youkou [Principles to implement agricultural multifunctionality payment]*. www.maff.go.jp/j/nousin/kanri/pdf/h29_tamen_yoko.pdf.

MAFF (Ministry of Agriculture, Forestry and Fishery). 2016. *Shuuraku einou jittai chousa [Survey of Community Farming Enterprises]*. www.e-stat.go.jp/SG1/estat/List.do?lid=000001169843.

McFarlane, Colin and Ben Anderson. 2011. "Thinking with Assemblage". *Area* 43 (2): 162–164. doi: 10.1111/j.1475-4762.2011.01012.x.

McElwee, Pamela D. 2012. "Payments for Environmental Services as Neoliberal Market-Based Forest Conservation in Vietnam: Panacea or Problem?" *Geoforum* 43 (3): 412–426. doi:10.1016/j.geoforum.2011.04.010.

McElwee, Pamela, Tuyen Nghiem, Hue Le, Huong Vu, and Nghi Tran. 2014. "Payments for Environmental Services and Contested Neoliberalisation in Developing Countries: A Case Study from Vietnam". *Journal of Rural Studies* 36: 423–440. doi: 10.1016/j.jrurstud.2014.08.003.

Müller, Martin. 2015. "Assemblages and Actor-Networks: Rethinking Socio-Material Power, Politics and Space: Assemblages and Actor-Networks". *Geography Compass* 9 (1): 27–41. doi: 10.1111/gec3.12192.

OECD (Organisation for Economic Co-operation and Development). 2001. *Multifunctionality: Toward an Analytic Framework*. Paris: OECD.

Potter, Clive and Mark Tilzey. 2007. "Agricultural Multifunctionality, Environmental Sustainability and the WTO: Resistance or Accommodation to the Neoliberal Project for Agriculture?" *Geoforum* 38 (6): 1290–1303. doi: 10.1016/j.geoforum.2007.05.001.

Rose, Nikolas. 1999. *Powers of Freedom: Reframing Political Thought*. Cambridge: Cambridge University Press.

Rural Development Bureau, MAFF (Ministry of Agriculture, Forestry and Fishery). 2017. *FY 2016 Tamenteki kinou shiharai koufukin no jissi joukyou [State of implementation of Agricultural Multifunctionality Payment]* www.maff.go.jp/j/nousin/kanri/attach/pdf/28_jisseki.pdf.

Sakamoto, Kiyohiko, Yong-ju Choi, and Larry L. Burmeister. 2007. "Framing Multifunctionality: Agricultural Policy Change in South Korea and Japan?" *International Journal of Sociology of Agriculture and Food* 15 (1): 24–45.

Tachikawa, Masashi and Kiyohiko Sakamoto. 2017. "What Constitutes 'Goodness' in Farming? Farming and Local Community in Neoliberal Context in Japan". *Journal of Asian Rural Studies* 1 (2): 134–144.

5 Assembling halloumi

Contesting the EU's food quality label policy in the Republic of Cyprus

Gisela Welz

Throughout Europe, many artisanal foods stuffs, produced in rural households and small family-run businesses, have become almost extinct. They are today at risk of disappearing altogether when the older generation of producers abandons production and there is no successor to take over. Some products – especially dairy and meat products such as cheese, sausages, and hams, but also wine and oil products – survive because they have made the transition to industrial mass production. However, in many areas of Europe, once traditional products ceased to exist decades ago.

To halt or at least slow down this development, the European Union decided, in 1992, to establish a quality label system for the protection of geographically specific food products. By reserving the use of the name of a product to an authorized group of producers, so-called geo-labels protect unique food products against copies from other regions or countries. This is intended to have a positive effect on domestic markets for artisanal food products, to safeguard the diversity of European food traditions, and to enhance the global competitiveness of European food products.

In general, European Union economic strategies, regulatory frameworks, and financial incentives tend to privilege large-scale industrial production. This certainly holds true for the agricultural sector where, for decades, the EU's Common Agricultural Policy has been determining what is being produced, where, and how much. But the European Commission also champions niche products such as ecologically grown and processed foods. Its rural plans initiate and reward small-scale sustainable development projects, and the European Union's geo-label program – as just mentioned – extends special copyright protection to artisanal and regionally specific 'origin foods'. In this chapter, a case study from the Republic of Cyprus demonstrates the interplay of these divergent and even contradictory policies, as well as with the goals of biodiversity maintenance, environmental quality and sustainable development.

Geo-labels as a regime of agri-environmental governance

Voluntary certification has become one of the major tools in agri-environmental governance (Forney 2016: 6). Often, it is communicated to consumers through quality labels and is monitored either by state authorities or by third-party private certifiers. The European Union's food quality labelling system is an early example of this policy. It gained considerable momentum with the 2004 and 2007 expansion of the European Union, because in many of the accession countries agriculture constituted a large sector of their economy. However, Southern European member states such as Spain, Portugal, and Italy also have applied for dozens of new geo-labels every year. To date, more than 1,500 products are certified – or waiting to be certified – across the European Union.

The pertinent European Union regulation distinguishes between two categories of protected names: the Protected Designation of Origin (PDO) and the Protected Geographical Indication (PGI). The inclusion of a new product in the public register of protected product names is announced in the *Official Journal of the European Union*. In addition, the product is entered into an online inventory that is publicly accessible.[1] In 2006, the regulation was updated and slightly modified. To be eligible for the PDO, among other things, a product has to meet the following conditions:

> The quality or characteristics of the product must be essentially or exclusively due to the particular geographical environment of the place of origin; the geographical environment is taken to include inherent natural and human factors, such as climate, soil quality, and local know-how; the production and processing of the raw materials, up to the stage of the finished product, must take place in the defined geographical area whose name the product bears.[2]

For the PGI, the requirements have been less strict. For a PGI, it suffices that one of the stages of production has taken place in the defined area. In both cases, however, elaborate and very precise product specifications form the basis for the European Commission's decision to include the product in its list of 'origin products' and to give the applicants the right to print the certification seal on the product label.

It is not particularly difficult to recognize the similarity to the French concept of 'terroir' at the core of these European regulations (Bérard and Marchenay 2007). Indeed, the European Union quality label system effectively adopted and integrated national legislation that was already in place in France and Italy. The fact that food products that have been awarded an EU quality label tend to fetch higher prices provides the main incentive for groups of producers who are applying for the certification of their products through the pertinent authorities in their countries, even if the expense incurred in the application process and the follow-up monitoring is often quite high. In striving to attain a quality label for a product, producers, distributors, government authorities and agricultural advisors have to engage in a huge coordinated effort, often lasting several years, in order to translate an unregulated product into the kind of standardized commodity that will be granted an EU quality label (Grasseni 2017).

In what follows, one specific case of the implementation of the EU's food quality label policy will be scrutinized. The attempt to secure a PDO for a speciality cheese called halloumi – traditionally produced on the island of Cyprus in the Eastern Mediterranean – generated a number of unexpected conflicts and contradictory effects. Public discourse and economic policy tend to interpret the geo-label programme as an attempt by the European Commission to strengthen marginal rural areas and to support small-scale producers who are not competitive in globalized markets. However, as the case presented below will show, the food quality programme is not immune to being hijacked by powerful economic actors who then push small-scale rural producers out of the market. Also, its effects – both intentional and accidental – are not necessarily in line with agri-environmental policy goals that are supposed to make agriculture and regional development in Europe more sustainable and ecologically sound. The case study is based on a period of long-term fieldwork in the Republic of Cyprus (Welz 2015) where I have been inquiring into regional development, food culture, rural tourism and heritage making since the mid-1990s.

Anthropology, policy studies and assemblage theory

Can the implementation of the food quality program lead to sustainability's demise? In order to discuss the case study detailed below, I will engage with recent conceptual developments in public policy analysis. Obviously, policies devised and decided upon by national governments or in supra-national bodies such as the European Commission become effective only when they are actually implemented on the ground, by regional administrative bodies, local organizations, farmers and consumers. 'Street-level implementation' (Cini 2009) is usually thought of as a linear 'top-down' process, applying previously determined regulations and thereby achieving politically desired goals. According to this conventional perspective in research, policy instruments such as the voluntary quality label PDO are considered to be politically neutral devices that have benign effects and are couched in terms of 'soft' law. Conversely, critical perspectives in political science have pointed out that such policy instruments often produce problematic effects. These may even contradict their more overtly stated goals (Bruno, Jacquot and Mandin 2006; Lascoumes and Le Gales 2007). More recent approaches in political science emphasize that policies do not become operational in isolation, but are part of a complex field of interacting strategies and implementations. Initially proposed by social anthropologists such as Cris Shore and Susan Wright, the Anthropology of Policy takes issue with conventional accounts of policy-making and policy-implementation that frame policies as rationally devised instruments which are put to work to achieve a politically desired outcome (Shore and Wright 1997; Shore, Wright and Pèro 2011). Researchers draw attention to the fact that while

> policies invariably attempt to capture [reality] in a singular and linear perspective, [this reality] is inherently non-coherent since it is made up of multiple layers that are frequently contradictory. [...] This is important if we

aim at understanding why politics and policies rarely succeed in engineering society. Unexpected events always take place.
(Mellaard and van Meijl 2016: 5)

More recent developments in anthropology engage with assemblage theory to deepen and further develop the notion that policies are neither linear nor one-dimensional but rather should be considered unpredictable and prone to generating multiple effects.

When globalization brought forms of practice and categories of social actors into the purview of anthropology that could no longer be easily conceptualized using conventional notions of 'society' and 'culture', anthropologists started casting about for new theoretical frameworks. The assemblage concept originated with French philosophers Deleuze and Guattari (DeLanda 2006) and was adopted in anthropology initially by Paul Rabinow, best known for his exegesis of Michel Foucault's work, and by George Marcus, a protagonist of the movement towards new approaches to ethnography (Rabinow 2004; Rabinow and Marcus 2008). Marcus considers assemblage thinking as "a working access to difficult and elusive objects" because it addresses "the problem of the heterogeneous within the ephemeral" (Marcus and Saka 2006: 102). Assemblage theory became hugely popular in anthropology and related disciplines in the aftermath of the publication of an anthology titled *Global Assemblages: Technology, Politics, and Ethics as Anthropological Problems* (2005), edited by Aihwa Ong and Stephen J. Collier. They argued that an "assemblage is the product of multiple determinations that are not reducible to a single logic. An assemblage is emergent. It does not always involve new forms, but forms that are shifting, in formation, or at stake" (Ong and Collier 2005: 12). This heralded a growing interest in global processes and a heightened awareness among anthropologists of the impact of scientific expertise, technologies, and policies on modern social practices and subject formations. Assemblage theory became influential in anthropology in many research areas, such as urban studies, biomedical anthropology and infrastructure research. In recent years, an increasingly intense dialogue between policy studies, anthropology and Science and Technology Studies also sharpened the attentiveness of researchers towards the interplay of human and nonhuman agency. This is conceptualized in a particularly intriguing manner in the 'policy assemblage' approach that combines critical perspectives on public policy in political science with the anthropological take on assemblage theory (Mellaard and van Meijl 2016; Adam and Vonderau 2014; Ureta 2014). According to these authors, a policy assemblage emerges when different categories of: social actors, technical devices, legal regulations, measurements, calculations and standards as well as substances, organisms and physical matter are brought into interaction within the framework of a policy.

Adulterated tradition

The ongoing and contested endeavours to attain a geo-label for halloumi cheese – that the Ministry of Agriculture, Rural Development, and Environment of the

Republic of Cyprus has been launching for some years – offers an exemplary case that allows us to scrutinize "the very processes through which policy is done, with all its complexity, ambiguity and contradictions" (Ureta 2014: 1). An application for a PDO to be awarded to halloumi cheese produced on the island of Cyprus is currently pending at the European Commission in Brussels. Halloumi is produced by curdling milk with rennet (Papademas and Robinson 2007). After pressing to remove the whey, it is re-cooked, which gives it its special organoleptic quality: halloumi is the cheese 'that grills but does not melt'. Its ingredients are fresh sheep or goat milk (or a mixture thereof), rennet, mint leaves and salt. An endemic lactobacillus has been discovered that makes the cheese unique to Cyprus (Lawson et al. 2001).

Up until the 1960s, the production of halloumi was a gendered activity that formed part of the subsistence economy of agrarian households. Groups of women would pool the milk that they had from the few goats and sheep that each family kept, collectively fill the cheese kettle, and cook halloumi in the cheese kitchen of one of their group. With modernization, growing prosperity and urbanization since the 1970s, the traditional collective cheese-making turned into a more professional and commercialized activity, with family-run operations producing the cheese in an artisanal fashion for regional consumers, supermarkets and restaurants. At the same time, halloumi developed into an important mass market commodity. Consequently, a significant proportion of halloumi cheese production was massively industrialized and transposed into high-tech modern factory settings. EU accession in 2004 and the transposition of tightened food hygiene regulations contributed to a process of consolidation in cheese production, with many small-scale producers being forced to close down and leave the market, while big dairy corporations increasingly not only dominated the domestic market but generated massive increases in production for export (Welz and Andilios 2004). Industrially produced halloumi from the Republic of Cyprus is now available world-wide, with the EU, the United States, Australia and the Arab world as major markets.

Already, in 2011, an earlier application in Brussels by the Cyprus government for a PDO status for halloumi cheese was rejected. One of the problems with this application (submitted in 2009) was that it appeared to lay claim to halloumi as being uniquely and exclusively Greek Cypriot. Historically, halloumi – called hellim in Turkish – is a traditional element of the habitual diet shared by both the Turkish and Greek populations of the island. The on-going, de-facto partition of the island in the aftermath of the 1974 invasion by the Turkish army – ostensibly to protect the Turkish minority from violence when Greek rightwing extremists overthrew the government and took power – is an enduring political problem that the European Union has not been able to solve. In Brussels, doubts were voiced as to whether it would be wise to certify such a contested product, and support the 'gastronationalism' (DeSoucey 2010) of the Greek Cypriot government. Members of the European Parliament had launched official enquiries at the European Commission implying that a designation of halloumi as an exclusively Greek Cypriot product would unfairly discriminate against Turkish Cypriot producers of the same product and, in a more general vein, contradict the European spirit of integration and inclusiveness.

However, the actual reason as to why the Ministry of Agriculture of the Republic of Cyprus had to abort the process was that the applicant organization – the cheese-makers' association – had cancelled their participation in protest at elements of the application. The association is dominated by a handful of powerful industrialists who between them produce most of the dairy products in the Republic of Cyprus and who have emerged as global players as most of their output is for export.

Traditionally, halloumi is a cheese produced either from a mixture of goat and sheep milk, or – in some regions of Cyprus – from goat's milk exclusively. For the industrial halloumi cheese produced for the global market, however, cow's milk is utilized, due to its much higher available volume and its lower price compared with sheep or goat milk. High-yield dairy cows had only been introduced to Cyprus on a large scale in the 1960s, so the claim that halloumi cheese that contains cow's milk may still be called traditional is hotly contested. National legislation that had been in effect since 1985 allowed for up to half of the milk in halloumi to be of bovine origin. This liberal interpretation of the ingredients that go into halloumi cheese evidently was connected to the increasingly high export value of halloumi, which persuaded the government to privilege the industrial rather than artisanal product with its significant admixture of cow's milk. In recent years, the quantity of halloumi production for export has skyrocketed. Industrial cheese-makers' annual revenue from halloumi has risen from about €60 million in 2012 to more than €100 million today.

Consequently, the first application process for a PDO for halloumi cheese foundered because the product specification that was being examined in the DG AGRI (the European Commission's General Directorate for Agriculture and Rural Development), determined that a cheese would need be made of at least 51% sheep and/or goat milk in order to be permitted to carry the name halloumi. This was in line with the above-mentioned domestic legislation already in place. Instead of applying for a PDO label for traditionally produced halloumi cheese made solely of sheep and/or goat milk, which would have left the industrially produced cheese uncertified and not permitted the carry the quality label, the Ministry went out of its way to accommodate the desire of the large corporations to have their entire output of halloumi cheese valorised by the sought-after EU quality label and, consequently, to be able to market it at a higher price. This is an interesting departure from the way the quality label policy has been enacted in many other European countries where it is often intensely local, sometimes almost forgotten food traditions that are only kept up by a handful of small-scale producers that are revitalized by the award of the geo-label. Also, most of the certified products carry names that explicitly refer to their regional origin. It is rare for nationwide products to be recognized as PDOs. Indeed, the officials working on the halloumi dossier in DG AGRI would have welcomed an application from the Cyprus agricultural ministry for a traditional cheese from a delineated local region within Cyprus. Considerable regional differences do exist between varieties of artisanal halloumi cheese within Cyprus, some of them as a consequence of the local vegetation that animals feed on (Osorio, Koidis and Papademas 2015), but the intention of the government of the Republic of Cyprus was to have the entire output of halloumi cheese valorised by the quality label.

The level of admixture of bovine milk permitted in the first application was identical to legislation that had been in place since the 1980s, which had allowed for halloumi to become what I call an 'adulterated' tradition. Yet, the industrialists turned down this option, arguing that even 49% cow's milk was not enough, and they needed a larger percentage. The large-scale producers claimed that the volume of sheep and goats milk produced in Cyprus was far too small to support their cheese production if they were required to keep the bovine ingredient below 50%. Apparently, they also rejected the close monitoring they would be subjected to, in order to safeguard compliance with this requirement. Previously, due to lenient controls, the lawful upper limit appears to have been habitually disregarded by some industrial producers.

A second application – submitted in 2015 – is now under scrutiny at DG AGRI and, in 2017, had already cleared most of the hurdles towards actual certification. This time around, it is also inclusive of the hellim cheese produced by Turkish Cypriots in the north of the island – provided that their production facilities fulfil European Union food safety requirements and are controlled by an internationally accredited certification body. The second application's product specification determines up to almost 50% bovine milk, again, as the acceptable level. As this is identical with the first application's text, why did the industrialists refrain from turning it down immediately? The reason is that the new application grants them a very generous grace period to phase in new levels. During a transitional phase of ten years, cheese that contains only 20% sheep and goat's milk and 80% cow's milk will be certified with the quality label and be permitted to carry the name halloumi. This compromise was the result of difficult negotiations – both in Nicosia and in Brussels. However, the industrialists are still not content! They protest that the available volume of local goat and sheep milk is far too low for them even to comply with the initially permitted 20% threshold, if they want to maintain their present high output of cheese, and perhaps increase it further.

Unlimited growth?

There is "[N]ot enough sheep and goats milk to match increasing exports of halloumi!" (Kades 2016) complained the head of the cheese-makers' association to the press last year. In order to secure the cheese-makers' support of the PDO application, the European Commission subsequently promised the Republic of Cyprus additional funds in order to greatly increase the available volume of sheep and goat milk in Cyprus. In October 2016, the Minister for Agriculture announced "that the government secured thirty-five million Euros for the implementation of policies that will help increase the production of sheep and goats milk to be able to meet the industry demands for the production of halloumi" (Andreou 2016). In 2017, the government has started to subsidize livestock farmers, in order to make them able to provide the greatly increased quantities of sheep and goats milk needed to replace bovine milk in the industrial production of halloumi cheese. EU funding and subsidies passed out by the agricultural ministry are projected to increase the number of sheep and goats by 80,000 over the next five years – growing from 370,000 to 450,000. Also, the Cyprus Agricultural Research Institute is engaged in increasing the milking productivity of goats and sheep. Experts in the field are convinced of the potential success of this option, resulting in higher volumes and higher quality of milk without having to increase the number of animals to such a high degree as envisioned.[3] Meanwhile, a new batch of subsidies directed to livestock farmers will give them €26 per head of animal if they use them for milk production and sell the milk to the dairy industry.

The increase in goats and sheep can be expected to place the environment, and especially the water supply, under added pressure. Cyprus, an island in the Eastern Mediterranean, already "faces major challenges regarding the environment, biodiversity, resource efficiency and climate change. Low rainfall, high temperatures and increased periods of drought are putting extreme pressure on scarce natural resources".[4]

The recent measures, aimed at enabling industrial producers to comply with the anticipated implementation of a more rigid definition of what goes into halloumi cheese, conflict with numerous agri-environmental policy goals. These include the EUs 2014–2020 Common Agricultural Policy for Cyprus and, in particular, the Republic of Cyprus's current EU-funded Rural Development Program (RDP). These policies place a strong emphasis on protecting the natural environment and biodiversity as well as promoting the sustainable management of natural resources and adaptation to climate change. Within the framework of the CAP's present funding period, 30% of direct payments to farmers in Cyprus are linked to what the EU calls environmentally friendly farming practices, such as crop diversification, maintaining permanent grassland and conserving 5% of areas of ecological interest. A budget of €132 million (of the close to €500 million to be spent over this seven-year period) is allocated within the Rural Development Program (RDP), which is designed to both create jobs in rural areas of Cyprus, "while protecting the natural environment and biodiversity (and) promoting the sustainable management of natural resources and adaptation to climate change".[5]

The increase in goats and sheep necessary to increase cheese production will further deplete water resources. Goats also pose severe threats to soil by exacerbating erosion. However, due to generous state funding for the construction of stables and fenced-in holding pens, year-round open range grazing is generally no longer the norm in Cyprus, and is only still to be found in some marginal areas in the mountains. So probably the worst effects of an increased goat population can be averted. But even now, evidence of desertification and increased incidence of dust storms and of brush fires can be observed in many areas.

According to the factsheet for the 2014–2020 Rural Development Program, "water supply and diffuse water and soil pollution from agriculture are major concerns [...]. The majority of underground aquifers are in less than good status. Irrigation water accounts for 70% of total water consumption" suggesting that this ought to be reduced rather than increased.

In public discourse in the Republic of Cyprus and particularly among the milk producers lobby, the sustainability of increasing the goat and sheep population is mainly problematized in terms of this need for more water for livestock farmers because of prevalent drought conditions and dependence on irrigation. Already now, a sizeable amount of the water supply of the island is produced by desalinization plants which rely on fossil fuel, with all the attendant problems. Politicians are now calling for additional subsidies for livestock farmers, to make up for the anticipated rise in water costs. The underlying premise of an 'economy of scale' and the notion of 'unlimited growth' are not questioned. Rather, the expectation is that the increase in halloumi exports, which has been rising by 10 to 15% annually in the past few years, should continue for years to come.

Discussion: a heterogeneous policy assemblage

The food quality policy's implementation in Cyprus will have consequences that are at odds with the sustainable development of agricultural production and may specifically threaten to exacerbate the consequences of climate change – namely desertification and lack of water. The EU's food quality strategy, however, is generally intended to be environmentally friendly and, in many cases throughout Europe, the geo-label protection is deployed to revive and strengthen ecologically sound and sustainable forms of agriculture and food production. Is the clash between the implementation of the EU's geo-label policy and agri-environmental policy goals accidental? Is it an anomaly that runs counter to the spirit of the European Union's geo-label programme? Or is it actually a strategic mix of policies which only serves to further advance the neoliberalisation of the Cypriot economy?

Sociologist Zsuzsa Gille (2016) has conducted extensive research into comparable cases in Hungary – a country which, like the Republic of Cyprus, acceded to the European Union in 2004. She argues that the European Union deploys a 'calculated mosaic' of policies that, at first sight, appear contradictory. In her study of the production and transnational marketing of paprika, she points out that protectionist policies – such as geo-labels which add value to authentic Hungarian paprika products – coexist with policies of deregulation that allow for a much looser definition of 'Hungarian paprika', so that producers are able to utilize admixtures of considerably cheaper ingredients imported from other countries in order to compete on transnational markets. Gille contends that the process of 'Euro-globalization' combines the 'protectionist capitalism' of geo-labelling with deregulated 'flexible production' (Gille 2009) in such a way as to hasten along the neoliberalisation of the agricultural sector in Hungary.

This juxtaposition of goals serves my wider argument that the complex issues and relationships that make up the halloumi case are best understood as a 'policy assemblage' as defined above – a heterogeneous network of multiple co-existing practices and materials (Mellaard and van Meijl 2016). This framing allows us to look at the constitutive effects (Dahler-Larsen 2014) of this heterogeneity. Two aspects of policy assemblages – their non-linearity and their multiplicity – deserve a closer look.

Non-linearity refers to the unexpected outcomes of policy implementations resulting from the interaction of human and non-human actors. Agricultural research in Cyprus today aims at making the existing goat and sheep population more productive in terms of milk production. The industrialists criticized existing practices, arguing that while "exports are increasing year after year to the tune of 15 to 20 per cent, bringing a revenue of €103 million in 2015, production of sheep and goats milk is falling" (Kades 2016). In my research, I found that this is indeed true. The reason is that it has become increasingly difficult for dairy farmers to rear and keep sheep and goats for milk. Milk production has become much more expensive for them due to the cost of an increase of concentrated feeds and due to the operational costs, maintenance and equipment for milking and milk storage, which has become very strictly regulated under phytosanitary regulations introduced by the European Union. It is more profitable these days to sell kids and lambs for slaughter than to keep and rear the female animals for their milk. It is surmised by the Ministry of Agriculture that if there is no intervention the number of milking animals will further decline.[6]

So, there is a very real decrease in available goat and sheep milk as a non-linear and certainly unintended effect of EU regulation. Such unexpected policy outcomes are due to the fact that policy implementation is never just "the application of plans well defined from the onset [but] the ever-shifting interlocking of multiple entities, both human and non-human" (Ureta 2014: 13). Indeed, the policy assemblage under discussion includes: goats and sheep, brush-covered hills, the life worlds of livestock farmers in remote villages, their culturally learned understandings of economic advantages and financial gains, but also expert knowledge about animal health, genetics and reproduction, as well as the consumption choices of middle class urbanites in Cyprus whose hunger for meat has greatly increased in recent decades.

In addition, policies always "exist in multiple versions as the same time" (Ureta 2014: 13). Clearly, the implementation of the EU geo-label policy in different European countries is framed by issues that have no, or only tenuous, linkage to agriculture and sustainability, resulting in a multiplicity of policy assemblages. In the Republic of Cyprus, the economic importance of cheese exports increased dramatically in recent years, as the country attempted to recover from the debt crisis of 2012/2013 along with the austerity measures imposed by the Troika. For this reason, also, the government subscribes to an ideology of economic growth, disregarding sustainability criteria. In turn, the claim by cheese producers that the employment that they provide contributes significantly to the recovery of the economy gives them a lever to put pressure on political actors. In addition to these economic issues, the striving for a geo-label acquired an added political salience which has to do with the European Union's hope for resolving the Cyprus conflict and the long-term division of the island.

The European Commission appeared especially enthusiastic on having the halloumi deal approved this time around, after the first application for the geo-label had failed in 2011. When the European Commission received the second application in 2014, "for the registration of the names Halloumi/Hellim as a Protected Designation of Origin", it welcomed the fact that "the application covers producers from the whole island and foresees the protection of the name in the two languages, Greek and Turkish".[7] During his July 2015 visit to the Republic of Cyprus, the European Commission's president Jean Claude Juncker reportedly emphasized the importance of the understanding reached in the halloumi issue between President Anastasiades of the Republic of Cyprus, and Mr Akinci, the leader of the internationally non-recognized Turkish–Cypriot polity in the north of the island. Juncker called it "highly symbolic" and a demonstration of the "willingness of the two parties to work together and build confidence" in his speech in Nicosia.[8] These sentiments were expressed within a wider context in which the latest attempt at reunifying the island, in negotiations under the auspices of the United Nations, were taking place. Unfortunately, these negotiations failed in 2017, and the Cyprus problem remains an ongoing and important issue for the European Union.

Policies are not simply implemented, but – according to assemblage theory – policy assemblages are enacted in different contexts. This means that "several performances of the same policy coexist in the different locations in which the policy is assembled" (Ureta 2014: 13). The regulatory space of food regimes therefore is highly uneven and cannot be understood as a straightforward transposition of EU and domestic policies.

Conclusion: sustainability and quality labels

Products that are awarded a PDO or PGI label throughout Europe have become focal points of regional development strategies that aim to revive artisanal skills and local knowledges and to re-install environmentally friendly sustainable types of production. In order to maintain and create employment opportunities in disadvantaged rural areas, new economic ventures that combine food processing, gastronomy, agro-tourism and the designation of cultural heritage are favoured by national governments and local political actors alike who compete either for EU funding within the framework of national Rural Development plans required by the Common Agricultural Policy, or for regional development subsidies that come under the umbrella of Structural Funds.

However, ethnologists and anthropologists have been critical of the programme because small-scale artisanal producers find it hard to achieve certification, are faced with added financial burdens and other requirements, such as costly inspections, and have to submit extensive self-documentation. Indeed, one of the consequences of the introduction of the programme has been that those small-scale producers who cannot comply with these complex demands eventually close down and leave the market altogether. Because the product specifications that have to be followed are often rigid, artisanal food is standardized, and this – according to critics – contradicts the inherent variability of vernacular products and practices (Bérard and Marchenay 2007). Another more recent line of criticism highlights the 'propertisation' of cultural commons that occurs when only certified producers will be allowed to market their products. Ultimately, they become sole owners of the intellectual property of how to make a traditional food product, something that before used to be shared by the entire community.[9]

In the case study presented in this chapter, however, another rarely discussed problem comes to the fore. Here, the attempt to add value to a food product by applying for a European quality label combines with powerful business interests to the detriment of resource efficiency and ecological sustainability. The European Union's quality label strategy requires production to follow traditional recipes and use regionally produced ingredients. The Republic of Cyprus could have applied for a quality label for cheese made exclusively of sheep and goat milk – or even only goat's milk – designating, for instance, a regional product such as Halloumi Pafitiko, which is a halloumi cheese from the Paphos area, or else a cheese made with milk from free-range grazing animals in highland and mountain areas of Cyprus (Osorio et al. 2015). This would have been in accordance with the general practice of applications for PDO throughout Europe. However, the insistence on having the entire output of industrial production valorised by a PDO meant that the applicants had to give the product only a semblance of traditionality. Reducing the volume of production, in order to adapt it to the available supply of goat and sheep milk, was not considered as an option. Instead, industrial producers demanded a massive increase of goat's and sheep milk production in order to maintain their trajectory of stupendous growth rates in recent years. This belief in unlimited economic growth is being combined with European Union policies that originally were geared towards sustainable, small-scale artisanal production. This conjuncture of conflicting intentions and measures generates a heterogeneous policy assemblage. Ultimately, the industrial dairy sector and its export markets, domestic consumer preferences, the island's attractiveness to foreign tourists, the landscape and climate of rural Cyprus, its vegetation, soil, and habitat quality, the livelihoods of local farmers, the water supply of an entire country, the microbial processes of cheese-making, food chain technologies and logistics, the genetic make-up of goat and sheep breeds indigenous to the island, will change and interact in ways that are hard to predict. This re-traditionalisation of halloumi will have a number of consequences that cannot be anticipated by any of the policy actors involved, neither in Nicosia nor in Brussels. What is fairly certain, however, is that rural populations and rural ecosystems will be adversely effected.

Notes

1 See the DOOR ('Database Of Origin & Registration') online resource of the European Commission http://ec.europa.eu/agriculture/quality/door/list.html?locale=en.
2 According to Regulation no. 2081/92 of 14 July 1992. See "Agricultural policy and rural development: Protected Designations of Origin and Geographical Indications" at http://ec.europa.eu/agriculture/rur/leader2/rural-en/euro/l1-3-2.htm.
3 The agricultural research units of the government, however, do recognize that it is not useful to only go for an increase of capital intensive livestock production. Experts point out that the traditional extensive forms of animal husbandry were much better adapted to the natural and climatic conditions, i.e. the possibility of using natural vegetation with roughage and silage production of rain-fed crops. Efforts are made to improve the milk yield of existing goat and sheep populations. Breeding, genetic improvement and improving the physiology of reproduction are cited. Local breeds are local fat-tailed sheep, the Cypriot type of Chios sheep, local goats (Machaira and Pissouri breeds) and the Cypriot type of Damascus goat. See Activities of the Livestock Production and Nutrition Section, Department of Agriculture, Ministry of Agriculture. www.moa.gov.cy/moa/da/da.nsf.
4 European Commission: Factsheet on 2014–2020 Rural Development Program for Cyprus, n.y., p. 2 https://ec.europa.eu/agriculture/sites/agriculture/files/rural-development-2014-2020/country-files/cy/factsheet-cyprus_en.pdf.
5 For information on goat and sheep breeding and livestock farmers' economic situation, see also Republic of Cyprus, Ministry of Agriculture Review Voluntary Coupled Support 2017–2020 www.paa.gov.cy/moa/paa/paa.nsf/0/21E16FB36BADFEFDC22580 600041B358/$file/CY_VCS%20review%202017-2020%20-%20Annex.pdf.
6 European Commission: Factsheet on 2014–2020 Rural Development Program for Cyprus, n.y., p. 2 https://ec.europa.eu/agriculture/sites/agriculture/files/rural-development-2014-2020/country-files/cy/factsheet-cyprus_en.pdf.
7 The European Commission: "Cyprus: Halloumi/Hellim cheese set to receive Protected Designation of Origin status" Brussels, 28 July 2015. European Commission – Press release europa.eu/rapid/press-release_IP-15-5448_en.pdf.
8 See Christou 2015. A stumbling block, however, was the fact that Republic of Cyprus does not exercise sovereignty in the areas on the other side of the Green Line. The question of which authority would inspect the production facilities in the North was solved when the European Commission decided to assign the task of quality control to a big transnational company active globally in the business of quality control, which will in the future monitor cheese production both in the government-controlled areas and in the North.
9 For ethnographic studies of PDO implementation that offer critical perspectives on its outcomes, see for instance DeSoucey 2010, Welz 2015, May 2016, Grasseni 2017.

References

Adam, Jens and Asta Vonderau. (eds). 2014. *Formationen des Politischen. Anthropologie politischer Felder*. Bielefeld: Transcript Verlag.

Andreou, Evie. 2016. €53m to Boost Halloumi Production. *The Cyprus Mail* 4 October 2016 http://cyprus-mail.com/2016/10/04/e35m-boost-halloumi-production/.

Bérard, L. and P. Marchenay. 2007. Localized Products in France: Definition, Protection and Value-adding. In: V. Amilien and G. Holt (eds), 'From Local Food to Localised Food', special issue, *Anthropology of Food* S2 (March). http://aof.revues.org/index415.html.

Bruno, Isabelle; Sophie Jacquot and Lou Mandin. 2006. Europeanization through its Instrumentation: Benchmarking, Mainstreaming and Open Method of Coordination…. Toolbox or Pandora's box? *Journal of European Public Policy* 13(4): 519–536.

Christou, Jean. 2015. EC Chief Breaks Deadlock in Halloumi/Hellim PDO Dispute. *The Cyprus Mail* 17 July 2015. http://cyprus-mail.com/2015/07/17/ec-chief-breaks-deadlock-in-halloumihellim-pdo-dispute/.
Cini, Michelle. 2009. Implementation. In: Michelle Cini (ed.), *European Union Politics*. Oxford: Oxford University Press.
Dahler-Larsen, Peter. 2014. Constitutive Effects of Performance Indicators. Getting Beyond Unintended Consequences. *Public Management Review* 16(7): 969–986. DOI: 10.1080/14719037.2013.770058.
DeLanda, Manuel. 2006. *A New Philosophy of Society. Assemblage Theory and Social Complexity*. London/New York Continuum Books.
DeSoucey, M. 2010. Gastronationalism: Food Traditions and Authenticity Politics in the European Union. *American Sociological Review* 75(3): 432–455.
Forney, Jérémie. 2016. Blind Spots in Agri-Environmental Governance: Some Reflections and Suggestions from Switzerland. *Review of Agricultural and Environmental Studies* 97(1): 1–13.
Gille, Zsuzsa. 2009. The Tale of the Toxic Paprika: The Hungarian Taste of Euro-Globalization. In: Melissa L. Caldwell, Elizabeth C. Dunn, and Marion Nestle (eds), *Food and Everyday Life in Postsocialist Eurasia*. Bloomington, IN: Indiana University Press. pp. 97–128.
Gille, Zsuzsa. 2016. *Paprika, Foie Gras, and Red Mud. The Politics of Materiality in the European Union*. Bloomington, IN: Indiana University Press.
Grasseni, Cristina. 2017. *The Heritage Arena. Reinventing Cheese in the Italian Alps*. New York; Oxford: Berghahn Books.
Kades, Andria. 2016. Not Enough Sheep and Goats Milk to Match Increasing Exports of Halloumi. *The Cyprus Mail* 21 April 2016. http://cyprus-mail.com/2016/04/21/not-enough-sheep-and-goats-milk-to-match-increasing-exports/.
Lascoumes, Pierre and Patrick Le Gales. 2007. Introduction. Understanding Public Policy through its Instruments – From the Nature of Instruments to the Sociology of Public Policy Instrumentation. *Governance. An International Journal of Policy, Administration, and Institutions* 20(1): 1–21.
Lawson, Paul, Photis Papademas, C. Wacher, E. Falsen, R. Robinson, and M.D. Collins 2001. Lactobacillus cypricasei sp. nov., Isolated from Halloumi Cheese. *International Journal of Syst. Evol. Microbiology* 2001 Jan.; 51(Pt 1): 45–49.
Marcus, George E. and Erkan Saka. 2006. Assemblage. *Theory, Culture and Society* 23(2–3): 101–109.
May, Sarah. 2016. *Ausgezeichnet! Zur Konstituierung kulturellen Eigentums durch geografische Herkunftsangaben*. Göttingen Studies in Cultural Property – Göttinger Studien zu Cultural Property No. 11. Göttingen: Universitätsverlag.
Mellaard, Arne and Toon van Meijl. 2016. Doing Policy: Enacting a Policy Assemblage about Domestic Violence. *Critital Policy Studies*. Published online: 16 June 2016. http://dx.doi.org/10.1080/19460171.2016.1194766: 1–19.
Ong, Aihwa and Stephen J. Collier (eds) 2005. *Global Assemblages. Technology, Politics, and Ethics as Anthropological Problems*. Malden MA/Oxford UK: Blackwell, pp. 173–119.
Osorio, Maria, Tassos Koidis and Photis Papademas. 2015. Major and Trace Elements in Milk and Halloumi Cheese as Markers for Authentication of Goat Feeding Regimes and Geographical Origin. *International Journal of Dairy Technology* 68(4): 573–581. DOI: 10.1111/1471-0307.12213.
Papademas, Photis and Richard K. Robinson. 2007. Halloumi Cheese: The Product and its Characteristics. *International Journal of Dairy Technology* 51: 98–103.

Rabinow, Paul. 2004. *Anthropologie der Vernunft. Studien zu Wissenschaft und Lebensführung*. Frankfurt a.M.: Suhrkamp.

Rabinow, Paul and Marcus George E. 2008. *Designs for an Anthropology of the Contemporary*. Durham/London: Duke University Press.

Shore, Cris and Susan Wright (eds). 1997. *Anthropology of Policy: Perspectives on Governance and Power*. London and New York: Routledge.

Shore, Cris, Susan Wright and Davide Pèro (eds). 2011. *Policy Worlds: Anthropology and the Analysis of Contemporary Power*. Oxford and New York: Berghahn Books.

Ureta, Sebastian. 2014. Policy Assemblages: Proposing an Alternative Conceptual Framework to Study Public Action. *Policy Studies* 2014. http://dx.doi.org/10.1080/01442872.2013.875150: 1–16.

Welz, Gisela. 2015. *European Products. Making and Unmaking Heritage in Cyprus*. Oxford and New York: Berghahn Books.

Welz, G. and N. Andilios. 2004. Modern Methods for Producing the Traditional: The Case of Making Halloumi Cheese in Cyprus. In: P. Lysaght and Ch. Burckhardt-Seebass (eds), *Changing Tastes: Food Culture and the Processes of Industrialization*. Basel: Schweizerische Gesellschaft für Volkskunde; Dublin: Department of Irish Folklore, University College Dublin, pp. 217–230.

6 From 'disciplinary societies' to 'societies of control'
An historical narrative of agri-environmental governance in Indonesia

Angga Dwiartama

Introduction

The last century has witnessed a major change in the way we practice agrifood relations and governance. Since the dusk of what Friedmann and McMichael (1989) termed the second food regime (c.1970s) and the presumably interwoven Green Revolution all around the world, there has been a pressing need for countries like Indonesia to reimagine their agriculture. Once an engine to achieve food security for the sake of the hundred millions of its population, concurrent streams of environmental repercussions, social unrest and economic crises have shifted agriculture into an entirely new meaning. Government, civil society, and of course academics, are now reassembling what it means to enact and govern agriculture, as well as advocating for new agricultural utopias in the country.

Perhaps like elsewhere in Southeast Asia, the 1998 Asian financial crisis, which in the case of Indonesia was followed by the collapse of the long ruling government under former president Soeharto, has become a turning point for Indonesia's agriculture, a reorganization phase that has yet to meet its finale (a term borrowed from the adaptive cycle of resilience thinking; see Dwiartama, 2014). Indonesia is now at a crossroads, and the many attempts of different actors to restructure the trajectory of Indonesia's agricultural policy are likely to only result in two things: a deadlock at the normative level and, yet, multiple facets of agricultural governance in the praxis (see Dwiartama et al., 2016).

This chapter attempts to document this transition period of Indonesia's agriculture. Inspired by Tania Li's book, *The Will to Improve* (2007a), the narrative of this chapter is centered on governance, none that has not been commonly discussed in a plethora of other papers. There is nothing unique about Indonesia in this sense. However, Li also precedes her book with an article on Deleuzian assemblage – and there she illustrates that the practice of assemblage comes hand in hand with Foucauldian governmentality (Li, 2007b). Whilst Li contextualizes her theoretical framing to a smaller community group that deals with forest management, this chapter attempts, if not ambitiously so, to expand the analysis to a wider point of references: the Indonesian agricultural society.

What then comes as a surprise is perhaps the manner in which seemingly separated modes of governance, each centered on the public, private and civil society sectors, coalesce into an unlikely assemblage driven by one common denominator: a transition from a disciplinary society to a society of control. The latter term is introduced by Gilles Deleuze (1995) in response to Foucault's disciplinary institution. Whereas the agricultural society of today, particularly in countries like Indonesia, is still partly governed by a Foucauldian disciplinary institution through incentives, taxation and formal procedures, there is currently a transition towards a 'free' agricultural society characterized by market signals, inclusiveness, virtual technology and morality. This mode of governance is in reality far from 'free,' but instead relies on dispersed power such that is depicted by the aforementioned Deleuzian 'society of control.' Yet a question remains: if such a society even existed, how can we distinguish it from the Foucauldian disciplinary society? And can there be a multiplicity of governance that shares the characteristics of each? In order to do so, I argue in this chapter that we ought to look into how agrifood governance was and is shaped across the history of modern Indonesia. Only then can we imagine whether such changes really exist.

This chapter will then come in two sections. The first section forms a historical narrative of the formation of agri-environmental governance in Indonesia that is based on a disciplinary society. This has extended over centuries, from the era of precolonial feudalistic societies across the archipelago, to the Dutch colonial despotism and the rise of authoritarian regimes post-independence. The next section discusses the present. Modes of governance emerge beyond capitalism or neoliberalism. Different societies attempt to engage with the Deleuzian society of control in such a way that a seemingly more democratic agricultural society is present, but only to the extent that each devolves control to the individuals.

Assemblage and societies of control: a theoretical context

This chapter aims to understand the assemblage of agri-environmental governance in a seemingly unorthodox way. I begin the theoretical framing with reference to Tania Murray Li (2007a, 2007b) whose works in Indonesia have made her among the prominent scholars in the field of Indonesian studies. Her study on a traditional upland community in *Lore Lindu* National Park in the Sulawesi Island attempted to explore the processes by which governance was enacted, and imposed, by the elites in order to open a way towards development and improvement. Her book, *The Will to Improve* (2007a), in fact stretched further to see how this foundation of governance was constructed during the Dutch colonial era. As per the title of the book, Foucauldian governmentality is seen as "a conduct to conduct" (Li, 2007a: x), a way for the government to improve the wellbeing of its society and the integrity of its ecology through *dispositif*, devices and interventions. These modes of governance, as they turned out, impacted the people that they sought to govern in unprecedented ways.

What is also of interest is the manner in which many different actors – Dutch colonial government, missionaries, Indonesia's public officials, technical experts, international donors, and political activists – have done what they thought were the right schemes to govern the local community. This is what she envisaged as the practices of assemblage (Li, 2007b). Referring to Deleuze and Guatarri's (1988) assemblage thinking, Li theorized an analytical framework to understand how assemblage is practiced amidst a seemingly unmanageable community forest. The moral of the story is by all means assemblage-minded: that the practice of governance is a process comprising heterogeneous elements, both of the actors/agents and the objectives, and that the results of this process are often capricious and ephemeral. Li's article (and book) elegantly juxtaposes the whole theoretical framing of Foucauldian governmentality and Deleuzian assemblage on the same page.

Gilles Deleuze, of course, was a good friend of Michel Foucault, and much of his thinking was influenced by the latter. In his book *Negotiations* (1995; *with a particular note on the last chapter*), Deleuze continued to link his ideas with those of Foucault by examining Foucault's disciplinary societies and reflecting this with the evolution of our current society. He distinguished the disciplinary society from what he termed a society of control, as much as Foucault himself contrasted the disciplinary society with the preceding sovereign society (see Foucault, 1977/1995). The society of sovereign was characterized by the era of colonialism and European imperialism prior to the eighteenth century and involved society's obedience to the law of the king, taxation for the peasants, and rule on death. This type of society was soon replaced by a new type of society that was founded on the growth of the Industrial Revolution. This society was regulated on the basis of the organization of space, time and people's activity by a single authority with the help of complex disciplinary systems. Society, as Foucault argues, transitions from one form to the other, to the point where even the disciplinary society would come to a crisis.

Deleuze elaborated further on what this transition should become. A society of control is something entirely different from its predecessor. In contrast with the disciplinary society that relies on spaces of enclosure (family, school, factory, prison, etc.) and discontinued productions, a society of control puts people under continuous control and surveillance. So, school is replaced by perpetual training and factories by corporations. A society of control is no longer governed by a centralized governing body that acts as a *panopticon*, but through dispersed power in the society as a whole – a condition whereby society becomes an agent in their own right. Furthermore, the type of capitalism that this society embodies is that of a higher-order production: "… it no longer buys raw materials and no longer sells finished products; it buys finished products or assembles them from parts. What it seeks to sell is services, and what it seeks to buy, activities" (Deleuze, 1995: 181).

A matter of concern in this chapter is modes of production, which shows differences between the two societies. The disciplinary society creates *moulds*, a situation where the governments, schools or factories create standards to which everyone is bound so as to be functional in the society. A society of control, on the other hand, creates *modulation*, where the production and reproduction processes do not stop in each institution, but are continuously connected between one module and another. Even an individual is no longer perceived as a single unit, but *dividual* – we become divisible data used for the sake of control (see Carolan, 2016 for a case of precision farming). People and space, in this case, are transient, fluid and always becoming. Control, as Deleuze (1995: 181) puts it, "is short-term and rapidly shifting, but at the same time continuous and unbounded, whereas discipline was long-term, infinite, and discontinuous." This resonates with Deleuze and Guatarri's (1988) idea of *assemblage*, which posits the way in which heterogeneous elements, be they people, institutions, and objectives, are entangled with one another and held together without ceasing to be heterogeneous. Of course, the two tenets come from the same persons. Yet, a point of interest is the slightly nuanced emphases of the two; while assemblage indicates no primacy of action or intention (everything happens due to the potentiality and exterior relationality of each element), a society of control relies on a deliberate, albeit dispersed, power such that is exerted by corporations (which are controlled by stockholders) in the modern capitalist system. This is perhaps one fracture point of the two theoretical framings.

Another fracture point that is critical to this chapter is the chronological sequence of the societal transitions. On one hand, Deleuze and Guatarri's conceptualization of assemblage pivots around transience, fluidity, and non-linearity. There is no predetermined trajectory of how a society develops, in contrast to a more structuralist understanding of our modern history (revisiting, e.g., Friedmann and McMichael, 1989). On the other hand, Deleuze's reading of his twentieth-century men indicates the use of a rather deterministic spectacle. It is as if to say that there is a certain shift from one realm to another, something that creeps into every space of enclosure and from which we cannot escape. Yet, Hardt and Negri (2000) argue that Deleuze's concept of control society is, in fact, negligible. In their argument, the emergence of such a society can best be seen as a generalization rather than an indicative transformation. For instance, Lavin (2009) confirms that the agrifood relations in the twenty-first century is still that of *disciplinary*, albeit on a different subject (consumers rather than producers).

In reference to the three different societies (sovereign, disciplinary and control) that are described sequentially, Indonesia's agricultural (and environmental) governance was arguably founded on the basis of the transition between those different constructions of societies. This can be observed, although vaguely, as corresponding with the history of Indonesia from the era of colonialism to the present day. The argument, thus, would follow: that if the early colonial era resembles a Foucauldian sovereign society and the time between the Industrial Revolution and the New Order Regime of post-colonial Indonesia resembles the disciplinary society, then Indonesia's agriculture is now transitioning to a Deleuzian society of control.

However, the finding shows that a transition is not necessarily discontinuous. Assemblage is being made in the very conceptions of societies that Deleuze posits. What has become of a society that simultaneously disciplines and controls? The framing of 'society of control' is, in this case, useful to the extent that it helps provide an analytical framing for the changing agricultural structure in Indonesia, although I also argue that an assemblage of 'disciplinary-control societies' can mutually exist. Focusing on various political and economic instruments related to Agri-Environmental Governance (AEG), the case will illustrate how an assemblage of heterogeneous elements shapes the way societies were governed during the course of history in Indonesia, and, consequently, how a multiplicity of agricultural society is conceived.

The face(s) of Indonesia's agricultural governance

The seeds of governance in Indonesia: upon a sovereign society

We now move back in time to understand how the assemblage of Indonesia's agriculture took shape centuries ago. Agriculture in Southeast Asia (including Indonesia) first and foremost pivoted around rice (Dwiartama et al., 2016). Studies have shown that the first rice was brought from mainland Asia and cultivated as a dryland crop in the form of swidden agriculture (Christie, 2007). The transition from dryland to wetland rice agriculture occurred between the ninth and tenth centuries in ancient Java. Throughout that period, rice became not only a major subsistence crop in Java, but also a market commodity and the basis of agricultural tax systems in several small kingdoms in the region. A sophisticated irrigation system was later developed that eventually reached its peak in the sixteenth century, before starting to disintegrate by the nineteenth century (Booth, 1985). Around the main cities, rice was also produced commercially and exported to other trade cities in the Indonesian archipelago, such as Malaka, Aceh, Ternate and Tidore (Reid, 1999). This narrative provides a hint to an early form of agricultural governance in pre-colonial Indonesia – one that is based on a society of sovereignty.

In the meantime, the story of spices, another prominent group of commodities from the archipelago, came with a different narrative. Spices had always been important to Europeans since they were introduced by the Ottoman Turks through spice trade. When the holy war inadvertently cut off the supply of spices, the Portuguese sailed a revered voyage in search of the Spice Islands, reaching India, Malaysia and finally the Spice Islands in the Moluccas in 1512 (Ricklefs, 2001; Milton, 1999). The success of the Portuguese was to be followed by the Dutch less than a century later when they arrived in the Moluccas in 1599. They took control of the spice trade in the region and from then on built a solid base for the growth of the *Vereenigde Oost-Indische Compagnie* (VOC) (1602–1800s), the first known multinational corporation to issue stock. Its main objective was to carry out colonial activities in Asia, with quasi-governmental powers such as to wage war, negotiate treaties, coin money and establish colonies. As a result, VOC brought ten-fold of profits from the spice trade, a performance that was never seen before in Europe (Ricklefs, 2001).

What then becomes a matter of concern is the way in which VOC governed its colonies and, consequently, the agricultural systems within them.[1] Dutch colonialism was moving towards a twin purpose: the display of power and sovereignty of the Dutch Empire and profit for the multinational corporation. This was done ultimately through iron-fist policies, heavy taxation systems and the display of brutal force to inflict fear, resembling the typical idea of Foucault's (1977/1995) sovereign society. One notable example is the Banda massacre, during which, in order to gain access to the monopoly of spices, the VOC's Governor-General, Jan Pieterszoon Coen, annihilated thousands of the Bandanese population, displayed executions of their leaders and elites, destroyed most of the well-distributed nutmeg smallholder plantations, and repopulated the islands with slaves to work on the VOC-acquired nutmeg estate (Hanna, 1978; Milton, 1999). A quote from the VOC's Governor-General perhaps sums up the idea:

> ... that trade in India must be conducted and maintained under protection and favor of your own weapons, and that the weapons must be supplied from the profits enjoyed by the trade, so that trade cannot be maintained without war or war without trade.
> (J.P. Coen, VOC's Governor-General, 1614 in Day, 1904: 46)

The disciplinary society of the Dutch East Indies

The cruelty of the Dutch occupation was not without contestation. Following 200 years of local resistance and the Anglo-Dutch war, VOC experienced a long period of mismanagement and native politics that opened ways for corruption, leading to its bankruptcy in 1800. The efficacy of the old sovereign society was challenged. The downfall of VOC was concomitantly signified by a restructuring of Dutch colonialism in Indonesia, or Dutch East Indies as it was known then. Java Island, and particularly Batavia (currently Jakarta), became the centre of calculation, not only because it was the capital and port city, but also because, after the local war, the influence of the Dutch colonial government was shrinking mainly to Java. It was at this moment that the agricultural landscape was altered and the crops were limited to a handful of industrial commodities imported from elsewhere (as driven by the Industrial Revolution in Europe). This restructuring proved to be pivotal to the beginning of a new wave of agricultural governance in the Dutch East Indies.

The basis for this new mode of governance was the Dutch policy on agriculture c.1830, namely the Cultivation System or *culturstelsel* (Ricklefs, 2001; Husken and White, 1989). The Cultivation System was basically an agricultural policy orientated towards the growing markets of industrial Europe. This is a perfect blend of a *sovereign* and *disciplinary* society. For the sake of efficiency, the Dutch implemented a replacement of the taxation system by enforcing villages to allocate 20% of their land to grow commercially tradable crops. They used local elites to collect the harvest from the farmers and implemented a commission system for this. On the other hand, landless farmers were obliged to work in state-owned plantation for a minimum of 66 days per year (Ricklefs, 2001). By means of this policy, the Dutch endeavoured to transform the region's farming system into an industrial estate with commodities opened to the world market; in Java this was done mainly through sugarcane, tobacco and indigo, whilst the outer islands contributed to perennial crops such as cocoa, coffee and tea. In the most arable area of *sawah*, particularly in Central and East Java, the peasants were forced to cultivate sugarcane during the dry period in rotation with rice.

The nineteenth-century Dutch East Indies were pretty much the golden boy of the Industrial Revolution. Dutch Cultivation System was seen as the benchmark for other cultivation systems in occupational colonies all around the world. A 'free' agricultural system, as opposed to the forced labor of slave plantation in the Caribbean (e.g., Mintz, 1986), was proven to be more effective. This benefitted, in my account, from that transition to a disciplinary society where power was no longer subject to the sovereign (ascending individualism), but exerted in hierarchy (descending individualism) (Foucault, 1977/1995). The state gained fame due to its estates and, consequently, increased profits from the export products, particularly from sugarcane (Fryer, 1957; Knight, 1988) and coffee (Money, 1860/2008). A book entitled '*Java; or How to manage a Colony*' (Money, 1860/2008). was published as a lessons-learned in the coffee estate to be copied elsewhere. The Cultivation System, furthermore, displaced subsistent farming with cash crop plantations, while at the same time shifting some of the staple foods, most importantly rice, into commercialization (Booth, 1985).

The disciplinary society of post-colonial Indonesia: a continuation?

A growing environmental and socio-political awareness in European societies during the culmination of colonialism also affected the Dutch East Indies and its agriculture. In response to European societies' protests against the uncivilized treatment of people in the Dutch colony (see e.g., Multatuli's famous book, *Max Havelaar*, 1860/1995), the Netherlands implemented the Dutch Ethical Policy in the early 1900s to boost the welfare of Indonesian people, particularly through education and agricultural infrastructure. During the implementation of this Ethical Policy, irrigated land in Java had expanded incrementally. Meanwhile, an educated middle-class opened up a spirit of nationalism, which ultimately led to the fight for independence (Ricklefs, 2001).

Indonesia claimed its independence in 1945 at the end of the Second World War and from then experienced a series of wars with the Dutch until the Netherlands finally acknowledged Indonesian sovereignty in 1949. But after that, the post-independence era was characterized by considerable political turmoil and an inflation crisis in the Indonesian economy. A closer look at what the society had undergone during this era exposes another, if not continued, mode of governance made on the basis of this disciplinary society. For instance, in the 1950s, Soekarno, the first president, made efforts to revitalize the agricultural sector by disciplining farmers in using 'national improved' seeds and artificial fertilizers; a period known as the 'proto-Green Revolution' (Hill, 2000). Fryer (1957) also documents the massive destruction of sugar factories during the war of independence in many regions in Java, a phenomenon typical to mass resistance in a disciplinary society. This is to be followed by another form of capitalism of concentration, as clearly depicted in the acquisition of factories and plantations from the Dutch.

After the fall of Soekarno, a new wave of supports and aid arrived at Indonesia's front gate. The 1965 crisis was neutralized during the coup, after which the new president, Soeharto, opened the country to foreign investment and aid (Sumarto & Suryahadi, 2007). The aid focused more on technical assistance toward the improvement of Indonesia's rice agriculture, in particular, and to some extent that of other plantation industries (sugarcane, coffee, cocoa, rubber, etc.). In the late 1960s, the government, with the help of FAO, restructured its agriculture through three strategies: (1) stabilizing the farm-gate price; (2) introducing High Yielding Varieties (HYVs) and technical assistance to farmers; and (3) giving subsidies for agricultural inputs and credit. The first strategy was carried out by Bulog (*Badan Urusan Logistik*, lit. State Food Logistic Agency), a government agency that functioned as a price stabilizer. The latter two strategies were accomplished by programs such as Bimas (*Bimbingan Masal*, lit. mass guidance), Sugarcane Smallholder Intensification Programme (*Tebu Rakyat Intensifikasi*, TRI), and the establishment of rural organizations in the form of KUD (*Koperasi Unit Desa*, lit. rural cooperatives) and BRI (*Bank Rakyat Indonesia*, a bank for small farmers in rural areas).

These devices, or *dispositif*, were there to guide Indonesia towards a new agricultural utopia built upon the spirit of the Green Revolution. It brought a positive result, whereby from 1970 to the 1980s, production for almost all main agricultural commodities soared and Indonesia was proudly labeled self-sufficient. However, as Li (2007a) also documented in forest conservation, this *will to improve* did not necessarily align with the will of local people. Many peasants were forced to comply with certain SOPs, grow particular HYVs, and organize in a particular government-driven farmers' union. Dwiartama (2014) recorded how an older farmer reminisced about the act of violence of officials, backed by the military, to ensure that no local varieties of rice were grown in strategic agricultural areas, sometimes to the extent that a whole paddy field was burnt to the ground. The disciplinary society reveals its true face, all under the shadow of improvement. As the agricultural society and ecology were pushed to the limit, it was a matter of time before the whole assemblage deteriorated once again.

Agri-environmental governance in a society of control

Public governance: the discourse

During the mid-1990s, Indonesia was starting to see declining vitality in the agricultural sector as an amalgamation of environmental problems arose (pest outbreaks, soil erosion, severe ENSO-related drought) simultaneously with the removal of agricultural subsidies (Gerard et al., 2001). Economic growth began to stagnate and Indonesia's resources began to deplete. The situation was exacerbated by the Asian Financial Crisis in 1997. Following this crisis, Indonesia, which was financially exhausted at that time, experienced a dramatic depreciation of its currency and a sudden collapse of its import-based manufactures (Gerard et al., 2001). The year 1998 was characterized by political turmoil, particularly by the fall of Soeharto and massive riots, forcing a fundamental reform, *Reformasi*, throughout the government's policies and structures. The economic crisis faced by Indonesia was relieved by IMF's financial assistance; but it came at a large cost – Indonesia was forced to rescind all tariff and non-tariff barriers, as well as direct subsidies of its agricultural commodities as a form of loan requirement from the international body.

The Asian financial crisis and its supplementary effects set course for a new face of Indonesian agri-environmental governance. Two changes were definitely pivotal. One was the democratization euphoria after the fall of an authoritarian regime, which dispersed powers to a wider range of actors. The government had lost its grip on farmers and agriculture, and so was required to devise new *dispositif* to satisfy the audience. Two was a stronger drive towards environmental sustainability to compensate for the degradation of its ecology. A growing awareness among the Indonesian middle class, as well as international consumers, with regards to healthier produce pushed the government to decree regulations that may reduce the amount of pressure on the environment. It is apparent that the new mode of governance was by no means a single authority of public officials. In some instances, the government had to juggle between an individual's right towards plant varieties (Act No. 29/2000 on PVP) and the ratification of Convention on Biological Diversity that protects the right of communities to biodiversity (Act No. 11/2013 on fair access to local genetic diversity); or between securing the use of chemical fertilizer (Government Regulation No. 8/2001), organic practices (Regulation of the Minister of Agriculture No. 28/2009), and Genetically Modified Organisms (Government Regulation No. 21/2005); or between a large-scale Food Estate (Presidential Instruction No. 5/2008 on economic focus) and nurturing groups of small-scale farmers (Decree of the Minister of Agriculture No. 273/2007). The apparatuses that were devised serve for the benefit of different, sometimes opposing, interest groups – be they seed companies, corporations, foreign investors, organic groups, peasants, indigenous communities, or consumers.

Deleuze (1995: 178) argues that despite the call for reforms in every enclosure, disciplinary institutions are in a terminal decline, waiting to be replaced by new forces knocking at the door. This was what happened during the *reformasi* era. Counterintuitive to what many Indonesians expected from the newly reformed government, there was a diminishing power of the state and a stronger one in private sectors and civil society. Another snapshot from Dwiartama's (2014) study shows how the role of agriculture extension officers was currently played by *formulator*, i.e., salespersons for industrial pesticides companies (reflecting the prediction of Deleuze whereby sales/marketing becomes the 'soul' of the new capitalism). There is a distrust among farmers towards public officials. Government no longer has the authority over farmers, particularly with the Act No. 12/1992 on Plant Production System (that took effect years after) allowing farmers to grow any commodity they wanted, in contrast to the compulsory practice of farming decades ago.

In response to the emerging society of control, public governance is now undergoing a moment of reassembling – re-devising ways of extending its power over society. Government becomes one of many other corporations, which act not through disciplines, but through continuous control and surveillance. One *dispositif* is the procurement and installment of a spatially based agricultural information system that monitors, records and overlays real-time farm data across all strategic agricultural regions. This set of data is then delivered to the public via the Ministry of Agriculture's website. *Everyone* is now able to monitor everyone else's agricultural landscape, understanding the changes in the environmental parameters to ensure the best time/way to plant – or at least that is the idea. What follows is a redefinition of a single unit of farm. A farm, just like a person in Deleuze's perspective, has become a *dividual*. Data on soil pH, ambience temperature, or rainfall is separated from the integrity of a farm and aggregated with data from elsewhere to produce trends (Carolan, 2016). The same might hold true for the *dividual* farmer, although it is not the government that plays this part, as I will show in the next subsection.

Another *dispositif* is a farmer certification process, i.e. an apparatus to standardize farmers' capacity and technical skills in farming in such a way that agri-environmental performance in every place will be at its most efficient. This is conducted under the Decree of the Ministry of Agriculture No. 120/2014. Farmers who are willing to be certified will benefit from access to government subsidies and incentives. In a way, the scheme resembles the idea of *moulding* farmers, a very typical trait of a disciplinary society. However, the manner in which this is done is quite the opposite. First, by participating in a certification scheme, farmers become entangled in a continuous process of modulation, through perpetual training rather than a discontinuous institution. To be certified, farmers need to participate in a program called *Sekolah Lapangan Petani* (field school for farmers). This is different from a formal school in the sense that it is a training process in specific aspects of farming that farmers can join through modules. Second, in providing certification for the farmers' profession, the government works together with, thus distributes the power of control to, a third-party certification body. It is not the government that fully exerts power. Farmer certification is particularly an extension of government's ratification of Good Agricultural Practice (GAP; No. 48/2013) as adopted from European Retailers' standards (see Campbell, 2005). It is corporations, in the hand of stockholders, all along that have the power of control. This is the basic premise of a Deleuzian society of control in the new age of capitalism.

Private vs. civil society governance

As said, the private sector plays an important role in the making of twenty-first-century agri-environmental governance in Indonesia. But what is this abstraction of 'private sectors'? Deleuze blames corporations, an abstract entity that exerts control, something that is "... short-term and rapidly shifting, but at the same time continuous and unbounded" (Deleuze, 1995: 181). In the case of Indonesia, control and surveillance can be exerted by a small start-up company in agriculture that collects personal data through networks of farmers and/or consumers, and uses this set of data to predict the behaviors of the masses – dissecting a *dividual* farmer. It can also be in the form of a consortium of large corporations that jointly extend their influence from one end (farmers) to another (consumers). The Roundtable on Sustainable Palm Oil (RSPO) is among the examples. It works using *dispositif* such as certification, branding and modulations to create coordination in the line of meta-production. Control is also distributed across the modulation, a representation of a post-Fordist industry where labor is not concentrated in one enclosure. In Indonesia, the *hilirisasi* policy (derived from resourced-based industrialization), where farm products are processed along the value chain, is best practiced by the private sector in a regional or global production network. As coordination is the key, farm machineries have now been replaced by virtual technology on the basis of computational algorithms.

Civil society also plays a part in this society of control, sometimes to the extent that it is indistinguishable from the so-called private sector. Alternative food networks and civil society in Indonesia are beginning to utilize the same *dispositif* as larger corporations, for examples certification, *dividual* data, network and virtual technology; using the same weapons to defeat the enemy (Dwiartama, in press). In one research site, I encountered a network that is now developing an alternative organic certification scheme for local farmers, in response to a controlling, sometimes exclusive, private certification system (due to the high cost and strict standards). The alternative food network also makes good use of the data shared by its willing members (location, age, products, production capacity, etc.) to control and monitor the performance of each and every one of them, for the sake of the satisfaction of the members and integrity of the network. This is done using smartphone applications and social media. Social media is a particularly effective apparatus to instill values to the network members. All members are now able to control and monitor everyone – reminding people to stay within the organic principles or excluding those who do not comply with the values. These attempts are in fact, from a Deleuzian perspective, the way a society of control works. It also aligns with Lavin's (2009) interpretation of Foucauldian disciplinary society that now targets an entirely different group of people: the consumers.

Private-driven agri-environmental governance in Indonesia, and probably elsewhere, is the perfect embodiment of an assemblage. Even the term 'private sector' is purely an assemblage of heterogeneous elements that might not hold together if not without a continuous negotiation between the entities. If we are to meld Deleuze's idea of 'society of control' and Deleuze–Guatarrian assemblage, then the post-reform era in Indonesia and the global neoliberal regime utterly exemplifies that the two are inseparable; a society of control is one that is built upon assemblage, ephemeral and rapidly shifting, but fluid and unbounded. Unlike the government that has a precise boundary, one cannot say for certain how a corporate entity looks. Conglomeration, partnership, union, acquisition, liquidation become the inherent characteristics of the global assemblage. Power is neither centralized nor dispersed; it is relational (Allen, 2004), and is used by societies to continuously control and discipline, produce and consume, mould and modulate.

Reflections

There are at least four wrap-up points that this chapter wants to highlight. First, disciplinary-control provides an alternative framing to the classic colonial-postcolonial world. The Dutch East Indies and post-independence Indonesia had a common mode of governance, both of which were based on a disciplinary society that was formed by hierarchy, concentrated productions, spaces of enclosure and moulds. Government acted as the panopticon, disciplining farmers through the hierarchy of extension officers, and implementing precepts vigorously. Farmers were merely producers of energy, as their ingenuity was suppressed by the "factory owners," allowing them to always start from zero in each of their enclosures. This in turn was replaced by a society of control that relies on dispersed mechanisms of surveillance, virtual technology and modular production, dividing people and farm into *dividuals*.

Second, revisiting the framework, there is perhaps no clear distinction either between sovereign, disciplinary and control societies. In every moment of Indonesia's history, we can witness governments being shadowed by corporations (VOC is a perfect example), discipline accompanies control, and an exercise of power used to both inflict fear and correct convicts. As Lavin (2009) argues, what changes perhaps is not the mode of governance itself, but the subject to which governance is enacted. It then appears as a multiplicity of agri-environmental governance, dovetailed with each other.

Third, understanding the framing through the perspective of assemblage helps to clarify how a society can both discipline and control. The last section of this chapter asserts the lucidity of assemblage within the society of control. Yet, even the disciplinary society was made of the same relationality; one shaped by actors who were separated across the hemisphere. There is no stability in the process, only 400 years or so of meta-stability. Deleuze (1995: 181) argues, of course, that a disciplinary society is "long term, infinite and discontinuous." Nevertheless, this long stability has never been the sole exertion of either the Dutch or the Indonesian government. In fact, the sovereign-disciplinary-control transition was arguably the result of ongoing contestation between various heterogeneous elements, each attempts to territorialize the agrifood landscape.

Lastly, what is the point of understanding agri-environmental governance through the perspective of a Deleuzian society of control and assemblage? In a way, it is about what one can learn from a shift in the current social relations and about preparing oneself from the inevitability that is creeping closely to every aspect of our life. It is not to say that a new system is better than the old one, but to understand how each has its own way of nurturing and contesting power – and how we (government, private sector, community, farmers or academics) should adapt and respond accordingly.

Note

1 This is not to say that there was no form of governance prior to VOC. Records of feudalistic agricultural systems during the pre-colonial Indonesia, as mentioned in the preceding text, were evidence that such a concept did exist. It is that of limitations of the paper's interest that more weight is put on governance during the colonial era onwards.

References

Allen, J. 2004. The whereabouts of power: politics, government and space. *Geografiska Annaler: Series B, Human Geography* 86(1): 19–32.
Booth, A. 1985. Accommodating a growing population in Javanese agriculture. *Bulletin of Indonesian Economic Studies* 21(2): 115–145.
Campbell, Hugh. 2005. The rise and rise of EurepGAP: European (re)invention of colonial food relations? *International Journal of Sociology of Agriculture & Food* 13: 6–19.
Carolan, Michael. 2016. Publicising food: big data, precision agriculture, and co-experimental techniques of addition. *Sociologia Ruralis* [Online First] doi: 10.1111/soru.12120.
Christie, J.W. 2007. Water and rice in early Java and Bali. In P. Boomgard (Ed.) *A World of Water*. Leiden: KITLV Press.
Day, Clive. 1904. *The Policy and Administration of the Dutch in Java*. London: Macmillan Publishing.
Deleuze, Gilles and Félix Guatarri. 1988. *A Thousand Plateaus: Capitalism and Schizophrenia*. London: Athlone.
Deleuze, Gilles. 1995. Postscript on control societies. In G. Deleuze *Negotiations 1972–1990*. (Translated by Martin Joughin). New York: Columbia University Press.
Dwiartama, Angga. 2014. *Investigating Resilience of Agriculture and Food Systems: Insights from Two Theories and Two Case Studies*. Doctoral dissertation. Dunedin: University of Otago.
Dwiartama, Angga, Chris Rosin and Hugh Campbell. 2016. Understanding agri-food systems as assemblages. In C. Rosin, P. Stock and H. Campbell (Eds.) *Biological Economies: Experimentation and the Politics of Agri-food Frontiers*. Abingdon: Routledge Publishing.
Dwiartama, Angga. in press. From initiative to movement: the growth and evolution of local food networks in Bandung, Indonesia. *Asian Journal of Social Science Studies*.
Foucault, Michel. 1995. *Discipline and Punish: The Birth of the Prison*. (Translated by Alan Sheridan). New York: Vintage Books (Original work published in 1977).
Friedmann, Harriet and Phil McMichael. 1989. Agriculture and the state system: the rise and decline of national agricultures, 1870 to the present. *Sociologia Ruralis* 29: 93–117.

Fryer, D.W. 1957. Recovery of the sugar industry in Indonesia. *Economic Geography* 33(2): 171–181.

Gerard, F., I. Marty and Erwidodo. 2001. The 1998 food crisis: Temporary blip or the end of food security? In F. Gerard and F. Ruf (Eds.) *Agriculture in Crisis: People, Commodities, and Natural Resources in Indonesia, 1996–2000.* CIRAD: Montpellier.

Hanna, W.A. 1978. *Indonesian Banda: Colonialism and its Aftermath in the Nutmeg Islands.* Philadelphia: Institute for the Study of Human Issues.

Hardt, M. and A. Negri. 2000. *Empire.* Cambridge: Harvard University Press.

Hill, Hal. 2000. *The Indonesian Economy.* 2nd edition. Cambridge: Cambridge University Press.

Husken, F., and Ben White. 1989. Java: Social differentiation, food production, and agrarian control. In G. Hart, A. Turton, B. White, B. Fegan and L.T. Gheen (Eds.) *Agrarian Transformations: Local Processes and the State in Southeast Asia.* Berkeley: University of California Press.

Knight, G.R. 1988. Peasant labour and capitalist production in late colonial Indonesia: The 'campaign' at a North Java sugar factory, 1840–70. *Journal of Southeast Asian Studies* 19(02): 245–265.

Lavin, Chad. 2009. Factory farms in a consumer society. *American Studies* 50(1/2): 71–92.

Li, Tania M. 2007a. *The Will to Improve: Governmentality, Development and the Practice of Politics.* Durham: Duke University Press.

Li, Tania M. 2007b. Practices of assemblage and community forest management. *Economy and Society* 36(2): 263–293.

Milton, Giles. 1999. *Nathaniel's Nutmeg.* London: Sceptre.

Mintz, Sydney W. 1986. *Sweetness and Power: The Place of Sugar in Modern History.* London: Penguin Publishing.

Money, J.W.B. 2008. *Java: or How to Manage a Colony.* Reissue Edition. Charleston, SC: BiblioBazaar (Original work published in 1860).

Multatuli. 1995. *Max Havelaar: Or the Coffee Auctions of the Dutch Trading Company.* Reissue Edition. (Translated by Roy Edwards). London: Penguin Classics (Original work published in 1860).

Reid, A. 1999. *Charting the Shape of Modern Southeast Asia,* Chiang Mai: Silkworm Books.

Ricklefs, M.C. 2001. *A History of Modern Indonesia since c.1200.* 3rd edition. Houndsmill: Palgrave Publishing.

Sumarto, S. and A. Suryahadi. 2007. Indonesia. In F. Bresciani and A. Valdes (Eds.) *Beyond Food Production: The Role of Agriculture in Poverty Reduction.* Northampton: FAO.

Part II
The politics of territorialisation

7 Assembling value in carbon forestry

Practices of assemblage, overflows and counter-performativities in Ugandan carbon forestry

Adrian Nel

Introduction

In the contemporary moment, characterised as the Anthropocene, assemblage approaches are increasingly lauded for their capacity to apprehend new social formations arising in relation to the multiple crises of capitalism, climate change and environmental degradation (Larner 2011). The valuation of nature is key to these new formations, with the creation of new 'valued entities', through calculative practices, that can be accounted for, costed and circulated in monetised and financialised forms (such as within a market in which they have a price) in order to attempt to fix certain outcomes (Bracking et al. 2014). Through this intensification of the neoliberalisation of 'nature' (Castree 2008) we have seen the rise of prices for carbon emissions and biodiversity offsets in varied contexts, as well as to land and water. Valuation structures and the new socio-natural assemblages that attend them have, however, been most prominent in regard to forestry, with the emergence of 'global' transnational projects and initiatives such as carbon forestry offsetting and REDD+. These policies aim to tackle global CO_2 emissions by saving forests for the good of the globe through particularly complex, multi-scalar interventions within the global south (Mwangi and Wardell 2012). Such new interventions in agro-ecological governance and the market logics which inform them, are both important to study and difficult to get to grips with. In this light assemblage approaches afford significant potential in examining the valuation of socio-ecological resources in particular localities, and the issues related to them (Fredriksen 2014).

However, applications of assemblage approaches to the forestry context have been somewhat limited and there is significant scope for refinement. While Li has notably applied an assemblage approach to community forestry management (Li 2007), there has only been one similar attempts in regard to carbon forestry (Whitington 2001), where uncertainties in carbon forestry are contextualised in terms of a diverse assemblage of agreements, conventional practices, durable artefacts and rules held among people who operate in very different contexts around the world. In apprehending transnational forestry assemblages Li advances an 'analytic of assemblage' which relates directly to theorisation in a way which does not highlight the resultant formation under examination, but its *making*; the 'hard work' required to draw heterogeneous elements together, forge connections (both spatially and temporally) and sustain them in the face of tensions and fractures (Li 2007, 264). Such accounts have however been criticised for being too formulaic and rigid (Featherstone 2011, 141); good at specifying the forms of what Bennett (2009) calls commodity enchantment, but lacking in specificity in outlining how assemblage 'takes place' through processual relationalities and orders which outcomes cohere in particular places. Thus in order to provide a more robust account others such as Fredriksen (2014) have argued for a focus on processes of territorialisation and deterritorialisation, and the forms of 'overflows' and feedback effects attendant to attempts at valuing nature. This is particularly relevant for the empirical material of this chapter, which considers how carbon forestry coheres in Uganda, as what might be termed a transnational, hierarchical (arborescent) territorialised assemblage, which promotes order and hierarchy and make claims to jurisdiction over social space (Rivkin and Ryan 1998, 378).

In this chapter, then, I utilise an assemblage approach in specifying how carbon forestry, in its manifestation as a contemporary assemblage that is simultaneously local and global (with, for example, multiple local level projects, transnational actors and institutional reconfigurations), is territorialised in a particular place, Uganda. I ultimately work towards the assertion that such an approach is useful in considering new forms of agro-ecological governance, in affording a space for making sense of how and where contestations, violence and resistances in and to forestry interventions occur, and how things might be different.

Towards an assemblage account of carbon forestry

With regard to carbon forestry specifically assemblage is important in circumventing the language of scale, beyond the problematic deployment of the 'local', 'national' and 'global' in carbon forestry, which presents a distraction from grounded everyday particularities and the 'hidden enfolded immensities' or 'terra incognita' of geography (Springer 2014, 1). Utilising concepts of hierarchy and *arborescence*, as well as more horizontal or rhizomatic conceptions of socio–spatial relations between localities, state bodies and multi-lateral institutions such as the UNFCC, assemblage accounts can describe connections with more clarity. They also allow a deeper consideration of given forest territories (such as Central Forest Reserves (CFRs) in Uganda or carbon project boundaries). Instead of viewing them as essentialised, natural entities, an assemblage approach connects how social structures give expression to territory, and how the historical and contemporary transformations affect both landscapes and the geographic imaginaries which relate to them. Assemblage also provides a useful framing to conceptualise how the heterogeneous entities involved in carbon forestry – people, trees, governance systems, forestry officials, methodologies and documentation, forest territories and so forth – interact, and is useful in connecting carbon forestry and market environmentalism to broader social processes in Uganda.

Foremost in specifying an assemblage account of how carbon forestry localises in particular places is the description of its two axes of co-functioning. First are the material and virtual practices, which do the work of drawing assemblages together. These can relate to the implicit or explicit authorising knowledges, principles, sets of practices or lines of organisation which set out what the carbon forestry assemblage should do, as well as a variety of material ensembles of things through which it is articulated, including: multiple interacting actors and landscapes; carbon financing from 'global' capital; trees; carbon contracts; state bureaucrats; maps; scientists; carbon quantifications; and project adjacent communities and both state and non-state actors, among others. Second are the axes of re-territorialisation and deterritorialisation. Territorilisation in this case relating to the establishment and governing of project areas, references areas and jurisdictions, and elements of unscalability, 'overflows' and deterritorialisation. Indeed, carbon forestry can be said to reflect these changes, as the chapter will demonstrate.

An adaptation of Li's description of *practices of assemblage* is useful in exploring the carbon forestry assemblage and the particular neoliberal environmentality that gives impetus to its formation. The first practice is that of 'problematization' – the often implicit framing of specific problems to be addressed (Li 2007). In this context the 'problem' of deforestation and emissions from deforestation and degradation is constructed and framed in such a way that it is subject to technological, political and ethical reflection and market *intervention*. Here practices of knowledge construction make the *governance imperative* of carbon forestry possible, by drawing from interacting appeals to authority based on the terms of the *global public good*, market authority and the *best available science* (Vaccaro, Beltran and Paquet 2013). Second is the practice of *forging alignments*, which entails the *enrolment and aligning* of diverse and varied actors into collaborations and partnerships (Li 2007). Enrolment is self-explanatory, while alignment in this case involves a coming to consensus (a programmatised neoliberal environmentality [Fletcher 2010]), that the assemblage is worth territorialising and defending – a practice that is always challenged and in-the-making, and never a completed accomplishment. The third practice is that of *rendering technical*, which here produces the 'resourcesness' of a carbon offset itself, through a contingent, mediated and contested process of resource making, commodification, and, as Tsing puts it, 'conjuring' (2005). The commodification of carbon is a 'fetishisation'; an abstraction of nature in both image and value so as to be integrated as a good into the market (Carrier and Macleod 2005). This is because carbon is an intangible 'environmental good', not a 'thing' in and of itself set apart from the complex practices which attempt to render it fungible and commensurable. Indeed, some villagers in western Uganda pointed out incredulously that they were 'selling the air'. This production entails the fundamental re-branding of the environment as a pool of resources involving the spectacular conjuring of profits, scale and ostensible benefits (Sullivan 2013; Igoe 2010).

In spite of the veracity of the three practices in this particular assemblage, the neoliberalisation of nature is anything but a smooth process, and is far from complete (Smith 2008). We should expect that, attendant to the process of territorialisation and intervention, there will be inevitable frictions, contestations and tensions. These 'overflows' (Callon 1998) are those things that are framed out of initial value calculations only to force their way back in as 'counter-performativities' unsettling the orders of initial valuation projects, just as contradictory social relations can emerge in relation to the rescaling activities themselves (Vaccaro, Beltran and Paquet 2013). While carbon forestry interventions attempt to rescale forestry governance, there are 'nonscalable' elements of assemblages of value that are made 'scalable' through the obscuring difference and specificity. Such efforts, however, can have unsettling potential (Bracking et al. 2014). Li focuses on the management of such tensions and contradictions (or more accurately overflows), less than their emergence, and argues there are practices that "attempt to present failures as the outcome of rectifiable deficiencies in technique, to smooth out contradictions and then devise compromises" (Li 2007, 277). The function is to keep the assemblage *governmental* as opposed to coercive, while constantly reifying (and at times policing) the line between coercion and governance. This is a dimension that is central to the carbon forestry assemblage, as the tension threatens the assemblage if bare-faced coercion is exposed, indicating communities often do not want or appreciate interventions or reject the problems' framings imposed on them (ibid.). Second, in the face of reality and its contradictions, the practice of *antipolitcs* addresses the ways in which actors in the assemblage attempt to frame 'unruly reality' so as to close down debate about the legitimacy of forest laws, and their unequal implications and distributive effects of projects, and re-pose political questions as matters of technique and science. The final practice that Li (2007, 284) describes is *reassembling*, and this has the closest link to processes of territorialisation and reterritorialisation of physical forestry spaces in this context. While other practices territorialise boundaries within the broader assemblage to exclude disruptive features or elements in favour of a preferred socio-technical-environmental arrangement, geographical territory in this case is implicated in reassembling. As Li states, reassembling occurs as disparate pre-existing elements and entities, such as forest territories or management structures, are drawn together, and taken up or redefined in the new assemblage. This includes the grafting of new elements onto the assemblage, as well as the reworking of existing elements (such as forestry territories) for new purposes. I now turn to how these practices cohere in Uganda.

The assemblage of carbon forestry centred on Uganda

Forests in Uganda have intimate linkages, connections and fractures with each of the other entities in the assemblage. Forests and woodlands cover only about

14% of the land area of Uganda. They are however intimately anthropogenic, where the formalization and gazettement of forest territories was gradual, unsystematic and often violent, with forced re-locations of many, including the Bennet peoples at Mount Elgon and the Batwa in the South Western Bwindi and Mgahinga forests (Tumushabe and Musiime 2006). Forests have also exhibited a long relationship to pre- and post-colonial systems of ecological control and agrarian use, which contributed to an approximate one quarter of Uganda's GDP in 2011 and provided 65% of employment in 2009 (World Bank 2011). They are perceived as cultural sites, 'sacred groves' and houses of ancestral spirits by some, and as an important source of subsistence agriculture through the 'opening of the forest'. Cultures of care and ecological control had evolved around forests, but later became strained due to colonisation, land competition and population pressure. Forests have also been interpreted by the colonial and post-colonial governments as sites of extraction and state formation, and by private interests as sites of accumulation. At the same time the *de jure* protected areas and reserves that eventuated from state enclosure were seen as a source of 'empty land' for increasing numbers of landless people (Baland *et al.* 2007), migrants, and displaced peoples from the civil wars and cross border conflicts, which made the management of protected areas in the region difficult (Nampindo, Phillips and Plumptre 2005). In fact, it is an 'open secret' according to some officials in the National Forestry Authority (NFA) that approximately 90% of Ugandan 'fortresses' (referring to an exclusionary conservation model) protected areas are 'encroached' or contested and the policy model is in many ways sorely embattled (Interviews, Kampala, July 2012). At the same time, however, the hierarchical sets of institutions and management practices that have emerged have a legacy of conflict and are characterised by highly unequal power differentials and overtly top-down structures, such that it remains unclear whether forestry policies and laws are acceptable to the local people or appropriate to the local situation (Turyahabwe and Banana 2008).

In considering carbon forestry as a tool of agro-ecological governance, Karsenty and Ongolo (2012) have suggested the inappropriateness of Reducing the Effects of Deforestation, Degradation (REDD+) projects for 'fragile states'. It has been remarked that – in the context described above – Uganda is a 'funny place to store carbon' (Lang and Byakola 2006). With high levels of poverty, pressure on resources from population growth and political conflict over land (Cavanagh 2013), there have already been tensions and evictions from contested protected areas under the auspices of new carbon forestry project implementation (Grainger and Geary 2011; Nel and Hill 2013; Lyons and Westoby 2014); and, in the face of these complications, the energy and investment required to draw carbon forestry together has been significant. I turn now to the practices that comprise and legitimise this effort, and the overflows and orderings that proceed from it.

Problematisation and authorising knowledges

The expressive, or virtual, components of carbon forestry relate to the geographic imaginary of global emissions that are to be sequestered in local sites for the *global public good*, a process of legitimisation sustained by appeals to scientific and market authority, and a problematisation or framing of deforestation and emissions from deforestation and degradation in such a way that they are subject to a *governance imperative* and technological, political and ethical reflection and market *intervention*. The *idealised–normative carbon form* that we are invited by project proponents to conceptualise does not merely relate to particular molecules released into the atmosphere, but to valuable Tonnes of Carbon Dioxide equivalent units (TCO_2) comprising a cumulative 'global' profile or edifice of emissions, which are disembedded and context independent of their source. Furthermore this framing constructs a space in which we can and normatively *should* 'offset' our emissions and carbon footprints as individuals or corporate persons, to institute flows of carbon finance across a general rural/urban divide from the 'economic core' of the Global North to the 'periphery' of the Global South (Sullivan 2014). This is an appeal to *market authority*, in which expression is given to the desire to politically construct the market as the preferred social institution of resource mobilisation and allocation (Swyngedouw 2005), a process that was already in motion more broadly in Ugandan forestry (Lyons and Westoby 2014).

In this context we are to re-imagine nature through the costs of its degradation (Corbera and Schroeder 2011). After deforestation (estimated at 7.3 million ha per annum) garnered particular focus as a primary climate mitigation vehicle in the IPCC's Fourth Assessment Report (2007), it follows within this environmentality that what we should do is make it make economic sense not to cut down a tree, or to afforest extensively. Payments for Ecosystem Services (PES) interventions have arisen in response to this exigency as schemes that operate on the assumption that market forces can offer an efficient and sustainable means of offering sustainable development objectives (IUCN 2007). These 'efficient' solutions are preferred to state 'command and control measures' of taxation and regulation as contemporary governments try to shield themselves from environmental decisions by voluntarily tying their hands to both placate markets and avoid public pressure. Nonetheless, interventions still necessitate significant institutional restructuring. At the local level appeals to legitimising legislation were required over the rights to carbon that had been established in the form of the National Forestry and Tree Planting Act of 2003 – where the protected Forest Estate is 'held in trust' for the people, and the biomass in 'private forests' is owned by the land title holder. It also required the implementation of programs such as Uganda's Ready for REDD+ process under the auspices of the UN-REDD project, a national REDD steering committee and a USAID funded SCRIPT project, which did the initial work of localising the concept of natural capital in the country by providing economic estimations of value for varied resources (Pomeroy et al. 2002). Other mediators involved in knowledge creation, such as the Forest Trends consultancy (2011), did scoping exercises and feasibility reports geared to ascertain the legal and institutional contexts for project creation, and ran 'sensitisation' workshops and project 'incubator sessions' for information dissemination.

Forging 'stakeholder' alignments

> Nothing in this space is easy; you do not align greedy, hungry and commercial in one neat little overlap quickly. You just do not.
> ((Interview, September 2012, Johannesburg) – Carbon Broker, Johannesburg)

There are a wide variety of actors drawn into the Carbon Forestry 'space' in Uganda, where different state, private sector and NGO actors are being responsibilised as agents of carbon sequestration in respective carbon forestry projects, gaining new normative roles through which they are able to either fund carbon sequestration through offsetting, facilitate reforestation and avoid deforestation through project implementation, or conform to specific neoliberal environmentalities (as, for instance, an individualised, rational homo economicus who is to be paid to conserve their trees) in order to utilise forest resources in desirable ways. Actors range from multi-lateral institutions, donors, national authorities and ministries, private companies, a variety of civil society and NGO groups and 'community' groups – all instrumentally manoeuvring and positioning to capture perceived new flows of carbon finance.

The World Bank, for instance, funds CDM activities through the purchase of credits, while Norway is the major REDD donor, after Norway withdrew funding from Uganda's National Forestry Association subsequent to its corruption scandals. International environmental NGOs (eNGO) enrol in carbon forestry schemes for a variety of reasons. Conservation NGOs such as the Jane Goodall Institute, for instance, aim to secure 'forest corridors' for chimpanzee habitats, whilst the Wildlife Conservation Society (WCS) are more concerned with maintaining tree stocks and local community 'co-benefits'. Such differences can be problematic when organisations combine in a single project with intermittent funding. There are also Voluntary Carbon forestry projects implemented by carbon providers, who broker and sell carbon credits, or projects and NGOs who market for themselves, leveraging funds from Corporate Social Responsibility (CSR)/'greening' flavoured offsets in the Voluntary Carbon Market. These projects, such as Ecotrust's Trees for Global Benefit project, deal with indigenous tree planting on 'private forest lands', in preference to alien, exotic species such as pines and eucalyptus. At the same time carbon forestry incorporates three of the 'big 4', international industrial plantations companies including Green Resources (and its local subsidiaries), Global Woods and New Forests, and the private equity funds and large institutional investors that invest in them. These include Agri–Vie, the International Finance Corporation (IFC) of the World Bank, HSBC and Citibank. The big 4 establish projects on their leased Central

Forest Reserves (which at times conflict directly with local community interests) to justify novel, additional carbon finance revenue streams from the World Bank's Afforestation/Reforestation Clean Development Mechanism (A/R CDM), for exotic pine and eucalyptus plantations on 'degraded forests', supplementing what they describe as narrow profit margins. In this respect, there is a clear bias towards foreign investors, NGOs and carbon developers, partnership linkages to local government, and minimal or at times tacit acknowledgement of local indigenous actors or specific community groups.

Key to forging alignments is the way in which contrasting positions can be reconciled into common objectives. The catch all or 'token object' of sustainable development is agentic itself in forging a common group consensus predicated upon making conservation 'pay'; ostensibly affording compensation for alternative land uses so that communities engaged with the projects will plant trees or avoid cutting them down. Furthermore, because of the discursive formation of a 'triple win' for conservation, development and commercialisation, carbon forestry projects can claim success even if, in meeting one aim, they flaunt the others. The Green Resources Bukaleba plantation project, for instance, makes the quite spectacular assertion that the overall objective of the project is to "contribute to mitigating climate change while meeting the growing demand for quality wood products from well managed plantation forests and contributing to sustainable environmental management, community development and poverty alleviation in Uganda" (Busoga Forestry Company Ltd 2015), while it is demonstrably the case that there have been negative social and environmental impacts of the project (Nel and Hill 2013; Lyons and Westoby 2014).

It is evident then that enrolment and alignment in the assemblage is not unproblematic. The actors also range across a variety of local, global and glocal scales, and axes of rural or urban spatial, ideological, institutional and political difference. They each have their own rhythms, flows of activity, and funding and short staffing cycles, which can become problematic within the long time horizons that carbon forestry projects adopt to be 'cost-effective' in mitigation activities (for instance, short staffing cycles within donors and NGOs leads to a loss of institutional memory and critical local knowledge). This extends to government positions where, as one project proponent put it, "as soon as somebody does something somebody doesn't want them to do, they generally get replaced and that is problematic ... you are permanently starting from scratch" (Nedbank executive, Interview, September 2012, Johannesburg). Some non-project actors actively oppose projects. Local politicians at election time, for instance, have promised communities land within the project areas at the Green Resources Bukaleba project, to the dismay of project implementers. Communities utilising tactics reminiscent of 'weapons of the weak' (Scott 1998) have burnt trees at the Global Woods, FACE Mount Elgon, Green Resources Bukaleba and New Forests projects. As such, alignments and collaborations can be held together across a continuum from tenuous (where projects are contested, tentative, exploratory and opportunistic) to persistent, institutionalised and durable.

Rendering technical – framing the area of intervention and performing carbon sequestration

The practice of rendering technical is the key to the framing of the area of intervention and the performance of carbon sequestration. Understood as made up of *calculative technologies*, carbon forestry interventions operate through a *biopolitical engineering of the social* to produce 'calculating individuals' engaging in 'calculable spaces', working to "represent the unruly array of forces and relations of the 'forest' as a bounded area in which *calculated will* produces beneficial results" (Li 2007, 270). There are mountains of documents (such as the all important Project Design Documents (PDDs)), thousands of hours of consultations, flights to various yearly COP meetings and conferences around the world, reams of media articles, promotional films, and much sweat and effort dedicated to continually producing the figures and discourse that go towards accomplishing this, and keeping carbon forestry in the international and national agenda. The terms utilised in this discourse are themselves complex: Safeguards, Drivers of deforestation and degradation, non-market-based approaches, reference levels, Measuring, reporting and verifying (MRV), results-based finance, non-carbon benefits, etc....

The projects themselves have a specific aesthetic form and must conform to an accepted *methodology*, or set of principles and practices delimiting the relevant prerequisites and procedures for a project to actualise its mitigation activities.[1] The varied technological interventions include (A/R CDM) projects that are generally large industrial scale initiatives, REDD projects that are generally more cognisant of community dynamics, and a range of Voluntary Carbon Market (VCM) projects. An obviously crucial part of this process is the *boundary setting* of projects, and the characterisation of the drivers of deforestation. The quantification of carbon benefits also requires the establishment and solidification of a hypothetical non-reality against which carbon sequestration changes can then be measured; a 'without project' or 'business as usual' scenario which must be projected into the future to substantiate what deforestation *would* have been like without the intervention. This is an integrative socio ecological project that homogenises the landscape under an 'ecosystem services' lens (Robertson 2012), and entails a compartmentalization (or parcelisation) of those various landscapes into fungible tracts capable of incorporation into markets.

The 'simpler' elements of quantification involve the calculations of the prospective amounts of carbon sequestered given the activities undertaken. In contrast to countries such as Tanzania, Uganda does not have nationwide 'baseline data' on deforestation or carbon stocks from which to draw. Projects thus set out to measure and quantify an estimation of the carbon sequestration, reliant on the relative projects' technical capacity and application of *appropriate* scientific knowledge though estimations of carbon storage (in tonnes of CO_2) and Above Ground Biomass (AGB) through sampling, measurements of tree diameters at breast height (DBH) and estimations. However, both calculation and qualitative judgment are co-implicated in evaluative practices such as carbon sequestration. Here the quantities of carbon are irrelevant without the situated agency of human users (who are paid) and stabilised as calculative agents who allow such technologies to 'travel', and be enacted when they are *translated* by intermediaries, or mediators who have the ability to influence and multiply difference (Callon 1986).

Carbon offsets are *performed* through acts of *certification*, *monitoring* and *verification* over time to prove their integrity and sustainability, and to ensure trust and protect revenue. Lansing (2011) details carbon verification as a technology of performance within uneven power relations, where various actors become stabilised as *calculative agents* to simultaneously maintain both the carbon offset as a commodity object and establish a field of action and communication that allows for such an object to be exchanged. There are thus a multitude of paid mediators and boundary actors who are instrumental in allowing carbon practices to travel in Uganda, and are crucial to the coherence of carbon forestry in conjuring 'meaningful and measurable economic benefits' which are also tax deductible for the off-setter. These actors include external consultants, arbiters or 'verifiers' from multinationals like SGS and TUV SUD who are primarily involved in the projects on plantations and central forest reserves, from local NGOs like Nature Harness or eNGOs like the Sierra Club. There are also boundary actors who move across projects, or between national forestry institutions and projects (for instance individuals previously employed by the NFA, who since the reforms and corruption scandals have moved into roles as project staff, or consultants for multilateral agencies such as the World Bank).

Finally, with the hard work of commoditisation performed, the move of marketisation is pursued, through an attendant labour of institution building, to re-embed the now abstracted carbon into an apparatus of surveillance and exchange. It also requires a financing mechanism to monitor, verify and assign monetary value to the newly produced commodity of carbon. To gain legitimacy, projects attempt to comply with independent *standards*, or more exactly 'eco-voluntary certification schemes'.[2] These differ widely; from a focus on community co-benefits, biodiveristy or accounting standards, but they enforce and produce the image of compliance requisite for legitimacy, and they also act as 'premium enhancers' and quality guarantees for 'gourmet offsets'. However, standards have been criticised for their inability to guarantee the types of biodiversity and social benefits projects claim, including in Uganda (Eklof 2012). Furthermore even the most ardent supporters of carbon finance would admit that assigning a 'proper' market value for environmental services constitutes one of the main challenges in the establishment of PES schemes (Mayrand and Paquin 2004), let alone questions of the sustainability of demand for carbon credits. A Nedbank South Africa broker who has been financing carbon forestry projects in eastern and southern Africa describes the capriciousness and spectacular nature of carbon finance starkly:

> None of these projects have inherent value. They are all captive relative to the emotional value they instil.... Three years ago they wanted REDD forestry. Easy. But this year they want REDD+ Rhinos (REDD with biodiversity

value) where you get bang for your buck to save the 368 Rhinos from being killed each year in the most horrible way. So once off sex and violence credits everybody is keen, as it gives marketing spin and hits the right buzzwords ... but buying the forestry credits for 10 years? Ain't gonna happen!

(Interview, September 2012, Johannesburg)

Overflows and counterperformativities: anti-politics and the management of failures and contradictions

The process of *rendering technical* results in certain *critical omissions* and *erasures* (Li 2007), and there are 'overflows' and counter-performativities to the project of valuation of carbon more broadly, some of which have already been suggested. Many problems are to do with the inherent limitations and contradictions of carbon forestry implementation. Not least are the financial constrains where a lack of demand for credits and declining carbon prices are evident, and Ugandan projects are struggling in this context,[3] often failing to live up to the expectations of participants. Second, the types of actors who are vocal in opposition to and advocacy against carbon forestry – using framings of green grabbing and human rights violations – are much less restrained than the 'friendly critics' and academics whom Li (2007) describes in relation to community forest management. Through online platforms, actors are readily able to disseminate their opposition (see reddmonitor.org), and this vast platform greatly increases their capacity to discredit projects on various grounds, even if the projects are well intentioned. As one project actor put it, "with carbon credits you could be the archangel Gabriel and still be accused of all sorts of things" (Director, Uganda Carbon Bureau, Interview June 2012). Apart from more open and vocal critiques, the contributions and concerns of civil society and more moderate eNGOs must be also subsumed into the discourse of REDD and carbon forestry to ensure their concerns are rendered technical, and contained. The establishment of 'safeguards' in line with UNFCCC and World Bank standards, consultation and participation plans, grievance mechanisms, best practice advocacy and attempts at institutional strengthening – all technologies meant to speak for the dis-empowered or allow them a voice (Carothers and Barndt 1999) – has occupied the time of many civil society actors in Uganda to little effect. In practice what this means is that contradictions are managed "less by technique than by compromise in its dual sense – [where actors] make compromises [in joining the carbon forestry debate] and in doing so become implicated, their positions compromised and critiques contained" (Li 2007, 279).

On closer examination, however, there are more subtle omission and erasures, which include the simplification of landscapes and complex processes driving deforestation, in the selective (de-) emphasis of regulatory, disciplining approaches in sovereign control over enforcing the boundaries of the protected areas of the Uganda forest estate, and in the overlaps this has with the new neoliberal environmentality (Fletcher 2010) and its simplistic depiction of exemplary 'communities' who are to receive benefits. Project boundaries are at times superimposed over contested de jure protected area boundaries where land conflicts are in progress, or delineated over what are simplistically described as private/local 'forests'. The Uganda Wildlife Authority (UWA) and NFA approach the issue of the contested territoriality of the forest estate with some trepidation, acknowledging the problem but at the same time attempting to cope with its everyday reality. The tension in keeping the assemblage governmental, as opposed to coercive, however, was laid bare in the eviction of 'encroachers' from the New Forest Companies' plantations and CDM project in Kiboga District of Western Uganda. Backlash against the project took the form of an Oxfam report that gained global attention, and elicited an international outcry following its publication (see Grainger and Geary 2011).

Contestations over protected areas (particularly CFRs), as well as the complexities of land tenure types[4] (when considering projects on so-called private land), are not adequately accounted for, or actively avoided, in carbon forestry project documentation. Similarly, in this spatial homogenisation there is a tendency to characterise and problematise abstract 'drivers of deforestation' as primarily centred around smallholder or encroacher clearances, or for 'timber extraction', and not macro and structural issues which underpin the problems in the forestry sector (see Mwenda and Tumushabe 2011). The result is both a focus of policy and funding in which timber planting is favoured over the planting of indigenous species for woodfuel or biodiversity conservation, and a selective focus on maintaining state forestry territories where they intersect with private sector interests. This often works against the interests of the rural poor through both direct violence and policies which conflate informality with illegality (Cavanagh and Benjaminsen 2015). However, it does dovetail with declining state and donor support for the maintenance of the forest estate in general, and even de-gazettement of protected areas for oil exploration (in the Aalbertine Rift) or for biofuels production (on the Ssese islands in Lake Victoria) (Carmody 2016).

Further tensions are indirectly managed, often through the application of practices of assemblage at work in *managing failure and contradictions* and in *antipolitics* to suppressing potential spaces of contestation and questions of unruly nature, by reframing of political issues and questions as matters of technique (Ferguson 1990) or obfuscating them in 'rituals' that are established and performed to normalise and lend validity to conservation practices, despite their contradictions (Büscher 2013). *Antipolitics* highlights that perceptions of 'self-evident' benefits, relating here to climate mitigation and avoided deforestation, have the ability to obfuscate the systemic political economy and ecology underpinning the 'problems' they delimit (Büscher 2013; Ferguson 1990). For instance, rather than leading to a questioning of the territoriality of the protected forest estate itself, the embattled state and degraded nature of forest territories described above paradoxically re-enforces the *urgent* governance imperative of carbon forestry and renders them ripe for a variety of interventions, including the ostensible reforestation, care, and protection deployed by an apparatus of state, private and non-governmental governance. Similarly, at the project level when tensions and overflows are experienced, the premise of PES is maintained, but on the proviso that further revisions and demanding preconditions need be in place for it to properly function. This only serves to give impetus to further rendering technical, but doing it better next time through more MRV, more effort to obtain Free and Prior Informed Consent, better governance, better market guarantees, which fail to address the core concern with REDD+ as a top-down intervention (Elson 2013). The first carbon forestry project in Uganda provides an example: where the FACE (Forests Absorbing Carbon Emissions) at Mount Elgon experienced tensions with communities and boundary disputes over the area (Lang and Byakola 2006) to such a degree that they resulted in the failure of the project in spectacular fashion (Cavanagh and Benjaminsen 2015). FACE's response to this predictable eventuality (the threat of which was clearly outlined in initial project documentation on the area), was to erase mention of the project on its website and documentation, and to rebrand under the name Face the Future.

Reassembling governance

Thus far I have suggested that the carbon forestry assemblage promotes a shift away from, or a reassembling of, the centralised control of the colonial and postcolonial state over forest territories. This happens through practices of rescaling of governance through processes of upscaling, downscaling and outscaling (privatisation, deregulation and decentralisation), towards what Swyngedouw (2005) calls 'governance-beyond-the-state'. A key part of this is the process of *downscaling* which carbon forestry accomplishes. This is the devolution of governance to 'local' projects such as the carbon forestry initiatives studied here, away from the resource poor, with 'hollowed out' national management bodies and local government actors (Jessop and Kennett 2004) that are nevertheless charged with oversight of non-state actors at the local level. This downscaling of functions does not, however, effectively extend to community groups, where limited decentralisation coupled with continued central control over natural resources, including forestry, undermines popular decision-making, local autonomy and weakens the government's poverty reduction strategies (Muhereza, 2006). Thus downscaling is limited to creating greater local differentiation and the incorporation of new social actors in the governance arena, many of them private and foreign, and this extends a process of the *outscaling* of governance functions.

First, with regard to outscaling there are changes to the way in which conservation is governed, through NGOs and the private sector, in dialogue with the state, even if they do not directly acknowledge their 'non-governmental governance' role. It is evident carbon forestry as a calculative practice re-produces state control, in the face of declining capacity and the increasing activity of non-state actors.[5] For local government actors, carbon forestry projects provide a degree of what they term 'facilitation' – resources and opportunities to achieve parts of their mandate. Such funds can go towards bolstering protected territories and generating resources for its managerial mandate, in a forestry sector that has been afflicted by corruption scandals that precipitated the removal of external donor support. These actors include the quasi-decentralised local/district government officials, District Forest Officers, Community Development Officers and District Environment Officers. Just as NGOs and multi-lateral actors take on governance roles, the state retains some modicum of co-ordination over their activities. While project proponents or private planters have become the 'prime movers' in carbon forestry and in the privatised contemporary arrangement, they come into friction with state actors over the degree of ownership and control between government and the non-governmental developers. What is clear, though, is that the state's role is limited and facilitatory within the emergent mode of neoliberal environmentality. By limited I mean that it is relegated to agenda setting, and facilitatory in that it is involved in the creation of a context within which some objectives such as carbon sequestration and industrial tree planting are possible, while the interests of others are marginalised. The voices of 'encroachers' (residents on Central Forest Reserves, some for over 40 years), for instance, are precluded from having their 'stake' in governance recognised, while more abstractly alternative communal, non-rational land uses, or mixed farming and agroforestry systems in forest territories (a system called *taungya* in Uganda) are regarded as illegitimate. The state still maintains its disciplining and law enforcing role, however, in a faltering attempting to maintain the integrity of the protected forest estate.

Another rescaling that undermines direct state control comes from the upscaling of governance functions to the multi-lateral level and to donors. Here state actors must be conversant in carbon forestry discourse and practice, and it is at this point that donor influence can find purchase. This was particularly evident in the development of the national REDD readiness proposal and its participation strategy in the country.[6] With regard to accountability in carbon forestry, Xavier Mugumya, the former head of the national REDD steering committee utilised a popular saying in Uganda, 'he who pays the piper calls the tune'. Upscaling is accomplished in part through institutional reconfigurations 'at home'. Changes included the implementation of national REDD readiness activities through World Bank funding, and a REDD Readiness Preparation Proposal (RPP) which included alterations to governance institutions, laws and policies to clarify 'carbon rights', and a call for the establishment of National Forestry Monitoring Systems, which in Uganda's case occurred in parallel to the neoliberal reform of the forestry sector, which focused on public-private partnerships in timber planting (Nel 2014). The institutional apparatus that governs carbon forestry now comprises the Ministry of Water and Environment (housing the National REDD steering Committee under the Forest Sector Support Department), the Climate Change Unit (the Designated National Authority for the CDM), and the NFA and UWA. In particular, the UNFCCC now holds a key position of authority in relation to the national environment sector and its relation to the global institution-building around climate change. This becomes visible when exploring the position and limitation of the newly created 'Climate Change Unit' within the Ministry of Water and Environment. To quote the head of the unit;

> People want to see a divide between the international and national processes ... [but] It is important for people to know that it is both.... You need to work with that international framework, that's where the UNFCCC remains to guide all of us to act and move in the same direction; but Uganda as you know also has a national development plan and a special chapter on environment sectors and one of them is climate change subsector where the government sets out objectives to address climate change.
> (Interview, Kampala, October 2012)

Although the CCU, and other nodes such as the national REDD steering committee may be small, they are powerful, have mediator roles in regard to the claims to territory and legitimacy that are brought to bear in the lodging, negotiation and accommodation of different actors in the hierarchical and yet contested assemblage, which, as I have described, perpetuates asymmetries in power relations to the detriment of the rural poor.

Conclusion: territory, flows and overflows

What an assemblage approach offers is a way to characterise the 'knots' and practices that hold the carbon forestry assemblage together, for it is certainly the case that, similar to Li's characterisation of the Community Forestry Management Assemblage, there is much work dedicated to cohering carbon forestry. Within the contemporary carbon forestry assemblage, a focus on practices of assemblage as derived from Li shows that the work of articulating carbon forestry and solidifying neoliberal environmentality is anything but complete; there is still, and always will be 'more work to be done'. While this approach is both intuitive and certainly useful, it begs both adaption to the carbon forestry context and the application of careful scholarship to describe how contradictions are dealt with: how they are either brought under the governmentality of the assemblage or are created as 'overflows' to the valuation of nature itself. The creation of consensus here requires actors to be responsibilised subjects under the terms of the assemblage. In this light we see that an assemblage is less a constituted 'thing', (Featherstone 2011, 141), to which Li's (2007) account is arguably susceptible, than a processual relationality which is useful for explaining the fractured and fissured ways in which entities cohere and operate in particular places.

When adapted and augmented, not least for context specificity, Li's assemblage approach has important insights for further agro-ecological research on territoriality and on flows and overflows. First, it is important to delve deeper into how the assemblage works spatially, in this case in reconfiguring forest territories, for as Massey points out, it is clear that entities articulate in and through space. Following Delaney we know that depending on how "a given *social order* [or as I read it, assemblage] is organised, certain territorial expressions will be possible and more or less serviceable and others will be less likely" (Delaney 2009, 207). We can afford due credit to state managerial attempts at land-use planning and forestry management, and to the aims of carbon forestry proponents, but must appreciate that technical interpretations and normative interventions are often 'utopian fictions' (Vandergeest and Peluso 1995) that cannot fully account for the becoming, or lines of contestation in forestry that make governance so difficult. In Uganda, what carbon forestry and market environmentalism *does* is to extend a shift – in essence a re-territorialisaiton – from territorial based governance to flow based governance around carbon (see Sikor et al. 2013). This itself builds an 'overflow' which indirectly undermines the territorial control of the Ugandan 'forest estate' in places where the assemblage does not attempt to 'make nature pay for itself' (Nel 2015).

Further identifying the overflows, counter-performative entities and non-scalable elements in the Ugandan and other carbon forestry contexts and systems might unveil how this and other assemblages rely on, perpetuate or exacerbate unjust social relations and the destruction of nonhuman nature (Fredriksen 2014, 7). Assemblage presents to us an ecological future that is open not closed, and brings us "face to face not with the essence of things, but with questions of power, ethics and politics" (Braun 2006, 206). In the face of such *immanence* made visible, this approach also opens a space for intervention and a more progressive alignment. We see that, while contemporary formations and the injustices they sustain might appear to be relatively stable, by making visible their *immanence* we can also see how contemporary alignments are always capable of becoming 'other'. As Deleuze (1992) so aptly put it, there is no reason to hope, nor fear, only to look for new weapons; and I would suggest there is further scope for considering how horizontal and rhizomatic forms of organisation between communities of trees and people might be more sustainable and point to a more positive socio-ecological future in Uganda.

Notes

1 Ugandan examples include the CDM approved methodology AR–AM0004 for the CDM projects, the Plan Vivo methodology for Ecotrust, or the Carbon Fix methodology at Kikonda CFR.
2 E.g. The Verified Carbon Standard (VCS) which incorporates the NARCG and Kibale FACE projects, and the Climate, Community and Biodiversity Alliance (CCBA) for the TFGB (and which Green Resources failed to achieve accreditation).
3 The Northern Albertine Rift REDD project is struggling to secure donor funding, and looking to Tullow Oil drilling in western Uganda for finance, the Ecotrust TFGB and FACE Kibale projects are selling few units, while the Green Resources Bukeleba project is struggling to sell their credits in the absence of compliance markets.
4 The four types of tenure include communal land, Mailo land, leasehold and freehold land.
5 While such conduits of state power in the new governance arrangement are 'lodged' in space, they exercise reach to draw in other actors (Allen and Cochrane 2010).

6 While the NFA (and by extension the MWE), was the official Designated National Authority (and could prepare Terms of Reference, sanction payment and receive reports), NORAD as the primary donor exerted significant influence. The donor withheld funding from state institutions for the preparation of the proposal, and NGOs were contracted to accomplish key tasks; the IUCN were contracted to prepare a consultation strategy (with the Bennet and Batwa peoples only – those defined as 'indigenous' in the country) and CARE to prepare a grievance strategy.

References

Allen, John, and Allan Cochrane. 2010. Assemblages of State Power: Topological Shifts in the Organization of Government and Politics. *Antipode*, 42(5): 1071–1089.

Baland, Jean-Marie, Frédéric Gaspart, Jean-Philippe Platteau, and Frank Place. 2007. "The distributive impact of land markets in Uganda". *Economic Development and Cultural Change* 55(2): 283–311.

Bennett, Jane. 2009. *Vibrant matter: A political ecology of things*. Chapel Hill: Duke University Press.

Bracking, Sarah, Dan Brockington, Patrick Bond, Bram Buscher, James Igoe, Sian Sullivan, and Phillip Woodhouse. 2014. *Initial research design: 'Human, non-human and environmental value systems: an impossible frontier?'* Leverhulme Centre for the Study of Value (LCSV) Working Paper Series NO. 1. Available: http://thestudyofvalue.org/wp-content/uploads/2013/11/WP1-Initial-Research-Design-final.pdf.

Braun, Bruce. 2006. "Environmental issues: global natures in the space of assemblage". *Progress in Human Geography* 30(5): 644–654.

Büscher, Bram. 2013. *Transforming the frontier: Peace parks and the politics of neoliberal conservation in southern Africa*. Durham: Duke University Press.

Busoga Forestry Company Ltd. 2015. Green Resources on sustainable development Available: www.youtube.com/watch?v=u0LTIc5kSOg [Accessed 11 December 2017].

Callon, Michel. 1986. "Some elements of a sociology of translation: domestication of the scallops and the fishermen of St Brieuc Bay. Power, action and belief". *A New Sociology of Knowledge* 32: 196–233.

Callon, Michel. 1998. "An essay on framing and overflowing: economic externalities revisited by sociology". *Sociological Review* 46(1): 244–269.

Carothers, Thomas, and William Barndt. 1999. "Civil society". *Foreign Policy* 117: 18–29.

Carmody, Padraig. 2016. "Globalisation, land grabbing and the present day colonial state in Uganda: Ecolonisation and its impacts". *Journal of Environment and Development* 25(1): 100–126.

Carrier, James G., and Donald V. Macleod. 2005. "Bursting the bubble: The sociocultural context of ecotourism". *Journal of the Royal Anthropological Institute* 11(2): 315–334.

Castree, Noel. 2008. "Neoliberalising nature: the logics of deregulation and reregulation". *Environment and Planning A* 40(1): 131.

Cavanagh, Connor. 2013. *Unready for REDD+? Lessons from corruption in Ugandan conservation areas*, Michelsen Institute. Available at: www.u4.no/publications/unready-for-REDD+-lessons-from-corruption-in-ugandan-conservation-areas/ [Accessed 12 June 2013].

Cavanagh, Connor, and Tor Benjaminsen. 2015. "Securitizing REDD? Problematising the emerging illegal timber trade and forest carbon interface in East Africa". *Geoforum*, 60: 72–82.

Corbera, Esteve, and Heike Schroeder. 2011. "Governing and implementing REDD+". *Environmental Science & Policy* 14(2): 89–99.

DeLanda, Manuel. 2006. *A New Philosophy of Society: Assemblage Theory and Social Complexity*. London: Continuum.

Delaney, David. 2009. Territory and territoriality. In *International Encyclopedia of Human Geography* edited by R. Kitchin and N. Thrift, 196–208. Amsterdam: Elsevier.

Deleuze, Gilles. 1992. "Postscript on the societies of control". *October* 59: 3–7.

Eklof, Goran. 2012. *REDD plus or Redd light?* Stockhom: Swedish Society for Nature Conservation.

Elson, David. 2013. Guest post: Presenting the great REDD perpetual motion machine – Part 1 | redd-monitor.org. Available at: www.redd-monitor.org/2013/06/13/guest-post-presenting-the-great-redd-perpetual-motion-machine-part-1/ [Accessed 14 June 2013].

Featherstone, David. 2011. "On assemblage and articulation". *Area* 43(2): 139–142.

Ferguson, James. 1990. "*The anti-politics machine: 'development', depoliticization and bureaucratic power in Lesotho*". CUP Archive.

Fletcher, Robert. 2010. "Neoliberal environmentality: towards a poststructuralist political ecology of the conservation debate". *Conservation and society*, 8(3): 171–181.

Forest Trends, 2011. *Creating new values for Africa: Emerging ecosystem service markets*. Washington DC.

Fredriksen, Aurora. 2014. *Assembling value(s) What a focus on the distributed agency of assemblages can contribute to the study of value*. LCSV Working Paper Series NO. 7. Available: http://thestudyofvalue.org/wp-content/uploads/2014/07/WP7-Fredriksen-Assembling-values.pdf.

Grainger, M. and K. Geary. 2011. *The New Forests Company and its Uganda plantations*. Washington DC: OXFAM International.

Igoe, James, 2010. "The spectacle of nature in the global economy of appearances: Anthropological engagements with the spectacular mediations of transnational conservation". *Critique of Anthropology* 30(4): 375–397.

IPCC, 2007. *EXECUTIVE SUMMARY – AR4 WGIII Chapter 9: Forestry*. London: IPCC.

IUCN, 2007. REDD-plus explained. Available at: www.iucn.org/about/work/programmes/forest/fp_our_work/fp_our_work_thematic/redd/redd_plus_explained/ [Accessed 17 March 2013].

Jessop, Bob and Patricia Kennett. 2004. Hollowing out the nation-state and multilevel governance. In *A handbook of comparative social policy* edited by Patricia Kennet, 11–25. Cheltenham: Edward Elgar Publishing.

Karsenty, Alain, and Symphorien Ongolo. 2012. "Can 'fragile states' decide to reduce their deforestation? The inappropriate use of the theory of incentives with respect to the REDD+ mechanism". *Forest Policy and Economics* 18: 38–45.

Lang, Chris, and Timothy Byakola. 2006. *A funny place to store carbon: UWA-FACE Foundation's tree planting project in Mount Elgon National Park, Uganda*. Moreton: World Rainforest Movement.

Lansing, David. 2011. "Realizing carbon's value: Discourse and calculation in the production of carbon forestry offsets in Costa Rica". *Antipode* 43(3): 731–753.

Larner, Wendy. 2011 "C-change? Geographies of crisis". *Dialogues in Human Geography* 1(3), pp. 319–335.

Li, Tania, M. 2007. "Practices of assemblage and community forest management". *Economy and Society* 36(2): 263–293.

Lyons, Kristen and Peter Westoby. 2014. "Carbon colonialism and the new land grab". *Journal of Rural Studies* 36 (3): 13–21.

Mayrand, Karel, and Marc Paquin. 2004. *Payments for environmental services: A survey and assessment of current schemes*. Montreal: Inisfera International Centre.

Muhereza, Frank. 2006. "Decentralising natural resource management and the politics of institutional resource management in Uganda's forest sub-sector". *Africa Development* 31(2), 67–101.

Mwangi, Esther and Andrew Wardell. 2012. "Multi-level governance of forest resources (Editorial to the special feature)". *International Journal of the Commons* 6(2), pp. 79–103.

Nampindo, Simon, Guy P. Phillips, and Andrew Plumptre. 2005. *The impact of conflict in northern Uganda on the environment and natural resource management*, Wildlife Conservation Society & United States Agency for International Development (USAID). Kampala: USAID.

Nel, Adrian. 2014. Sequestering market environmentalism: Geographies of carbon forestry and unevenness in Uganda. PhD Thesis submitted to the University of Otago.

Nel, Adrian. 2015. "The choreography of sacrifice: Neoliberal biopolitics, environmental damage and assemblages of market environmentalism". *Geoforum* 65: 246–254.

Nel, Adrian, and Douglas Hill. 2013. "Constructing walls of carbon – the complexities of community, carbon sequestration and protected areas in Uganda". *Journal of Contemporary African Studies* 31(3): 421–440.

Mwenda, Andrew and Godber W. Tumushabe. 2011. *A political economy analysis of the environmental and natural resources sector in Uganda*. Kampala, Uganda: The World Bank.

Pomeroy, Derek, Herbert. Tushabe, Polycarp Mwima, and Panta Kasoma. 2002. *Uganda ecosystem and protected area characterisation*. Institute of Environment and Natural Resources (MUIENR). Kampala, Uganda: Makerere University.

Rivkin, Julie and Michael Ryan. 1998. *Literary theory: An anthology*. Oxford: Blackwell.

Robertson, Morgan. 2012. "Measurement and alienation: Making a world of ecosystem services". *Transactions of the Institute of British Geographers* 37(3): 386–401.

Scott, James C. 1998. *Seeing like state: How certain schemes to improve the human condition have failed*. New Haven: Yale University Press.

Sikor, Thomas, Graeme Auld, Anthony J. Bebbington, Tor A. Benjaminsen, Bradford S. Gentry, Carol Hunsberger, Anne-Marie Izac, Matias E Margulis, Tobias Plieninger, HeikeSchroeder and Caroline Upton. 2013. "Global land governance: from territory to flow?" *Current Opinion in Environmental Sustainability* 5(5): 522–527.

Smith, Neil. 2008. *Uneven development: Nature, capital, and the production of space*. Athens: University of Georgia Press.

Springer, Simon. 2014. "Human geography without hierarchy". *Progress in Human Geography* 38: 402–419.

Sullivan, Sian. 2013. "Banking nature? The spectacular financialisation of environmental conservation". *Antipode* 45(1): 198–217.

Sullivan, Sian. 2014. "The natural capital myth; or will accounting save the world? Preliminary thoughts on nature, finance and values". *Leverhulme Centre for the Study of Value* (LCSV) Working Paper Series No. 3 Available: http://thestudyofvalue.org/wp-content/uploads/2013/11/WP3-Sullivan-2014-Natural-Capital-Myth.pdf.

Swyngedouw, E. 2005. "Governance innovation and the citizen: The Janus face of governance-beyond-the-state". *Urban Studies* 43(11): 1991–2006.

Tsing, Anna L. 2005. *Friction: An ethnography of global connection*. Oxford: Princeton University Press.

Tumushabe, Godber and Eunice Musiime. 2006. *Living on the margins of life – the plight of the Batwa communities of South Western Uganda*. Kampala: Advocates Coalition for Development and Environment.

Turyahabwe, Nelson and Abwoli Banana. 2008. "An overview of history and development of forest policy and legislation in Uganda". *International Forestry Review* 10(4): 641–656.

Vaccaro, Ismael, Oriol Beltran and Pierre Alexandre Paquet. 2013. "Political ecology and conservation policies: Some theoretical genealogies". *Journal of Political Ecology* 20: 255–272.

Vandergeest, Peter and Nancy L. Peluso. 1995. "Territorialization and state power in Thailand". *Theory and Society* 24(3): 385–426.

Whitington, Jerome. 2001. "The prey of uncertainty: Climate change as opportunity". *Ephemera* 12, 113.

World Bank. 2011. World Bank Indicators. Uganda – Agriculture. Available at: www.indexmundi.com/facts/uganda/agriculture [Accessed 4 February 2014].

8 Not defined by the numbers

Distinction, dissent and democratic possibilities in debating the data

Karly Burch, Katharine Legun and Hugh Campbell

Introduction

On 12 March 2011 the first of four explosions took place at Tokyo Electric Power Company's Fukushima Daiichi Nuclear Power Plant (hereafter TEPCO's nuclear power plant). As TEPCO's radionuclides fell onto farmlands and into fishing waters, urgent interventions in the governance of the agrifood system became one of the main tasks of the Japanese government. Under the Japanese Food Sanitation Act, the government is legally liable for ensuring that food harmful to human health is not consumed by citizens (MHLW 2011a). Japan's Food Safety Basic Law of 2003 (hereafter the Basic Law) was created following the outbreak of bovine spongiform encephalopathy (BSE) in 2001. The Basic Law represented an overhaul of previous food safety laws, using a risk analysis framework to prove to the public that foods circulating in the agrifood system are both *anzen* (safe in a technical, objective sense) and *anshin* (safe in a psychological, subjective sense) (Tanaka 2008; also see Sternsdorff-Cisterna 2015; Hall 2010). Under the framework set forth by the Basic Law, management of food safety became the role of government ministries, and food safety laws were to be based on scientific assessments conducted by a new, independent body: the Food Safety Commission. In short, the establishment of the Basic Law in 2003 advanced science as a governance tool to ensure safety and rebuild the public's trust in the agrifood system (Tanaka 2008), and yet, the deployment of scientific claims does not necessarily enact the feelings of *anshin* so desired.

In the days following TEPCO's nuclear disaster, the Ministry of Health, Labour and Welfare (hereafter Ministry of Health) was given the responsibility of managing radiation in the food system. However, with no pre-existing legally binding standards, the government needed to quickly decide on how to manage radionuclides in the domestic food supply. In the chaos of the aftermath of the disasters, the Ministry of Health did not consult with the Food Safety Commission before deciding on allowable limits. Instead, the Ministry of Health announced its chosen 'provisional regulation values' on 17 March, five days after the first nuclear explosion (MHLW 2011a, 2011b). The values were adopted from the Nuclear Safety Commission of Japan's 'Indices Relating to Limits on Food and Drink Ingestion', originally developed in 1980 following the

1979 Three Mile Island nuclear disaster in the United States (Umeda 2013). The 'provisional regulation values' would use radionuclides cesium-134, cesium-137 and iodine-131 as indicators for radioactivity in food and drink. In Japan, radioactivity in food is measured in Becquerels[1] per kilogram (Bq/kg) or litre (Bq/l). The provisional regulation values for cesium-134 and cesium-137 were set at 200 Bq/kg for drinking water and dairy products, and 500 Bq/kg for other foods. For iodine-131, limits were set at 300 Bq/kg for drinking water and dairy products,[2] and 2,000 Bq/kg for vegetables and fishery products (FSCJ 2011b; also see FSCJ 2011a; Hamada and Ogino 2012; Hamada et al. 2012 for an overview of the food safety regulations).

From the outset, the numbers were contentious, in part because they appeared much higher than the common understanding of what constituted dangerous levels of radioactivity. At the time of TEPCO's nuclear disaster, international recommendations for managing the disposal of low level radioactive waste had an exemption level for radioactive cesium-134 and cesium-137 set at 100 Bq/kg. That is, anything over 100 Bq/kg required regulatory control (and was thus classified as radioactive), while anything under 100 Bq/kg was no longer classified as radioactive (IAEA 2004, 13). While the logic of these numbers may have made sense within the nuclear industry, it was difficult for some members of the public to understand why the government claimed it was acceptable for citizens to consume foods containing 500 Bq/kg – this appeared to be levels of cesium-134 and cesium-137 five times higher than the materials stored in drum cans labelled as nuclear waste (Mother's Revolution Network 2013).

Given the ambiguity of the numbers and their conflicting interpretations, establishing new guidelines presented a significant challenge. From March 2011 to February 2012, debates on the provisional values ensued amongst factions of the Japanese government and included two opportunities for public comment. The Ministry of Health eventually promoted decreasing the allowable individual effective dose[3] of radiation from 5 millisieverts (mSv)/year to 1 mSv/year.[4] To ensure this effective dose, the proposed radioactivity levels in food were calculated to be 100 Bq/kg for 'general foods'. For baby food and milk the standards were reduced by half (50 Bq/kg), and for drinking water by one tenth (10 Bq/l). While the Ministry of Health was eager to enforce the proposed 'new standards',[5] citizens and radiation protection experts did not share the same enthusiasm. The various numbers seemed to illuminate, or possibly provoke, deepening divisions between those wanting lower standards and those wanting more leniency. When looking at responses from the second public comment period, over three-quarters of the commenters (1,449 out of 1,877) demanded even stricter standards (MHLW 2012a). On the other hand, experts within the Radiation Council felt that the new standards were unnecessarily stringent and, though they eventually approved their adoption, wrote a report strongly critiquing the government's proposal (see Kimura 2012).

Recommended standards for radiation protection have developed within a complex international network of scientists, government and industry actors with its own political, economic and philosophical underpinnings. Following TEPCO's nuclear disaster, these recommendations were translated into numerical standards and deployed throughout the food system in an attempt to ensure food safety and manage the public's perception of a newly re-vitalized actor: the radionuclide. In this chapter, we will explore the agentic quality of these numerical standards, following the numbers from their historical beginnings, to their intended use as regulatory tools, and finally to the ways in which politicians and the public actually interact with these numbers once they enter agrifood assemblages. By following the numbers and elaborating their participation in relationships between the government and citizenry, we hope to reveal how the political, economic and philosophical values embedded within the numbers not only work to stabilize practices, but to further entrench systems of power. However, the numbers can also instigate disagreement and dialogue, and generate dissenting socio-technical communities. While governments may condemn dissent as a challenge to national unity, we argue here that the dissent generated through standards indicates a type of public political engagement that is valuable for democracy. The agency of numbers disrupts government attempts at complete control over governing processes.

Numbers for debate when the matter is messy

The release of radionuclides from their secure containment vessels inside TEPCO's nuclear power plant and into the wider environment can be characterized through what Callon and his colleagues (2009, 28) refer to as "overflow". Overflows point to an instance when something usually confined to a technical space (both physically and philosophically) spills over into the "big world" – the wider, unconfined environment with its various actors and complexities (ibid., 48). Overflows spark controversy and unleash a sense of uncertainty within society, making them both technical and social in nature. Unlike risks which are calculable and represent "a well-identified danger associated with a perfectly describable event or series of events" (ibid., 19), uncertainty refers to situations in which

> we cannot anticipate the consequences of the decisions that are likely to be made; we do not have a sufficiently precise knowledge of the conceivable options, the description of the constitution of the possible worlds comes up against resistant cores of ignorance, and the behavior and interactions of the entities making them up remain enigmatic.
>
> (Ibid., 21)

Overflows often lead to a state of uncertainty as the technical knowledge and skills used to manage materials within controlled, isolated spaces – spaces of "secluded research" – must be applied to the management of the materials that have escaped into "the wild" (ibid., Chapter 2). In other words, while the various behaviours and functions of such materials may be well-known and managed within laboratory-like spaces, they can become unruly and unpredictable in more complex environments. Thus, the laboratory knowledge about these materials is both foundational – as stable and public information – and inadequate – as it is unable to foresee the range of behaviours the material performs as it travels through a vibrant and dynamic world. In these conditions, science is necessary, but also necessarily limited, and a source of power in its deployment and through its contestation.

The actor at the centre of the controversy being examined in this chapter is the *radionuclide*, an unstable isotope that releases energy or particles in an attempt to transform itself to a more stable state. This process of emission (the activity of the radionuclide) is referred to as *radioactivity* or *radioactive decay*. The particles or energy released in the process of radioactivity are termed *radiation*. Through their activity, radionuclides do not simply disappear, but continue to transform themselves into different (daughter) isotopes, a process that ranges from seconds to millions of years. *Ionizing radiation* is the type of radiation that has the power to damage living tissue, making the radionuclides that emit ionizing radiation those of most concern following a nuclear disaster. What complicates the management of radionuclides, however, is their imperceptible nature: they cannot be seen, smelled or tasted, so require very sensitive technical equipment able to identify them through their activity.[6]

Within the highly technical assemblage of TEPCO's nuclear power plant, the activity of radionuclides was harnessed to heat fuel rods, which boiled water to produce energy that was transported from rural communities of Fukushima prefecture to the metropolis of Tokyo. However, when released into the wild, radionuclides travelled with weather patterns around the globe, with some of the highest concentrations deposited into the Pacific Ocean and onto areas of north-eastern Japan (Stohl *et al.*, 2012). TEPCO's radionuclides may become lodged in soil, travel up into plants, and into the bodies of livestock animals. They may travel through the ocean where fish and seafood incorporate the unstable actors into their bodies. Vegetables, meat and seafood possibly containing these unstable isotopes are then harvested and shipped around the country, and around the globe, to be made into meals where they have the potential to enter eaters' bodies. In short, radionuclides move fluidly and imperceptibly though a range of mediums and can easily wind up in a variety of foods.

The vulnerability of the agrifood system to the intrusion of external forces highlights the benefits of conceptualizing it as an assemblage of relations among human and non-human components (DeLanda 2006, 1–25). The newfound presence of TEPCO's radionuclides in Japan's food system created a situation in which all actors in the agrifood network – from farmers, to distributors, to consumers – became concerned with exchanging goods that potentially contain the life-threatening actors. Assemblage thinking is useful for exploring how heterogeneous collections of actors interact with each other within what we will refer to as the agrifood assemblage. TEPCO's radionuclides destabilized Japan's agrifood assemblage, threatening its identity by making it difficult to ensure the safety of the food its actors exchange. But they are also a particular kind of actor in their relative novelty, instability, and the ways that they are largely imperceptible but for their manifestations as malaise or disease. For this reason, the visibility of their actions is highly dependent on numbers; but those numbers also define their role in the assemblage. In this sense, the relationships between radionuclides and numbers can be seen to generate social and political outcomes.

In discussing the functioning of techno-economic networks, Callon (1991, 135 emphasis in original) highlights how vibrant actors are sometimes treated as passive intermediaries in order to stabilize and define an assemblage, specifying that *"actors define one another in interaction – in the intermediaries that they put into circulation"*. A text, food product, technical instrument, form of knowledge or skill held by a human, or currency are examples of intermediaries. Intermediaries define the relationship between the actors who exchange them, as in the case of food being circulated within the agrifood assemblage, or knowledge on radiation protection circulated within the nuclear assemblage. Additionally, each intermediary has its own network, but is able to travel to different assemblages and networks to be exchanged by actors there. These networks – each with their own political and economic values – may create intermediaries that replicate the values of their networks. We will go on to argue that while intermediaries seem to be docile subjects of human control and manipulation, they in fact always maintain their role of vibrant actor, dynamically involved in acting and instigating action among other actors in an assemblage.

Knowledge on radiation protection was inscribed into numbers which were deployed as standards to stabilize Japan's agrifood assemblage. We believe that viewing Japan's agrifood assemblage as a techno-economic network with the goal of exchanging food that is both *anzen* and *anshin* will be useful in exploring the Japanese government's attempt to stabilize the agrifood assemblage following the disruptive overflow of TEPCO's radionuclides in 2011. In their quest to circulate 'safe food' and manage the unstable and imperceptible actors, government officials incorporated intermediaries designed within the nuclear assemblage – in this case numerical standards – into the agrifood assemblage. However, because these intermediaries were created within the nuclear assemblage, the process of translation becomes essential for them to be intelligible to actors in the agrifood assemblage – though the agency of the intermediaries themselves makes outcomes unpredictable.

While all actors concerned with an overflow have the potential to become active participants in the unfolding of the controversy, their ability to participate may be limited depending on the political processes at play. Callon *et al.* (2009) distinguish between two forms of democracy that could be used to manage overflows: "delegative democracy" and "dialogic democracy". Delegative democracy refers to traditional forms of representative democracy where "experts" and "professional politicians" are enlisted as the representatives responsible for creating policies for the public – who receive the identity of "layperson" and "ordinary citizen" (ibid., 119–123). Callon *et al.* (ibid., 121) argue that in "delegating the production of knowledge to specialists, who are granted an almost exclusive monopoly moreover, delegative democracy purges political debate of all uncertainty regarding possible states of the world". However, the agency of numerical standards complicates processes of delegation which offers little space for dialogue among concerned actors. To account for uncertainty and provide a space for all actors to engage in discussions on techno-scientific issues, Callon et al. (ibid., 146) propose the process of dialogic democracy – the "dynamic process of constitution of the common world, which is a deliberately open, future world". Unlike delegative democracy where the production of knowledge and decision-making is reserved for experts and politicians, dialogic democracy proposes the creation of "hybrid forums" where diverse groups can collaboratively discuss technical options.

The approach proposed by Callon and his colleagues bears similarities to the work around deliberative democracy. Deliberative democracy suggests that engaged discussion among invested parties be central to the democratic process. While this seems relatively simple, the approach is nuanced in the ways that it elaborates what can be considered engaged, invested discussion. Gutmann and Thompson (2004) as well as Fung and Wright (2003) stress the importance of opposition in having fruitful discursive engagement, as well as the necessity of having a clear governance object, such as standards, that people understand. Understanding requires not only technical knowledge, but the ability for people involved to see how decisions will influence their everyday lives. In this sense, it is important that people who are affected by decisions have experiential knowledge about potential outcomes. Moreover, it is important to have contrasting viewpoints, requiring participants to justify their positions. Only from a foundation of knowledge, practice, and disagreement can members of the public meaningfully advocate for their personal and communal interests and develop a truly democratic and fair solution.

Here, we can see the potential for work on non-humans and deliberative democracy to link up. Having an understanding of non-humans and a voice in their public representation is a part of the deliberative democratic process. That understanding must come from interactive, lived practice – a grappling with those non-humans in a practical space where assemblages of daily life are enacted. As we elaborate, numbers translate the messiness and invisibility of radionuclides into a fixed set of standards to stabilize the existing agri-environmental governance assemblage. Numbers have also been brought into everyday life where they have created disturbances, and have precipitated the types of conflict, discussion, and new socio-technical assemblages that are integral to what we call a *deliberative public*. However, the existence of a deliberative public does not ensure the emergence of deliberative democracy. That is, without democratic processes bringing diverse voices into the political fold, it is possible to have a deliberative public that has not yet been enacted into deliberative democracy.

The role of the Japanese government in the management of radionuclides is an example of a delegative approach – acceptable standards move decision-making from the citizenry to the state, but also reduce complex information into uniform categories for the sake of stabilizing and accelerating desirable behaviour. Standards are often used in techno-economic networks to standardize translations and processes as a way to reduce transaction costs and foster cooperation among assemblage actors (Callon 1991). In the case of food, finding a way to quickly mark food as safe and erasing any nuances of that designation allows for food to continue to be purchased at a reasonable pace. This not only supports the continuation of an unaltered economic system, but also supports the continued legitimacy of the delegative process itself. When standards created purely with the input of 'experts' are used to manage an overflow, they become tools for the entrenchment of systems of delegative democracy. In some cases, standards can be a "means for obfuscating what is at stake and of concentrating decision-making in the hands of a technoscientific elite that falsely claims to have the answers" (Busch 2011, 285). So, not only do standards and their blunt categorization enable speedy exchange, they also solidify relations of power in the process. Indeed, pointing out the Japanese government's rigid use of numbers following TEPCO's nuclear disaster, Higuchi (2016, 112, 121) discusses how in both the realms of evacuation and food safety, numerical standards were used as a way to "monopolize knowledge and decision-making" processes, creating a situation where "there was no means by which to know risks other than the official inspection".

Radiation in the wild and attempts at delegating containment

Since radiation became a point of concern, it has been a bane to contain, both physically and politically. The effects of radionuclides on the environment and the body have been difficult to establish, and as a result, metrics of risk have been and continue to be a point of discussion. In the early 1900s, the field of radiation protection emerged as a multidisciplinary form of science that uses units from physics and applies them to biology with the goal of evaluating how radionuclides interact with human bodies (Taylor 1971, 22). This new field also adopted concepts such as "tolerance dose" developed in toxicology. While multi-disciplinarity is usually viewed in a positive light, there were, and remain, some fundamental obstacles to combining the disciplines of biology and physics. According to Whittemore (1986, 9), the

> complex variety of functions of various bodily parts was at odds with the uniform units contained in the basic definition of dose. More significantly, the use of concepts from physics fostered the popular belief that analysis of radiation should result in a single, quantifiable 'safe' limit.

In short, translating and inscribing complex science into concrete numerical values may be useful for regulatory purposes, but risks invisibilizing the uncertainty that existed, and continues to exist, in the always evolving field of biology (see Goodhead 2010). The first 'tolerance dose' was set by the International Committee on X-Ray and Radium Protection (ICXRP)[7] in a 1934 meeting, with the uncertainty of the underlying science explained with qualifiers and assumptions that were not, however, visible within the numbers themselves: "The evidence available at present *appears to suggest* that *under satisfactory working conditions* a *person in normal health* can tolerate exposure to x-rays to an extent of *about* 0.2 international roentgens (R) per day" (Taylor 1971, 16 emphasis added).

While science on the subject developed over the twentieth century, this nebulous interaction between an unstable material and active human bodies continued to hamper the establishment of clear guidelines for safety. By the 1940s, the genetic threats of ionizing radiation presented by geneticist Hermann Muller[8] were widely accepted, and it became clear that radiation protection standards should address both *deterministic*[9] and *stochastic effects*[10] for both the nuclear workforce and members of the public. Deciding on a per-capita 'dose' for the public which took into account the uncertainty of stochastic effects "was clearly a controversial subject and one involving a great deal of basic philosophy in addition to basic science" (Taylor 1971, 25). This meant that along with scientific data, a procedure or philosophy for making decisions in the face of uncertainty was necessary. Though activities of the ICXRP, including any capacity for ongoing re-evaluation and updating of their standards, were put on hold from 1937 to 1950, deliberations continued among members of the United States National Committee on Radiation Protection (NCRP). A former head of the NCRP, Lauriston S. Taylor (1971, 25) explains how the group's subcommittee on external exposure used a policy of consensus and omission to deal with uncertainty: "[a]s a matter of committee policy any controversial questions were debated and argued out until agreement was reached; when agreement could not be reached the item at issue was omitted". According to Taylor (ibid.), the NCRP's philosophy for managing uncertainty was eventually adopted by the ICXRP, now the International Commission on Radiological Protection (ICRP). Thus, uncertainty in the science of radiation protection became manageable through the adoption of assumptions and omissions to compensate for gaps in understanding.

However, overflows of radionuclides into the wild caused disturbances in the lives of the public and called the uncertainties and assumptions behind the radiation protection standards back into public debate. Nuclear bomb tests had been continuing throughout the world since World War II, and one controversy in particular both revealed the dangers of ionizing radiation and brought it directly to Japanese dinner tables. On 1 March 1954, a Japanese fishing boat was caught in the fallout of a US hydrogen bomb test in the Marshall Islands which resulted not only in the visible illness of many of the young male crew members, but in the contamination of Japan's air, water and food (Higuchi 2008; Lapp 1958). In particular, the presence of anthropogenic radionuclides in tuna – a staple food in Japan at the time – raised concerns and became a symbol of the overflow. The controversy, named the 'Lucky Dragon Incident' after the name of the ship, created a public uproar and release of anti-nuclear sentiment among people in Japan, especially housewives who did not want to feed the

US's radionuclides to their families. As it would again do in 2011, the Japanese government decided to deploy numerical standards to reassure the public of the safety of consuming the US's radionuclides. Through discussions with the US government and taking into consideration possible economic consequences for the fishing industry, Japan decided to base its standards on the maximum permissible doses recommended at the time. However, once out in the wild, the values began to operate beyond their original intent, enabling evaluations which "subscribed to the concept of a biomedical tolerance threshold" that "in effect 'normalized' the presence of human-made radionuclides in foods below the threshold as 'safe'" (Higuchi 2008, 344–345). The use of such numerical standards created an "illusion of certainty"[11] in which the layers of uncertainty known by scientists were no longer accessible in the data being presented.

Given the perplexity of establishing 'safe levels' of radionuclides within secluded spaces, it is no surprise that the need to expedite standards after the 2011 overflow was a considerable challenge. However, like the process of erasing complexity in scientific data, the social and political messiness around standards was erased through a delegative political process following a highly linear path. Following the onset of TEPCO's nuclear disaster, the Japanese government undertook its assigned role of translating the radiation protection recommendations into numerical standards to stabilize the food system and ensure the 'safety' (*anzen-sei*) of foods as required by its Food Sanitation Act (MHLW 2011a). Upon setting provisional limits, the Ministry of Health followed the protocols of the Basic Law and requested that the Food Safety Commission conduct an investigation into the adequacy of the chosen standards. The Food Safety Commission issued an interim report on 29 March 2011 and then convened a working group to discuss the standards. The group met between 21 April and 26 July 2011, and released a draft report that was opened for the first round of public comments on 29 July. In agreement with the contemporary scientific consensus, the draft report suggested that a cumulative effective dose[12] of more than 100 mSv (not including normal background levels) could be detrimental to human health. However, explaining the uncertainty in predicting health effects for exposures under 100 mSv, the Food Safety Commission recused itself from the responsibility of defining such risks (see FSCJ 2011d). In other words, by making decisions based on the certainty of harm at a particular level, uncertainty at lower doses was compartmentalized from the discussion and erased from public processes. Even after receiving 3,089 comments in the first public commenting period, mostly from people criticizing the proposal and calling for even stricter standards (FSCJ 2011c), the Food Safety Committee went along with its initial recommendations (FSCJ 2011d; Higuchi 2016). The result of these standards being institutionalized is that anything below a level clearly identified as harmful – which was translated into anything below 100 Bq/kg for most food – would be determined 'safe' (*anzen*) for human consumption.

Not defined by the numbers: distinction, dissent, and deliberative publics

Despite the difficulty in choosing acceptable levels for exposure to radiation, metrics were institutionalized and became the rule by which actors in the food assemblage oriented their activities. The work of measuring radioactivity was given to local governments in 17 prefectures where transgressive levels – according to government standards – of cesium-134 or cesium-137 had been found (MHLW 2012d). The numerical results of these measurements were, and are, posted online for those with the time and ability to search.[13] Because all responsibility for measurement was delegated to pre-sale processes conducted by local governments, for the majority of supermarkets business went on as usual. For everyday people, shopping at supermarkets meant trusting that the food being sold was under the government's limit of 100 Bq/kg of cesium-134 and cesium-137. But what were people to do if they did not agree with the 100 Bq/kg limit? Or if they did not trust in the government's ability to prevent foods over 100 Bq/kg from entering supermarkets? Drawing on observations and interviews carried out in 2016,[14] we argue that some members of the public did not simply accept the standards, but through a range of techniques, built an assemblage we are calling a *deliberative public*. These members of the public sought out alternative sources of information, found new ways to translate, spread and discuss technical data, and developed communities for testing food and sharing results. In this way, the standards adopted by the state can be seen to have defined an appropriate subject position as part of a delegative approach, and yet some members of the public developed strategies that demonstrated that they were 'not defined by the numbers'.

One method used by the public to get around government standards was the mobilization of different sources of data to act as a proxy for potential contamination. Supermarket food labels are not legally required to provide information on radiation measurements; however, labels on fresh foods – fruits, vegetables, seafood, meat and rice – are required by law to indicate the food's prefecture or country of origin (MAFF 2009). Therefore, due to the lack of available information on radionuclide content at the point of purchase, some people began using labels of origin to discern between foods that – according to government testing results and mandate – may contain radionuclides, and those from prefectures where no testing was taking place. Maps of the fallout distribution of cesium-134 and cesium-137 – especially the map created by Professor Hayakawa (2012) of Gunma University – were also utilized by people to decipher whether or not a prefecture's food products may be susceptible to contamination.

This practice of using geographic information to establish food safety was further elaborated by a group called OK Food for processed foods. Established in 2011, the group has been writing blog posts[15] with information on the place of origin of ingredients in a number of popular processed foods sold in Japan. Users of the blog may choose the food category of their choice – salt, miso, sake, mayonnaise, yogurt or soy sauce, just to name a few – and find the photos of a number of processed foods as well as a list of their ingredients and corresponding place of origin. OK Food's book (2012), roughly translated as *Identify Foods Not Contaminated with Radioactivity*, was published in June 2012 and promotes itself as being useful "at the supermarket!" and helpful for people "to buy ingredients [they] feel comfortable (*anshin*) eating, everyday!". A number of interviewees mentioned that the book or blog helped them in their initial attempts to navigate the processed food aisles, and this form of circulating strategy for avoiding contaminated foods illustrates how deliberative publics began piecing together other documents and information sources to develop contextualized knowledge of food that enabled people to better negotiate their purchases.

However, circumventing the official information is not the only strategy people used to negotiate subjugation by standards – some used state-released technical data in ways that would enable them to be more easily contested. The Ministry of Health publishes spreadsheets of test results, but these lack the types of context and presentation easily navigable by the general public. Some people transformed these data and presented it to the public in ways that are both palatable and easy to digest. One example of this is the book *Eat? 745 Measurement Results for Radioactive Cesium in Food* (Chidai 2013), which combines test results for particular food items measured by the Ministry of Health along with beautiful illustrations, warning levels, information on the foods measured including their main areas of cultivation, among other details. The book also includes "Becquerel-free recipes your body will love" and simple tips for avoiding radiation reminiscent of the Environmental Working Group's (2017) yearly list of the 'dirty dozen' designed as an easy way to help shoppers avoid purchasing foods with high amounts of pesticides. Another example of a group salvaging and revitalizing the Ministry of Health's data is the online food store White Food. The Hokkaido-based food store visually portrays government-produced data on a 3D map[16] showing which foods are tested in which prefectures, and also presents a bar graph with the average amounts of Bq/kg found for each tested item, as well as the number of samples from which cesium-134 or cesium-137 were detected. The shop uses the GC2520 by Canberra,[17] a germanium semiconductor with the capacity to measure levels of cesium-134, cesium-137 and iodine-131 down to 0.5 Bq/kg. Given these capabilities, the shop has set its own radiation standard for the food it sells at 0.5 Bq/kg for cesium-134, cesium-137 and iodine-131.[18]

While standards generated by food retailers may not inspire total confidence in the integrity of such processes, the shop also participates in the circulation of information outside its walls, cooperating with a Citizen Radiation Measuring Station (CRMS)[19] with a germanium semiconductor. These complex networks of information, and their legitimacy and transparency in the eyes of consumers, shapes how consumers negotiate relationships to the numbers and facilitates more informed and engaged decision-making. In other words, it becomes the fabric of a distinct subject position, shaped by numbers in response to the state numbers. Take, for example, the experience of one mother who, after evacuating from the Kanto region to the Kansai region, began volunteering at a local CRMS and orders food from a company that tests for radiation:

> Once dried shiitake mushrooms from Kyushu were measured and it was announced that three Becquerels was detected. Well ... we had bought that dried shiitake. About one kilogram of shiitake had been measured ... and there were three Becquerels. The normal amount we eat in something such as soup is about five. We would only use about five [at a time] ... so, even if [the kilogram] was contaminated with three Bequerels, when we eat it, it will only be a very small amount of contamination, so I think it is probably okay. We will eat them. Well ... even more than discovering the contamination, I really have faith in the company I purchased them from for reliably sharing the facts. I feel comfortable (anshin) buying food from a place like that.
>
> (Interview, May 2016)

Her careful negotiation with numbers as low as three-Becquerels establishes a rejection of state standards, a new distinction against those standards, and a coherent logic of dissent. These kinds of distinctions – created through the mobilization of new numbers – also provide a shared language for new forms of community science and opportunities for informed and engaged processes that include the public. Sharing data and cross-checking is a common practice among CRMSs to provide for more robust data. There are many CRMSs using scintillation detectors which, though much more affordable than germanium semiconductors and therefore the only option for many, are only able to measure levels of cesium-134 and cesium-137 down to approximately 1.5 Bq/kg – though the exact level of precision depends on the substance and amount of time measured. This is why the sharing of results online and through meeting with other CRMS volunteers and members is so important, and we can see how the technology inspires the diffusion of knowledge through crosschecking. One CRMS volunteer in the Kansai region who measures food with a scintillation detector explained how much he appreciates the data shared online by people with germanium semiconductors for allowing him to see the values that lurk beneath his numerical results, the activity of radionuclides at a level of sensitivity his machine is not capable of detecting. Thus, the impetus to measure, share, and document has also generated new collaborative platforms.

Minna No Dēta Saito (Everyone's Data Site) is an example of a group trying to create an online record of test results of food items from CRMSs around the country. Any CRMS that wants to join the group must pass a specific set of standardized tests to ensure proper calibration and functioning of their measurement devices. The group has also been active in collecting soil samples to determine concentrations of cesium (especially cesium-134)[20] in areas around the country. In order to maintain some record of fallout, the group put together a soil-measuring project where a number of member CRMSs from around the country joined in the effort. The results are presented on an interactive map on their website (Everyone's Data Site 2017). Through documenting science generated by the public and translating it into an easily accessible forum, the group is providing a platform for better engaging in deliberation. That is, they are creating a clear object to debate and inviting engagement with it.

The optimism we ascribe to the emergence of a kind of deliberative public is paired with a caveat: if deliberation fails to be considered a legitimate governance process, it will remain a form of marginalized, individual self-governance. This is a risk that is particularly acute when people who do pursue alternatives and vocalize their concerns are not only silenced, but framed as irrational and a threat to national identity (see Kimura 2016). The method of decision-making based around categorizing food risks by prefecture, for example, was almost immediately chastised in public discourse and people choosing foods based on prefecture were accused of spreading *fūhyōhigai* (harmful rumours that lead to economic damage). Advertisements advocating people "support by eating" filled the airwaves and foods from tsunami and nuclear disaster-stricken areas were promoted at government supported sales events (see Minister of Agriculture, Forestry and Fisheries, and Minister of State for Consumer Affairs 2011; MAFF 2011). In September 2012 the Japanese government introduced the 'Action Plan for Consumers to Feel at Ease (*Anshin*)' to address the decrease in food sales from disaster-stricken areas (CAA 2012). The plan outlined various strategies for ending damage from 'harmful rumours' through improved risk communication[21] and informational meetings at approximately 2,000 preschools and nursery schools throughout Japan. The basic premise of the argument was that consumers were making decisions that were 'baseless', that is, no scientific inquiry had been undertaken to prove there was in fact radiation contained in those specific products. But without data on radionuclide content provided at the point of sale, how could people who did not agree with the 100 Bq/kg standard be expected to make an informed decision? It was within such a simultaneously harsh and hazy environment that some people began producing and using numbers as a way to deliberate safety and cut through accusations that their personal food decisions were 'baseless' or discriminatory.

Conclusion

In this chapter, we have recognized that governments face significant difficulties when developing numerical safety standards for exposure to dangerous matter, particularly for something as intangible and unstable as radionuclides. Something as overflowing and uncontainable as radiation presents particular challenges for states who aim to provide security and peace for their citizenry through the reproduction of the integrity of physical and social worlds. A nuclear disaster can bring that challenge to the fore, and has the potential to radically alter the flow of food and the speed of commerce, and even has the potential to disrupt governance relations. It can both expose once obscure elements of agrifood assemblages and enable new political assemblage in response to overflowing uncertainty. As we've suggested in this chapter, attempts to stabilize overflows through coherent metrics pose a particular kind of challenge for both states and publics. Numbers are presented as passive intermediaries, transforming active and unstable radionuclides into elements that can be controlled and manipulated by human activity. Under this guise, the solidity of numbers seems to provide a perfect tool for delegative processes: they assist in stabilising the chaotic effects of an overflowing problem by becoming the anchors around which a state response to crisis can be secured.

However, the agentic quality of these numerical standards becomes evident when exploring the deliberation practices of some members of the public. As numbers become an anchor for state response to an overflow, they simultaneously become an anchor for public contestation and engagement. For those who make up deliberative publics, numbers have generated the types of discussions and socio-technical assemblages that enact alternative forms of decision-making. Community groups, the circulation of alternative knowledge, and testing stations all suggest that debates over numbers can precipitate informed and engaged scientific and political decision-making, and a more deliberative form of democracy. People have discovered ways to find new sources of information, transform technical information into something with which the public can grapple, and generate new platforms for documentation and dialogue. These processes are necessary components of deliberative democracy: the development of clear information that enables people to understand the ramifications of policy, and an infrastructure that allows invested parties to work collaboratively towards transparency.

Seen through this lens of assemblage and democracy, the radionuclide and its need for a numerical proxy is an overflowing problem that, through the uncontrollability of overflows, has the potential to actually enable greater democracy and opportunity for citizens to participate in broader conversations about state energy and risk. While it appears that the Japanese government has been successful in using numerical standards to more fervently entrench delegative political processes in the service of business as usual, once released, these numbers have traversed beyond the purview of their creators, catalysing the deliberative public assemblage. As this chapter indicates, infrastructures for deliberative engagement have been built around these safety standards and the relations among the various actors – government, radionuclides, numerical standards and deliberative publics – will continue to unfold in the coming years. As the silencing effects of rigid numerical standards are enlivened, reworked and made more visible through deliberative knowledge networks, richer and more diverse conversations on both the *anzen* and *anshin* aspects of food safety are possible. With this in mind, we believe that deliberative publics can contribute to widening discussions on food safety and its enactment within a vibrant, material world.

Notes

1 "1 Bq represents a rate of radioactive decay equal to 1 disintegration per second" (USNRC 2017).
2 Milk used for powdered baby formula was not to exceed 100 Bq/l.
3 "Effective does expresses biological damage to an individual" following exposure to radiation (Martin and Harbison 1996, 28). The effective dose "takes into account the type of radiation and the sensitivity of particular tissues and organs to that radiation" (Grupen 2010, 291).
4 The new standards would only be based on the activity of cesium-134 and cesium-137. Iodine-131 would no longer be measured due to its short half-life.
5 See Ministry of Health (2012b) for an overview (in English) of the 'new standards' effective on 1 April 2012.
6 See Martin and Harbison (1996) and Grupen (2010).
7 The ICXRP was established in 1928. For a discussion on the historical development of international expert committees for radiation protection see Boudia (2007) and Clarke and Valentin (2009).
8 Muller's research from the 1920s on fruit flies revealed that even small doses of radiation could cause damage to reproductive cells (Walker 2000, 3).
9 Deterministic effects can be lethal and acute and usually involve the "killing or gross malfunction of cells. These effects have a dose threshold below which they do not occur and above which the severity of the effect increases with dose" (Cooper 2012, 82).
10 Stochastic effects are those, including cancer or hereditary effects, that result from low doses of exposure to ionizing radiation (Cooper 2012, 82).
11 See Whittemore (1986, 5).
12 Cumulative effective dose is an estimated effective dose received over a person's lifetime.
13 See Ministry of Health (2012c) for an example designed for English speakers.
14 Insights and data in this section are derived from Karly Burch's experience of living six years in the Kansai region of Japan, including ethnographic fieldwork carried out for her PhD thesis in 2016. The fieldwork was conducted in two stages, the first from March to June and the second from September to November 2016. Guided by the principles of institutional ethnography, fieldwork involved an ethnographic inquiry into people's engagement with food following the 2011 nuclear disaster, and an investigation into the material forms (texts) that organize people's everyday food-related experiences.
15 OK Food's blog can be found at http://okfood.blog.fc2.com.
16 The maps can be found at https://news.whitefood.co.jp/news/foodmap/6937/.
17 Photos of the device and its measuring capabilities can be found at www.whitefood.co.jp/store/kensa.html?_ga=1.116016322.516374308.1491118440.
18 As mentioned previously, the Japanese government no longer tests for iodine-131 based on an assumption that, due to its short half-life, it is no longer a concern.
19 See Kimura (2016, especially Chapter 4) for an overview of the numbers and locations of CRMSs in Japan until February 2014.
20 Cesium-134 has a half-life of two years, compared with cesium-137 with a half-life of 30 years, so its presence in food samples is an indicator that the radiation came from TEPCO's disaster and not previous overflows from Chernobyl or hydrogen bomb tests. For people measuring radiation in food, the disappearance of cesium-134 means it will be difficult for them to identify whether or not the radionuclides actually originated from TEPCO's nuclear power plant.
21 See Ministry of Health et al. (2012) for an example of one of the government's educational hand-outs.

References

Boudia, Soraya. 2007. "Global Regulation: Controlling and Accepting Radioactivity Risks". *History and Technology* 23 (4): 389–406. doi:10.1080/07341510701527443.

Busch, Lawrence. 2011. *Standards: Recipes for Reality*. Cambridge, MA: MIT Press.

Callon, Michel. 1991. "Techno-Economic Networks and Irreversibility". In *A Sociology of Monsters*, edited by John Law, 132–161. London; New York: Routledge.

Callon, Michel, Pierre Lascoumes, and Yannick Barthe. 2009. *Acting in an Uncertain World: an Essay on Technical Democracy*. Translated by Graham Burchell. Cambridge, MA: MIT Press.

Chidai. 2013. *Eat? 745 Measurement Results for Radioactive Cesium in Food [Taberu? Shokuhin Seshiumusokutei Dēta 745]*. Tokyo: Shinhyoron Publishing Inc.

Clarke, R. H., and J. Valentin. 2009. "The History of ICRP and the Evolution of Its Policies". *Annals of the ICRP* 39 (1): 75–110.

Consumer Affairs Agency, Government of Japan (CAA). 2012. *Action Plan for Consumers to Feel at Ease [Shōhisya Anshin Akushon Puran]*. www.caa.go.jp/adjustments/pdf/120914message-2.pdf.

Cooper, John R. 2012. "Radiation Protection Principles". *Journal of Radiological Protection* 32 (1): N81–N87.

DeLanda, Manuel. 2006. *A New Philosophy of Society: Assemblage Theory and Social Complexity*. New York: Continuum.

Environmental Working Group (EWG). 2017. "Dirty Dozen: EWG'S 2017 Shopper's Guide to Pesticides in Produce". www.ewg.org/foodnews/dirty_dozen_list.php.

Everyone's Data Site [Minna No Dēta Saito]. 2017. "Map of 17 Municipalities and Prefectures [17 Token Mappu]". www.minnanods.net/soil/pref17_colored/map17.html.

Food Safety Commission of Japan (FSCJ). 2011a. *Emergency Report on Radioactive Nuclides in Foods*. www.fsc.go.jp/english/emerg/emergency_report_radioactive_nuclides.pdf.

FSCJ. 2011b. *Graphical Explanations of 'Emergency Report on Radioactive Nuclides in Food'*. www.fsc.go.jp/english/emerg/graphical_explanation_radiofoods.pdf.

FSCJ. 2011c. *On the Results of Public Solicitation of Opinions and Information Regarding (the Draft Report on) the Review on the Food Safety Evaluation of Health Effects Due to Radioactive Substances in Food [Shokuhin Ni Fukumareru Hōshasei Busshitsu Ni Kakaru Shokuhin Kenkō Eikyō Hyōka Ni Kansuru Shingi Kekka (An) Ni Tsuite No Goiken, Jōhō No Boshū Kekka Ni Tsuite]*. www.fsc.go.jp/iken-bosyu/iken-kekka/kekka-risk_radio_230729.pdf.

FSCJ. 2011d. *To All Concerned in Overseas: Remarks from the Chairperson of Food Safety Commission of Japan (FSCJ) About the Assessment of the Effect of Food on Health of Radioactive Nuclides in Foods*. www.fsc.go.jp/english/emerg/remarks_fsc_chair.pdf.

Fung, Archon, and Erik Olin Wright, eds. 2003. *Deepening Democracy: Institutional Innovations in Empowered Participatory Governance*. London; New York: Verso.

Goodhead, Dudley T. 2010. "New Radiobiological, Radiation Risk and Radiation Protection Paradigms". *Mutation Research/Fundamental and Molecular Mechanisms of Mutagenesis* 687 (1–2): 13–16. doi:10.1016/j.mrfmmm.2010.01.006.

Grupen, Claus. 2010. *Introduction to Radiation Protection*. Berlin, Heidelberg: Springer Berlin Heidelberg. doi:10.1007/978-3-642-02586-0.

Gutmann, Amy, and Dennis Thompson. 2004. *Why Deliberative Democracy?* Princeton, NJ: Princeton University Press.

Hamada, Nobuyuki, and Haruyuki Ogino. 2012. "Food Safety Regulations: What We Learned from the Fukushima Nuclear Accident". *Journal of Environmental Radioactivity* 111 (September): 83–99. doi:10.1016/j.jenvrad.2011.08.008.

Hamada, N., H. Ogino, and Y. Fujimichi. 2012. "Safety Regulations of Food and Water Implemented in the First Year Following the Fukushima Nuclear Accident". *Journal of Radiation Research* 53 (5): 641–671. doi:10.1093/jrr/rrs032.

Hall, Derek. 2010. "Food with a Visible Face: Traceability and the Public Promotion of Private Governance in the Japanese Food System". *Geoforum* 41 (5): 826–835. doi:10.1016/j.geoforum.2010.05.005.

Hayakawa, Yukio. 2012. "Radiation Contour Map of the Fukushima Daiichi Accident, 7th Edition." www.hayakawayukio.jp/pub/2012/0727A.pdf.

Higuchi, Toshihiro. 2008. "An Environmental Origin of Antinuclear Activism in Japan, 1954–1963: the Government, the Grassroots Movement, and the Politics of Risk". *Peace & Change* 33 (3): 333–367. doi:10.1111/j.1468-0130.2008.00502.x.

Higuchi, Toshihiro. 2016. "Radiation Protection by Numbers: Another 'Man-Made' Disaster". In *Learning from a Disaster*, edited by Edward D Blandford and Scott D Sagan, 109–135. Stanford University Press.

International Atomic Energy Agency (IAEA). 2004. *Safety Guide No. RS-G-1.7: Application of the Concept of Exclusion, Exemption and Clearance. IAEA Safety Standards Series*. Vienna. www-pub.iaea.org/MTCD/publications/PDF/Pub1202_web.pdf.

Kimura, Aya Hirata. 2012. "Standards as Hybrid Forum: Comparison of the Post-Fukushima Radiation Standards by a Consumer Cooperative, the Private Sector, and the Japanese Government". *International Journal of Sociology of Agriculture and Food* 20 (1): 11–29.

Kimura, Aya Hirata. 2016. *Radiation Brain Moms and Citizen Scientists: The Gender Politics of Food Contamination after Fukushima*. Durham: Duke University Press.

Lapp, Ralph E. 1958. *The Voyage of the Lucky Dragon*. New York: Harper & Brothers.

Martin, Alan, and Samuel A. Harbison. 1996. *An Introduction to Radiation Protection*. Boston, MA: Springer US. doi:10.1007/978-1-4899-4543-3.

Ministry of Agriculture, Forestry and Fisheries (MAFF). 2009. *Everyday Food and Dietary Habits [Mainichi No Shoku to Shokuseikatsu]*. www.maff.go.jp/j/pr/annual/pdf/09p3.pdf.

MAFF. 2011. "Information of Utilizing Agriculture, Forestry and Fisheries Products and Foods Made in the Devastated Areas of the Great East Japan Earthquake". www.maff.go.jp/e/support_action/list.html.

Minister of Agriculture, Forestry and Fisheries, and Minister of State for Consumer Affairs. 2011. "Eat to Support! Cabinet Minister's Message [Tabete Ōen! Daijin Messēji]". www.maff.go.jp/j/shokusan/eat/tabete/message.html.

Ministry of Health, Labour and Welfare (MHLW). 2011a. *Press Release: Handling of Food Contaminated by Radioactivity (Relating to the Accident at the Fukushima Nuclear Power Plant)*. www.mhlw.go.jp/stf/houdou/2r9852000001558e-img/2r98520000015apy.pdf.

MHLW. 2011b. *Handling of Food Contaminated by Radioactivity: Reference*. www.mhlw.go.jp/english/topics/foodsafety/dl/110318-1.pdf.

MHLW. 2012a. *Minutes for the Subcommittee on Food Safety in the Council on Drug and Food Safety [Yakuji Shokuhin Eisei Shingikai Shokuhin Eisei Bunkakai]*. www.mhlw.go.jp/stf/shingi/2r9852000002bzxb.html.

MHLW. 2012b. *New Standard Limits for Radionuclides in Foods*. www.mhlw.go.jp/english/topics/2011eq/dl/new_standard.pdf.

MHLW. 2012c. *Monthly Report of Test Results of Radionuclide in Foods Sampled Since 01 April 2012: April 2012*. www.mhlw.go.jp/english/topics/2011eq/dl/Apr2012data.pdf.

MHLW. 2012d. *Press Release: Revision of the 'Concepts of Inspection Planning and the Establishment and Cancellation of Items and Areas to Which the Restriction of Distribution and/or Consumption of Foods Concerned Applies'*. www.mhlw.go.jp/english/topics/2011eq/dl/food-120712-2.pdf.

MHLW, CAA, FSCJ, MAFF. 2012. *Food and Radiation Discussion: New Standards [Tabemono To Hōshaseibusshitsu No Hanashi: Atarashī Kijyunchi]*. www.maff.go.jp/j/press/syouan/johokan/pdf/120912-03.pdf.

Mother's Revolution Network [Okāsan Kakumei Nettowāku]. 2013. *Mother's Anti-Radiation Revolution: 22 Ways to Protect Your Family [Hahaoyatachi No Datsuhibaku Kakumei: Kazoku Wo Mamoru 22 No Hōhō]*. Fusosha Publishing Inc.: Tokyo.

OK Food. 2012. *Identify Foods Not Contaminated with Radioactivity [Hōsyanō Osen No Nai Shokuhin Wo Miwakeru Hon]*. Tokyo: Takarajimasha.

Sternsdorff-Cisterna, Nicolas. 2015. "Food After Fukushima: Risk and Scientific Citizenship in Japan". *American Anthropologist* 117 (3): 455–467. doi:10.1111/aman.12294.

Stohl, A., P. Seibert, G. Wotawa, D. Arnold, J. F. Burkhart, S. Eckhardt, C. Tapia, A. Vargas, and T. J. Yasunari. 2012. "Xenon-133 and Caesium-137 Releases into the Atmosphere From the Fukushima Dai-Ichi Nuclear Power Plant: Determination of the Source Term, Atmospheric Dispersion, and Deposition". *Atmospheric Chemistry and Physics* 12 (5): 2313–2343. doi:10.5194/acp-12-2313-2012.

Tanaka, Keiko. 2008. "Seven Samurai to Protect 'Our' Food: The Reform of the Food Safety Regulatory System in Japan After the BSE Crisis of 2001". *Agriculture and Human Values* 25 (4): 567–580. doi:10.1007/s10460-008-9152-y.

Taylor, Lauriston S. 1971. *Radiation Protection Standards*. Part of the Chemical Rubber Co.'s CRC Monotopics Series. London: Butterworths.

Umeda, Sayuri. 2013. "Japan: Legal Responses to the Great East Japan Earthquake of 2011". *The Law Library of Congress, Global Legal Research Center*. www.loc.gov/law/help/japan-earthquake/Great-East-Japan-Earthquake.pdf.

United States Nuclear Regulatory Commission (USNRC). 2017. "Glossary: Becquerel (Bq)". www.nrc.gov/reading-rm/basic-ref/glossary/becquerel-bq.html.

Walker, Samuel J. 2000. *Permissible Dose*. Berkeley: University of California Press. doi:10.1525/j.ctt1pprpn.

Whittemore, Gilbert Franklin Jr. 1986. "The National Committee on Radiation Protection, 1928–1960: From Professional Guidelines to Government Regulation". Cambridge, MA: Harvard University.

9 Media, decentralization, and assemblage responses to water quality deterioration in Uruguay

Diego Thompson

Water quality deterioration, governance, and assemblage responses in Uruguay

Since 2003, after the financial crisis that affected Uruguay in 2001–2002, the country began a process of economic growth driven by increased Foreign Direct Investment (FDI). Changes in the economic development promoted by recent governments have focused mainly on agriculture and extractive industries with great impact on water quality. Soybean production, wood pulp to make paper, and mineral extraction have been some of the main items recently promoted by the State and its major institutions (mostly located in the capital, Montevideo). There have been some similarities between these developmental changes and what the "dependency school" described with reference to Latin American development and its local impacts on the economy and the environment during the 1970s. Recent economic growth and some of the new development approaches have focused on "modernization" and "catch up" with developed countries based on the exploitation of natural and primary resources, with significant impact on water quality which has gained greater public visibility in recent years.

Recent economic transformations and their social and environmental consequences can be located in three main regions: Southwest; South or Central (Montevideo and its metropolitan area); and East (Tejera 2014). Communities from these different regions have been differently impacted, creating new debates on how different social actors and Uruguayan communities perceive, respond, and collaborate to address environmental problems such as water quality deterioration due to excess of nutrients, use of agrochemicals in agriculture, and climate change. Water quality deterioration has gained great importance to the point of being qualified by various government authorities as a "major environmental national problem." The social "construction" of this "national environmental problem" has been influenced by different actors and media coverage especially from the capital of the country (Montevideo), where almost half the population lives. In some communities of the Southwestern region of the country, problems related to deterioration of water quality had been observed since the 1990s. This region was the epicenter of agricultural transformations in the late 1990s and beginning of the 2000s. However, public debate on environmental conditions of water quality has gained significance only in the last few years, reaching its peak in 2015, when it had extensive media coverage from different views regarding the conditions of basins and drinking water supplied by *Obras Sanitarias del Estado* (OSE). Since then, the quality of drinking water and algae blooms of potentially toxic bodies of water cyanobacteria, have sparked unprecedented debates at the national level with focus on perceptions and responses to these problems.

Social studies on how environmental changes are perceived by different communities have historically had a very important role in the study of human interactions with the environment. Perceptions of environmental changes that are seen as negative and/or "problems" locally – many times – transcend the geographical and social boundaries of the community, understood as a social system in a specific geographic location where local people satisfy their concerns and needs through organizations and institutions (Flora and Flora 2013).

The challenges for community perceptions and responses to water quality deterioration have been increasingly blurred due to increased ties (real or virtual) with different geographically distant actors and realities. Social ties or social capital of communities can be classified into internal links (*bonding social capital*) or links with external actors (*bridging social capital*) (Flora and Flora 2013). The perception that the community has of itself and its natural environment responds to both internal and external social ties. Communities are strongly influenced by external links, meaning that environmental events occurring elsewhere have great significance and effect locally. Thus, perception of water quality deterioration and its effects on local responses depends on external linkages of communities. To understand what happens locally, it is critical to explore relationships between external actors and the local community (Flora and Flora 2013). As a result of different processes and social ties (economic, political, and cultural, among others), certain environmental conditions may be perceived as risks or as representing a state of crisis for some communities but not for others (Hannigan 2014; Thompson 2014). These processes and external links are dynamic and take multiple forms. Actors from the civil society, government, and the private sector influence how environmental problems are perceived locally and also possible responses.

In Uruguay, mass media nationwide and its information have had a great influence on social constructions of water quality problems and their possible risks. Different means of media and communication reflect and influence how different actors think and manifest themselves on different subjects such as science and/or environmental issues and risks (Ching 2010; Dolnicar and Hurlimann 2010; Boyd and Paveglio 2014). Mass media often transmits and/or responds to economic, political, or cultural views, having a critical role in covering specific geographic localities (Howe 2009) and highlighting environmental issues and the (selected) communities in which they occur. Information transmitted by media not only influences how environmental problems are perceived locally, but also plays a critical role in the social and geographical selection (community) where environmental problems are highlighted. Media coverage of some environmental problems can thus expose the nature of external links (*bridging social capital*) of certain communities, providing information about external actors and their role in local perceptions and collective responses.

Collective social mobilization or agency at the local level can make environmental changes more visible and promote structural changes to improve communities and promote greater participation by different local actors (Thompson 2014). It is critical to examine the factors that influence the perception of environmental problems and how collective agency takes place, especially in communities that are experiencing significant transformations and/or possible risks (Wright and Boudet 2012). The analysis of ties between communities and different regional or national actors can help to understand the genesis of the perception of environmental problems and collective social mobilization. External ties of communities (*bridging social capital*) and the role of mass media influence local perceptions of water quality, and geographically establish different levels of importance of where resources (from outside and within communities) are mobilized through different types of governance.

Governance is composed by structures and inclusion of different actors with different viewpoints on decision-making processes. It can include the participation of multiple actors to identify priorities and local resources to develop solutions through collaboration (Gates 1999). Literature on natural resource management and adaptation (Tompkins and Adger 2004), theory of the commons (Armitage 2008; Berkes 2008), and community resilience and climate change adaptation (Adger, Lorenzoni, and O'Brien 2009; Ensor and Berger 2009; among others), highlights the importance of external links of communities through decentralized and multi-level governance and/or network governance, and how it can facilitate transfer and flow of resources used for local adaptations to environmental problems such as water quality deterioration. Adaptations to environmental changes can be sustainable and be successful when they include participation through local decision-making to mobilize locally available resources and meet local priorities, but also taking into account the regional context and community links with external actors (Adger 2003; Adger et al. 2009; Ensor and Berger 2009; Ashwill, Flora, and Flora 2011). Decentralized governance or decentralization policies and programs can contribute to empowerment and adaptation to water quality deterioration.

Similarly to other Latin American countries, recent Uruguayan governments have tried to change their centralist approaches to allow more active participation of local actors in new government organizations and institutions (Piñeiro 2004; De Barbieri and Zurbriggen 2011; Zurbriggen 2011). These new approaches, programs, laws, and actions to decentralize decision-making processes see communities as critical units of change in specific territories and involve local actors in territorial and regional planning (Piñeiro 2004; De Barbieri and Zurbriggen 2011; Berdegué et al. 2012), while developing local responses to environmental problems through community empowerment.

Empowerment of communities means that the community (governments, local groups and residents), rather than departmental or national government institutions, make decisions about their resources and implement what is decided at the local level (IAPP 2007). Empowering local actors through decentralization involves decision-making in the hands of the local population. The empowerment of communities may be an alternative to the historical centrality of key players and is crucial for mobilizing locally available resources that may be useful to respond to water quality problems.

As part of these governmental initiatives, Uruguay created *Municipios* (City Councils in the U.S.) that focus on urban areas of communities and *Mesas de Desarrollo Rural* (MDRs, or Roundtables for Rural Development), which focus on their rural areas. These decentralization initiatives have emphasized the empowerment of small rural communities through collaborative efforts and the creation of new public-private alliances. These new types of decentralized governance structures and processes have had important roles for communities dealing with water quality deterioration (Thompson 2014, 2015). However, the historical dependency that Uruguayan communities still have with municipalities and national government institutions centralized in the capital (Montevideo), represents a major challenge to their capacity for decision-making on locally available resources (Thompson 2015). Communities financially depend on departmental and/or national institutions to carry out their responses. Governmental institutions often operate under centralist paradigms, being reluctant to delegate authority to communities (Head 2007) because they are not sure how public resources received will be administered locally.

In Uruguay, most of the communities depend on regional (i.e., *Intendencias* (departmental governments)) or national institutions (i.e., ministries) for monitoring and access to scientific information related to water quality and other natural resources. The dependence of communities on government actors and the scientific community in regard to the situation of natural resources can limit how local actors perceive environmental problems and their eventual responses (Thompson 2014, 2015). The dependency that communities have on key external actors to access financial capital and knowledge limits decision-making processes and empowerment promoted by decentralization programs such as *Municipios* (Thompson 2014, 2015).

This chapter investigates how media attention and decentralization of governance facilitated the construction of new assemblages composed of different actors working on specific environmental problems (i.e. water quality deterioration), leading to better community access to new external resources used for adaptation. The assemblage approach enriches the existing literature on governance and environmental matters as a form of critique as well as offering new possibilities for exploring the alignments or societal wholes between actors without losing aspects of potential agency (McFarlane and Anderson 2011). Collective responses emerging from the changing alliances to address water quality within the new assemblages can facilitate new social-spatial relations and forms (McFarlane and Anderson 2011). By comparing different geographical regions of Uruguay, this chapter explores the role of media and existing spaces for decision-making processes created and facilitated by new decentralization policies and programs, on the creation of assemblages to address water quality deterioration.

Methods

Collection of data used in this chapter began in 2011 and 2012. Through interviews with local informants from communities of Southwestern Uruguay, I began to explore environmental challenges experienced by communities of this region. During my field work from November 2012 to February 2013, staff of *Intendencias* provided contact information of local key actors, and then I used purposive snowball sampling to identify other major actors involved in local decisions at the community level. The participants I initially selected provided other contacts for key stakeholders involved in communities of that region. To address diverse viewpoints on community matters, I included market, state, and civic actors with diverse roles at the local level. In total, 43 participants were interviewed in Dolores and in Nueva Palmira, two of the communities of that region explored in this chapter (see Table 9.1). Using two semi-structured questionnaires,[1] I collected data to provide information about environmental challenges including water quality deterioration that these communities faced from increasing changes in agriculture and climate change. In addition, I explored the role of *Municipios* and *Mesas de Desarrollo Rural*. I utilized participant observation to gather similar data at one public meeting of the Municipio of Dolores and one public meeting of the *Mesa de Desarrollo Rural* ("Round Table for Rural Development") of Soriano.[2] In addition, I collected 85 on-line articles of two major Uruguayan (on-line) newspapers published between 2013 and 2016. Initially, I searched the term "water" and then I selected those articles that directly addressed water quality deterioration as a problem for communities of the regions explored in this chapter. I began content analysis of the articles looking at public statements about how communities from Southwestern Uruguay and communities from the South and the East, differently experienced water quality deterioration, community responses, and the role decentralization programs as well as centralized actors on local responses. This allowed me to establish a chronological order of the main water quality problems publicly discussed by different actors in the country, how water quality deterioration was addressed

Table 9.1 Interviewees in each of the communities

Types of actors	Nueva Palmira	Dolores
State	4	7
Market	6	7
Civic society	10	9
TOTAL	20	23

differently by communities and regions, and what factors influenced the creation of new assemblages to address water problems.

Assemblages and responses to water quality deterioration

Southwest: Nueva Palmira and Dolores

During the last two decades, communities of Southwestern Uruguay have observed significant deterioration of water quality mainly in the basins of Uruguay River, Black (*Negro*) River, and San Salvador River (among others) (Thompson 2014). In 2011 and 2012, some of these communities, such as the port town Nueva Palmira (NP, Colonia), had important collective mobilizations which prompted community responses and the re-assembling of actors in relation to water concerns. Local collective actions focused on the demand of external resources from the departmental (*Intendencias*) and the national government (ministries) which could help to alleviate water quality deterioration problems due to the intensification of agriculture and the growth of local port operations.[3] In NP, local mobilizations became more visible as well as multiple environmental problems including deterioration of water quality in Uruguay River and Higueritas Creek. Within the new assemblage of water and environmental governance, in December 2011, multiple local actors (*Municipio*, workers' unions, journalists, environmentalists, and NGOs) created the Work Group for Nueva Palmira (*Grupo de Trabajo por Nueva Palmira* (GTNP) (civil organization)).

> On December 11 of 2011, we, the citizens of Nueva Palmira, marched together to demand quality of life. In this peaceful march, over 2,000 people joined us in a symbolic embrace of our city. Our record of fighting for environmental issues is now very strong through the organization of various committees and working groups which promoted social consciousness. We, together as a community, are capable to mobilize resources and the right people, with local professionals willing to work and committed to their people with the Municipio, because will be our children who will suffer tomorrow the mistakes of today.
> (Nueva Palmira, April 18, 2012 – Report Submitted to the National Senate)

> With all the multiple problems we have, like infrastructure, health problems, and (air and water) pollution, last year the neighbors cut the highway (to the port) and we started working together instead or working as multiple commissions, and we said we are 'Grupo de Trabajo por Nueva Palmira.'
> (Nueva Palmira, December 20, 2012, Local Civic Actor – Co-founder and Member of GTNP)

The GTNP and the *Municipio* demanded the development of the Land Use Plan of Nueva Palmira (the first of Colonia) which was developed by the *Intendencia* of *Colonia*. This plan included local concerns and a plan of responses to environmental problems raised by multiple local actors in public meetings organized by the *Intendencia* and the local *Municipio* (Thompson 2014, 2015). The *Intendencia* of Colonia as well as the recently created *Municipio* had important roles in organizing and supporting local public meetings to address the multiple environmental challenges that the community was experiencing. The *Municipio* and the GTNP organized new spaces for public participation which made water quality deterioration (and other environmental problems) more visible at the local level. These new assemblages of local actors in collaboration with the *Intendencia* had minimum coverage by the mainstream media and received little attention from key government institutions located in Montevideo. The lack of attention and responses received from governmental institutions, led various local actors (working under GTNP) to gather their own scientific information about drinking water quality. Locally collected information included data from the local water processing plant of *Obras Sanitarias del Estado* (OSE) and statistical data from the local hospital about illnesses that could be related to air and/or water quality deterioration (Thompson 2014). Although the local *Municipio* and GTNP made environmental problems more visible through public meetings, they needed more scientific information to legitimize their claims and to get more resources and active involvement from national legislators and governmental institutions responsible for water management and environmental control. Local actors not only depended on external resources to monitor water (and air) quality, but they also needed to present evidence to legislators and government institutions from Montevideo that these environmental problems really existed. A member of GTNP stated:

> When we go to Montevideo to see people from government institutions to address the problems of the community, we have to show information and data, otherwise, they ignore or reject us.
> (Nueva Palmira, December 20, 2012)

Resources demanded by the GTNP and the local *Municipio* from departmental and national governments included the

> construction of a sewer system, the improvement of solid waste management, the improvement of drinking water quality, the improvement of the river (River Plate) water quality, the cessation of construction on a new barge port for soybeans (from Paraguay) in front of the beaches of the community, and the installation of a permanent office to monitor the natural environment of the community.
> (GTNP. Report Submitted to the National Senate on April 18, 2012)

Major media coverage publicised claims from residents of NP made when the main access to the local port was blocked by local protesters, risking economic profits of both the companies involved and the State. The main national news on the environmental problems of NP focused on the local opposition ("conflicts") to projects developed in the port, but with little attention to the environmental problems locally experienced. Nueva Palmira was generally described by government actors as a center of national development. The public image of Nueva Palmira as a community "booming" and an example of economic development was reproduced by the mainstream media, causing great unrest among local people who felt ignored and left without any resources. One of the members of Local GTNP who was a historian noted:

> The common feeling among local citizens is that the national government helps agriculture and port-related entrepreneurs but not residents of this community (…). When we listen to the national authorities on the news, saying that our community is a regional development center, we get angry because this is not how people perceive it here.
> (Nueva Palmira, February 20, 2013)

In NP, interviewees said that the environmental problems of this community were ignored by institutions and policy makers in Montevideo for not having "great political power or reputable local representatives" manifested in regional and/or national elections (Field Notes, December 2012). Most of the interviewees claimed that local environmental problems were neglected by the media coverage and public attention from social and centralist governmental actors, who responded to pressures and political interests in specific communities but not in others.

Dolores (Soriano) is located in the same Southwestern region, a few kilometers from NP. According to interviewees, this community had experienced water quality problems in the San Salvador River since the 1990s, which were identified and discussed by various local actors in the late 1990s (Thompson 2014), before the expansion and intensification of agriculture at the beginning of the 2000s. Claims and local debates about the water quality of the San Salvador River during the 1990s mainly focused on the problems that could exist with the local sewer system; but problems such as algae bloom were observed and worsened during the early 2000s. In 2012, a local ecologist commented:

> Today, you do not see a stream or watercourse without algae bloom and tremendous pollution.
> (Dolores, December 6, 2012)

According to local actors interviewed in 2012, the existing water and environmental governance assemblages failed to address the issues that the community was facing. Some people attributed the lack of local interests and collective responses to environmental problems to the economic benefits that intensification of agriculture and multinational companies had brought to the community. A local ecologist and a local farmer member of the Round Table for Rural Development said:

> Now, people here do not have motivations to make complaints about the environment because they now are economically fine. They think environmental problems happen outside the community and that they not have any 'weapons' or tools to defend their environmental situation.
> (Dolores – Local Ecologist, December 6, 2012)

> When things go wrong, people work together as in the (significant drought) crisis of 2001, but when they (farmers) do well like now, they do not work together (…). When you are well and things could be solved collectively it does not happen because people do not get together.
> (Dolores – Local Farmer and Member of MDR, December 3, 2012)

Problems related to algal blooms have recently became a notorious local issue that has motivated the re-assembling of water and environmental governance to include multiple local actors and the support of the *Municipio* and national elected officials from the department of Soriano. In this community, claims made by some local actors on water quality were not publicly visible and had no significance until 2015, after similar problems were observed and identified by the national media for communities of Southern and Eastern Uruguay.

On June 7, 2015, during the council of national ministers held in this town, various local actors collectively mobilized to express their concerns in a letter delivered to the minister of Ministerio de Vivienda, Ordenamiento Territorial y Medio Ambiente (MVOTMA), claiming that the community needed to know if water pollution existed and if drinking water consumed generated any health problems (Rojas 2015). In Dolores, the creation of new local alliances and responses regarding water quality occurred after water quality problem became a visible "national problem" in 2014–2015. New spaces for participation created by the *Municipio* and MDRs had made water quality deterioration more visible at the local level (Thompson 2014, 2015). However, dependency of the community on external resources (i.e., scientific information) from regional and national institutions limited the capabilities of the assemblages emerging within these new decentralization programs to develop their own adaptive responses and solutions to water quality deterioration and other environmental problems (Thompson 2014, 2015).

Only 1 percent of the articles analyzed from the press referred to communities of the Southwest, which was the epicenter of agricultural transformations with significant water quality deterioration, and which, according to some interviewees from Dolores, began to be observed in the late 1990s. Local mobilizations and the emergent assemblage in this community were influenced by the national media, which focused its coverage on the algal blooms observed in communities of the South and East of the country.

South and East: La Paloma, Santa Lucia River Basin, and Sauce Lagoon

Media coverage and social construction of environmental problems in Southern and Eastern Uruguay acquired unique characteristics, considering the importance of some communities in these regions for different types of centralized stakeholders from Montevideo. The Southeastern region of Uruguay is the main region for vacation and recreation during the summer for much of the population of the country (especially from Montevideo) and tourists from abroad. Communities from Southeastern Uruguay have strong ties with outside actors, mainly from Montevideo. These external links of communities facilitated the relatively rapid emergence of public discussion of water quality deterioration at local, regional, and national levels, due to media coverage and the attention of policy makers, scientists, and other key actors from Montevideo.

Since 2012, residents of La Paloma (Rocha) have expressed concerns about the situation of seawater quality at La Aguada beach as a result of the expansion of the port of this community. The problems of water quality observed locally were accompanied by other concerns that transcended the interests and concerns of local people. In 2013, several people collectively mobilized to protest the possible environmental risks from the construction of a roadway for timber trucks to the port. Local mobilizations and protests by various social organizations against some development projects in the area led to socio-political conflicts between various local, departmental, and national actors. These events had immediate and extensive media coverage by the press of Montevideo and social media (Facebook, Twitter, etc.). Social mobilizations in response to environmental issues (and safety) from the transit of timber trucks to the port were led by important local actors such as the local *Municipio* and tourism entrepreneurs, with great support from local people as well as a "floating" population (visiting or temporarily living in this locality) and social organizations from Montevideo. The social composition of La Paloma is unique in that the number of its residents who come from other departments and other countries is above the national average (Abrahan et al. 2014). Thus, this community has strong external links. In 2013, social mobilizations in La Paloma transcended the local population, involving different actors from other places who were linked to this community. As a result, protests and social events were covered by press and media from Montevideo. Consequently, these events and the environmental issues related to water quality became part of national news.

Since 2013, various government actors (OSE, *Dirección Nacional de Medio Ambiente* (DINAMA), etc.) have expressed concerns about the condition of water quality in the Santa Lucia River, affected by high levels of phosphorus concentration. The supply of drinking water for Montevideo and surrounding communities is mainly based on the resources of the basin of this river. The "water problem" of the Santa Lucia River has been widely covered by Uruguayan mainstream media, especially by the press of Montevideo. In March 2013, drinking water was contaminated in Montevideo. In the summers of

2013–2014 and 2014–2015, Montevideo's beaches were closed for swimming because of the high concentration of toxic algae bloom and cyanobacteria. These events created concerns regarding the water quality of the Santa Lucia River basin, leading to community mobilizations of different local stakeholders, including local *Municipios*, businessmen, and environmental groups linked to the different communities and neighborhoods affected. Consequently, various government agencies developed multiple measures to reverse water pollution and minimize potential future risks in this basin, although the results of these responses are still under discussion by various stakeholders including the scientific community, political actors, and civil society groups.

Between March and May 2015, residents of Maldonado complained about the quality of drinking water extracted from the Sauce Lagoon. This lagoon supplies water to about 130,000 inhabitants during most of the year and 400,000 people during the summer months. Like what has been observed in the basin of the Santa Lucia River and other parts of the country, natural and anthropogenic changes have caused excessive amount of nutrients and the presence of chemicals that affect drinking water before it is processed. Changes in water quality drew public attention from the media due to complaints by consumers of drinking water in communities of this region. Like the water problems in La Paloma and Santa Lucia River basin, this case had a huge media impact at the national level with immediate response from various government institutions. Given the cultural, economic, and political importance of this region, as one of the main tourist destinations in the country and the region, media coverage of this issue and responses by the State rapidly occurred. As in the case of the Santa Lucia River basin, it would be interesting to explore if water quality problems had been observed by local actors, previous to being observed in drinking water consumed by locals and tourists or visitors in the communities of this region.

The water problem events that occurred during 2013, 2014, and 2015 especially in communities of Southern and Eastern Uruguay disrupted existing water and environmental governance assemblages by attracting the attention of national governmental actors and eliciting new governmental responses based on existing legislature and policies to regulate water management and quality in different regions of the country.

Responses and emergent water management assemblages

Media coverage of local observations of and responses to water quality deterioration, motivated institutional responses and the emergence of new assemblages at local, regional, and national level, which were based on the existing policies for water management and control. In 2009, Uruguay developed the *Política Nacional de Aguas*,[4] which included constitutional rights of access to drinking water and sewer systems and different aspects of sustainable water management and planning with the participation of the civil society and other actors (among other aspects). In 2011, a new law[5] established the creation of the *Dirección Nacional de Aguas* (DINAGUA) as part of the MVOTMA. Its main goal has been to develop a national plan for water management at the national and regional level but with an important focus on local communities and their *Municipios*. The *Política Nacional de Aguas* facilitated the creation of the *Consejo Nacional de Agua, Ambiente y Territorio* (CNAAT) as part of the MVOTMA. It was established that the CNAAT had to be comprised equally of governmental representatives and members of the civil society. It was under the direction of the MVOTMA and included representation from the *Ministerio de Ganadería, Agricultura y Pesca* (MGAP), *Ministerio de Industria, Energía y Minería* and *Ministerio de Defensa Nacional*, through their dependent institutions working on biodiversity, water, soil, energy, and meteorology, among others. The creation of the CNAAT aimed to promote the participation of different actors at national, regional, and local level, establishing the *Consejos Regionales de Recursos Hídricos* (CRRH) and *Comisiones de Cuenca y de Acuíferos* (CCAs). The role of CCAs has been to facilitate regional and local participation of different types of actors from civil society (including the *Municipios*) and to advise the CRRH on water management and planning in each specific region and/or community. The MVOTMA and the MGAP have also organized the *Juntas de Riego* (*Juntas Regionales Asesoras de Riego*), which have aimed to coordinate collaboration between private and public actors in water management of irrigation systems.

Laws created in 2008 and 2009 for regional sustainable development[6] and the implementation of decentralization programs[7] which including the creation of *Municipios* have complemented the new efforts to facilitate active participation of different actors at different levels in the re-assembling of water management. Despite these efforts, the coordination, facilitation, and promotion of civil participation in decision-making processes with regard to water quality still represent a challenge for the actors involved.

The increasing public debate on water quality deterioration at the national level has led to additional responses from national governmental institutions, which have planned and developed new types of participation and collaboration to address this problem in different regions of the country. In 2016, DINAGUA developed the *Plan Nacional de Aguas* (PNA) which has been shared with regional and local actors through the CCAs. This plan includes general guidelines and goals (until 2030) for management of water resources for the whole territory of the country. The PNA highlights the importance of governance and the role of new institutional collaborations in water management by strengthening the role of multiple actors that currently participate at the CCAs and by facilitating civil involvement in water issues. The PNA includes short-term and long-term projects for water management which will be implemented through new types of institutional collaborations (MVOTMA 2016). One of the main points of the PNA has been the creation of the *Panel Ciudadano de la Deliberación Ciudadana sobre el Agua* (Deci Agua). Deci Agua is composed of scientists from the University of the Republic and an advisory board composed of multiple experts working on water issues in Uruguay. Public participation through citizen involvement in specific workshops and the professional collaboration promoted by Deci Agua aims to develop information that can be integrated into the PNA.

Conclusions

Emergent assemblages of water governance in Uruguay reflect the perceptions of water quality deterioration and governance that are specific to communities if we compare regions over time. Environmental problems related to water quality in the Southwest (Nueva Palmira and Dolores) had less media coverage (from the capital) and did not become part of the "major environmental issues" in the country. While in both communities there were local actors working to denounce and improve issues related to water quality, the external linkages of these communities with key stakeholders of interest and/or links with communities did not provide enough media coverage and active involvement by national institutions working in relation to water quality or other locally important environmental problems (Thompson 2014, 2015). The local assemblage created in NP did not sufficiently accumulate resources used for addressing water quality (and other environmental) problems. It should be noted that many of the problems associated with the appearance of algal blooms, visible in different parts of the country, had been observed in NP and Dolores for several years already. These communities are in a very productive agricultural region, which was the focus of attraction for agricultural expansion during the late 1990s and early 2000s. Water quality problems in these two communities became part of the national news only after similar problems were highlighted for communities of the South and the East. In Dolores, local water management reassembled to address water quality problems after national news highlighted similar problems in the South and the East.

Publicized problems associated with water quality deterioration in the South and the East, including La Paloma, and communities that depend on water supply from the basin of the Santa Lucia River and the Sauce Lagoon, are examples of how environmental problems at the local level may become of interest not only for affected communities but also for "external" actors with strong links and/or interests therein. Water quality problems detected in these three cases became part of the "national environmental agenda" through significant coverage by the press and social networks, and by drawing the attention of important government actors (DINAMA, OSE, MGAP, etc.) who responded to many local demands and, in the process, broadened the assemblage to regional and national scales to address water problems. Strong external ties of affected communities and interests of stakeholders mainly located in the capital facilitated the flow of external resources that local *Municipios* could use to deal with this and other environmental problems. In all of the cases, new decentralization programs and spaces for public participation such as *Municipios* and sometimes MDRs had important roles facilitating local discussion on environmental problems and making them more visible at local level.

Although the risks and negative effects of environmental problems associated with water quality are often perceived at the local level, lack of attention by external actors and media coverage may adversely affect the legitimacy of local environmental claims, the resources to which communities had access

(Thompson 2014, 2015), and the coherence of specific assemblages. Construction and social legitimization of locally observed environmental problems can be significantly influenced by social relations and ties of each community but also by historical centralism in governance. Centralism of certain private actors, state and civil organizations with specific interests (cultural, economic, political, etc.) can influence the identification and legitimization of environmental problems in certain communities and ignore or omit other environmental problems that are perhaps perceived as "uninteresting" or ignored in other communities or regions. This can be critical because many times the communities most affected by environmental problems are those with fewer resources, perpetuating environmental inequality and community dependency. This also raises the question of what are the economic, political, and/or cultural factors that attribute greater regional or national impact to some locally observed environmental problems than others, and consequently greater attention from centralist government institutions which could facilitate appropriate resources and assemblage responses to solve these problems.

In Uruguay, the historic dependency of communities and recently created decentralization programs on departmental and national institutions (i.e., *Intendencias* and ministries), negatively influences the detection of environmental problems and possible solutions through empowerment or the capability to decide how locally available resources can be used. New efforts by the Uruguayan government and the University of the Republic to decentralize environmental governance have great potential not only in improving local capacities to identify environmental problems but also in monitoring and controlling natural resources of communities through new assemblages. At the same time, some government institutions centralized in Montevideo, such as DINAMA and MGAP, have promoted "individual" environmental control at the local level, but centralized state bureaucracy and lack of resources and socio-cultural barriers at local levels may negatively influence these efforts (Thompson 2014).

Many communities do not have the links and/or sufficient resources to make visible and legitimate environmental claims locally, so new decentralization programs can have an important role in facilitating the scientific and technological resources (centralized in a few state institutions) for environmental monitoring and control in their new spaces for public participation. This could imply better coordination of various local, regional, and national actors on monitoring environmental changes at the local level. Unlike previous assembling to address water quality (and other environmental) problems, the emergent assemblages facilitated by CCAs and the PNA working on water management and control in different regions and communities of the country, may represent important opportunities for communities. They can improve the coordination of different types of actors from different levels, provide resources (i.e. technology, funding, scientific information), and promote community empowerment and participation. This re-assembling promoted by the national government can actively work with communities through the existing decentralization programs such as the *Municipios*. This will need to involve cultural and long-term social changes, not only within centralist institutions but also within the local population which needs to be aware of and responsible for how natural resources are managed and controlled.

Notes

1 One questionnaire for *Intendencia* staff and another (similar) questionnaire for other actors from the market, state, and civil society involved in the communities.
2 Dolores was under its jurisdiction. This meeting was organized in Mercedes.
3 The second most important port in the country, after Montevideo.
4 Law No 18.610.
5 Law No 18.719.
6 Law No 18.308, Ordenamiento Territorial y Desarrollo Sostenible 2008.
7 Law No 18.567, Descentralización Departamental y Local y Participación Ciudadana 2009.

References

Abrahan, Manuela, Florencia Beder, Gustavo Cánepa, and Sebastián Goinheix. 2014. "La Paloma y Nueva Palmira: Trayectoria Histórica y Datos Socioeconómicos Actuales." In *Nuevos Desafíos y Respuestas de los Actores Sobre el Desarrollo Local, La Paloma y Nueva Palmira Frente a Propuestas de Inversión*, edited by Altaïr Magri, Manuela Abrahan and Leticia Ogues, 95–110. Montevideo: Universidad de la República. Uruguay.

Adger, Neil W. 2003. "Social Capital, Collective Action, and Adaptation to Climate Change." *Economic Geography* 79(4): 387–404.

Adger, Neil W., Irene Lorenzoni, and Karen L. O'Brien (eds). 2009. *Adapting to Climate Change. Thresholds, Values, and Governance*. Cambridge, UK: Cambridge University Press.

Armitage, Derek. 2008. "Governance and the Commons in a Multi-level World." *International Journal of the Commons* (2): 7–32.

Ashwill, Maximillian, Cornelia Flora, and Jan Flora. 2011. *The Adaptation Coalition Toolkit, Building Community Resilience to the Social Dimensions of Climate Change*. Social Development Unit Latin America Caribbean Region. Washington, DC: The World Bank. (www.preventionweb.net/files/25378_adaptationcoalitiontoolkitbuildingc.pdf).

Berdegué, Julio A., Anthony Bebbington, Javier Escobal, Arilson Favareto, M. Ignacia Fernández, Pablo Ospina, Helle Munk Ravnborg, Francisco Aguirre, Manuel Chiriboga, Ileana Gómez, Ligia Gómez, Félix Modrego, Susan Paulson, Eduardo Ramírez, Alexander Schetjman, and Carolina Trivelli. 2012. "Territorios en Movimiento: Dinámicas Territoriales Rurales en América Latina." *Documento de Trabajo #11*. Programa de Dinámicas Territoriales Rurales. Retrieved on August 15, 2012 (www.rimisp.org/proyectos/index_portada_noticia.php?id_proyecto=180).

Berkes, Fikret. 2008. "Commons in a Multi-level World." *International Journal of the Commons* 2(1): 1–6.

Boyd, D. Amanda and Travis B. Paveglio. 2014. "Front Page or "Buried" Beneath the Fold? Media Coverage of Carbon Capture and Storage." *Public Understanding of Science* 23(4): 411–427. doi: 10.1177/0963662512450990.

Ching, Leong. 2010. "Eliminating 'Yuck': A Simple Exposition of Media and Social Change in Water Reuse Policies." *Water Resources Development* 26(1): 111–124. doi: 10.1080/07900620903392174.

De Barbieri, María and Cristina Zurbriggen. 2011. *Acción Colectiva, Gobierno y Territorio: experiencias Cono Sur*. Montevideo: FLACSO.

Dolnicar, Sara and Anna Hurlimann. 2010. "Water Alternatives – Who and What Influences Public Acceptance?" *Journal of Public Affairs* 11(1): 49–59.

Ensor, Jonathan and Rachel Berger (eds). 2009. *Understanding Climate Change Adaptation, Lessons from Community Based Approaches*. Rugby, UK: Practical Action Publishing.

Flora, Cornelia B. and Jan L. Flora. 2013. *Rural Communities: Legacy and Change*. 4th ed. Boulder, CO: Westview Press.

Gates, Christopher. 1999. "Community Governance." *Futures* 31: 519–525.

Hannigan, John. 2014. *Environmental Sociology*. 3rd edition. New York: Routledge, Taylor and Francis Group.

Head, Brian W. 2007. "Community Engagement: Participation on Whose Terms?" *Australian Journal of Political Science* 42(3): 441–454.

Howe, Peter D. 2009. "Newsworthy Spaces: The Semantic Geographies of Local News." *Aether* 4: 43–61.

IAPP (International Association for Public Participation). 2007. "IAP2, Public Participation Spectrum." Retrieved on October 14, 2013 (www.iap2.org/associations/4748/files/IAP2%20Spectrum_vertical.pdf).

McFarlane, Colin and Ben Anderson 2011. "Thinking with Assemblage." *Area* 43(2): 162–164. doi: 10.1111/j.1475-4762.2011.01012.x.

Ministerio de Vivienda, Ordenamiento Territorial y Medio Ambiente (MVOTMA). 2016. "Plan Nacional de Aguas. Propuesta" Montevideo: MVOTMA.

Piñeiro, Diego E. 2004. "Movimientos Sociales, Gobernanza Ambiental y Desarrollo Territorial Rural." RIMISP. Agosto de 2004. Retrieved on August 12, 2012 (www.rimisp.org/FCKeditor/UserFiles/File/documentos/docs/pdf/0534-005165-pineirodocumento1rimisp.pdf).

Rojas, Daniel. 2015. "Vecinos de Dolores al Gobierno: Contaminación está Trayendo Cáncer." *El País*, June 7, 2015. Retrieved on December 23, 2015. (www.elpais.com.uy/informacion/vecinos-dolores-gobierno-contaminacion-trayendo.html).

Tejera, Rafael. 2014. "Regiones de Concentración de Tensiones Desde La Recuperación Económica (2003–2013)." In *Nuevos Desafíos y Respuestas de los Actores Sobre el Desarrollo Local, La Paloma y Nueva Palmira Frente a Propuestas de Inversión*, edited by Altaïr Magri, Manuela Abrahan and Leticia Ogues, 85–92. Montevideo: Universidad de la República, Uruguay.

Thompson, Diego. 2014. "Environmental Stresses and Community Responses in Four Communities of Southwestern Uruguay." Doctoral Dissertation, Iowa State University. Copyright ProQuest, UMI Dissertations Publishing 2014: (http://search.proquest.com/docview/1659795213).

Thompson, Diego. 2015. "Community Adaptations to Environmental Challenges under Decentralized Governance in Southwestern Uruguay." *Journal of Rural Studies* 43: 71–82.

Tompkins, Emma. L. and Neil W. Adger. 2004. "Does Adaptive Management of Natural Resources Enhance Resilience to Climate Change?" *Ecology and Society* 9 (2): 10.

Wright, Rachel A. and Hilary S. Boudet. 2012. "To Act or Not to Act: Context, Capability, and Community Response to Environmental Risk." *American Journal of Sociology* 118(3): 728–777.

Zurbriggen, Cristina. 2011. "Gobernanza: una Mirada desde América Latina." *Perfiles Latinoamericanos* (38): 39–64.

10 The "dirty dairying" campaign in New Zealand

Constructing problems and assembling responses

Ismaël Tall and Hugh Campbell

Introduction

Agriculture in New Zealand is subject to considerable political and media attention due to its large economic contribution and, more recently, its highly visible environmental impacts. Dairy farming has experienced rapid growth and intensification during the last 30 years, and has come under heavy criticism from different sources: from the public to environmentalists and NGOs. The key crisis has emerged around water pollution. Rivers, lakes, streams, lagoons and wetlands are slowly deteriorating and dairy farming and its accompanying industry are increasingly being targeted as the main actors held accountable for this crisis. This particular entanglement of political forces and contradictory interests around the economic and environmental outcomes of dairy farming went through a major transition in the early 2000s through what has become known as the "dirty dairying" campaign.

This chapter will respond to the dirty dairying crisis by putting together new ideas around assemblage thinking with older theoretical framings that seek to uncover the way in which public and agri-environmental problems are socially constructed. We will examine the way in which the politics of rendering the connections between farming and farmed environments more visible has also made them more able to be politicized and responded to. At the heart of this new rendering is the assemblage approach which forms a central theme of this book collection.

Tania Li provides a prominent account of community forest management as assemblage which demonstrates the network of relationships that stabilizes and enables a particular enduring human relationship with land-based resources. In this chapter, we want to explore three of these elements – "rendering technical", "anti-politics" and "re-assembling". Thus, we shall reveal the way in which the multiple elements of the relationship between intensive dairy farming and water quality in New Zealand can be understood, both in composition and in its socio-political elements, as an assemblage, in order to explain particular environmental governance responses as a form of "re-assembling".

In order to disentangle this environmental and social imbroglio we will first explore the agricultural policy and the importance of dairy farming in New

Zealand. Second, we will examine the historical origin of the "dirty dairying" campaign. Third, we will address the theoretical background of assemblage by using the case of diffuse (or non-point source) water pollution. Fourth, the effects of the expression "dirty dairying" will be presented. As a discourse that shapes a new representation of reality, this term creates a new ontological connectedness between farming and the environment which then enables new governance responses to take shape. Finally, we will linger on the dynamics of "re-assembling" revealed in the particular framing of, and responses to, water pollution, showing the re-appropriation by authorities and industry of a certain association of ideas in order to come up with governing tools.

The neoliberal transition in New Zealand agriculture

New Zealand agricultural policy demonstrates a very peculiar characteristic: in many respects, it is almost non-existent! In 1984, the Fourth Labour government removed the main instrument of state intervention into agriculture – the subsidies allocated to farmers – and started deregulating the large government commodity export boards that controlled the exporting of key goods like wool, meat and dairy products. Afterwards, pastoral farming changed dramatically with the resultant slow decline of the sheepmeat and wool export sectors in favour of dairy farming which relentlessly moved towards its current status as the economically dominant farming land-use in New Zealand.

Agriculture has entered a new phase of intensification since the 1980s reforms: stocking units per hectare, animal productivity per hectare, and agricultural inputs such as feed, pesticides or fertilizers, have increased dramatically (MacLeod and Moller 2006). Dairy farming has both intensified as well as become more geographically extended. It was located primarily in the North Island regions of Waikato, Taranaki and Manawatu and, while it is still a very important part of those regions' identities, has spread through the South Island – particularly in Southland and Canterbury – where widespread conversions from sheep farming to dairying have occurred (Forney and Stock 2014). Today, a dairy farm has an average herd size of 419 cows, up from 113 cows in 1975/1976 (LIC and Dairy NZ 2016). Sheep farming, on the contrary, has suffered a slow decline. The national sheep flock has declined from 70 million in 1982 to only 27 million in 2016 (Statistics New Zealand 2017). The growth of the dairy industry has followed a path of institutional consolidation. The pre-neoliberal structure of multiple grower-owned processing cooperatives supplying the monopoly-exporting New Zealand Dairy Board (NZDB) gave way to a rapid amalgamation of cooperatives. This process culminated in 2001 with the legislated transition of the export functions of the NZDB to a new mega-cooperative – Fonterra – which had emerged from the final amalgamation of the remaining two large dairy cooperatives. Fonterra consolidated the supply and export functions of the dairy industry for the first time – purchasing over 90% of dairy products and is credited with being the largest dairy export organisation in the world (Muirhead and Campbell 2012).

Today, several colliding interests and trajectories around dairying have a high level of visibility in public debate. First, although the national economy has benefited from dairy intensification, its consequences have become a significant source of concern for environmental groups. The recent intensification of agriculture (and dairy farming in particular) is seen as being responsible for the decline of water quality in waterways. After many decades in which agriculture was not a key target of environmental concerns, the influence of diffuse pollution from agriculture on water quality is now seen as the most compelling environmental issue in the eyes of the public (Hughey, Cullen and Kerr 2016). Second, New Zealand's deregulated agricultural sector has become a testing ground for "market-led" and/or voluntary approaches to environmental management – including the complex issues around water pollution. Stakeholders from different social and political groupings (government, industry groups, NGOs, iwi[1]) gathered in 2009 to form the Land and Water Forum, which has been tasked with providing recommendations to both national government and regional councils in relation to freshwater management. Third, despite the absence of agricultural policy per se, farmers are indirectly affected by several other pieces of legislation, in particular the Resource Management Act 1991 (RMA), which applies to natural resources and land use. While the farmed environment is only lightly regulated by international standards, this Act and the regulations it imposes are a source of considerable resentment from farmers. In this sense, the environmental problem in agriculture, seen within a wider transition towards neoliberal governance, provides two compelling questions that we will explore in this chapter: how did a politically passive relationship between farming and the environment become problematized, and what kinds of new governance response are being assembled to respond to this new farming ontology?

Historical background of the dirty dairying problem

Our argument opens with the compelling need to clarify one quite singular ontological characteristic of New Zealand farming. For most of the twentieth century, farming was never the subject of an environmental critique. The environmentalist movement that emerged in New Zealand after the 1960s tended to focus on a range of causes that never seemed to include farming as a threat to the environment (O'Brien 2013). This contrasts greatly with the "contested countryside" accounts of environmental conflict in Europe. Put simply, farming and the wider environment never existed within the same ontological space. While this curious ontological separation will be examined at more length in other publications, it also forms the essential pre-condition to all that follows in this chapter.

After these many decades in which farming activities had rarely been questioned, the separated worlds of farming and the environment were about to collide in a compellingly powerful conflict. In June 2001, several local newspapers published advertisements for a public interest campaign openly showing hostility towards dairy farming as a perpetrator of environmental harms. The campaign originated with Fish and Game, an NGO for fishing and hunting enthusiasts, and represented a dramatic entry into policy debate by a previously moderate organization. The campaign created the loaded expression "dirty dairying", clearly associating dairy farming and environmental degradation (Blackett and Le Heron 2008). This represented a profound ontological challenge to a world that was founded on the separation of farming and environmental concerns. The campaign placed two concepts – dairy intensification and degradation of water – into the same political space and went on to criticize the lack of management of this problem by regional councils, the responsible local authorities for natural resource management.

A quote from Fish and Game's Chief Executive Bryce Johnson summarizes the strong impact achieved by the organization with the coinage of the discursive coupling "dirty dairying" (Fish and Game as quoted in Ryan 2014, 5):

> If I had to pick one issue since the beginning of the new millennium for which Fish & Game New Zealand could claim the credit for having successfully forced onto the political stage, it would be the plight of New Zealand's natural water. The catalyst for this was our 'dirty dairying' campaign, the success of which took everyone by surprise. It obviously touched a public nerve that was looking for expression, and went viral.

In the "Dairy Farming & The Environment" position statement that underwrote the advertising campaign in newspapers, the organization addressed the core logic of their demand for more environment-friendly agriculture:

> Habitat protection is critically important to the achievement of Fish & Game's statutory duty. We realised long ago that if the habitat is looked after then the animals that rely on that habitat will largely look after themselves.

And:

> [a]ny activity that degrades the quality and/or extent of this habitat is therefore a threat to sports fish and game populations and Fish & Game is obliged to challenge its adverse environmental effects and those specific activities and agencies that cause it.[2]

It is not surprising that Fish and Game sought to protect fishing and hunting interests; what is more curious is that these interests had remained unprotected for so long. The ontologically challenging element of the campaign (and its broad support across New Zealand) was that there was no dispute on the basic scientific dynamics under consideration, rather that something that was previously held in the realm of the "uncertain" and "invisible" had been identified and problematized. The fundamental claim that water pollution is caused by dairying is *essentially* confirmed by research on land use effects on water composition (that affect water quality). There is clear evidence that New Zealand has undergone a significant intensification of its agricultural systems (MacLeod and Moller 2006) and this intensification can be correlated to an altered water composition (see Davies-Colley 2013 for a list of environmental studies). We deliberately use the term "essentially" in a conditional form, because water pollution is a wider problem – a result of its diffuse and transversal characteristics. Furthermore, as we will go on to argue, water degradation concerns the multiple and diverse values that are socially attributed to specific waterways. The scientific discussion of the contribution of dairy farming to water pollution is not, however, what primarily interests us here; it is rather the way this "wicked" problem was problematized. What we see here is an example of a private problem (rivers being allowed to exist in poor quality to allow for the continuation of private farming activities) that then became translated into a public problem through the "dirty dairying" campaign. In order for this translation to happen, a non-problem became reconstructed as a problem. Such reconstruction, particularly in the light of the prior passivity of this ontological space, provides a compelling subject for an assemblage-based approach to understanding and enacting agri-environmental governance.

The uncertainties of water

Before we undertake a more detailed analysis of the ontological realignment of the "dirty dairying" problem, we must briefly return to Li's concept of assemblage. Li proposes an assemblage definition that goes beyond the Foucauldian concept of problematization – albeit while taking great inspiration from it – by giving analytical primacy to specific *practices* of governance. She demonstrates her particular approach to assemblage through an analysis of community forest management which combines elements such as: material things, socially situated objects, objectives, knowledges, discourses, institutions, laws, etc. Her assemblage framework comprises six kinds of practice: forging alignments, rendering technical, authorizing knowledge, managing failures and contradictions, anti-politics, and re-assembling (Li 2007a).

Among the six practices related to assemblage, we choose to concentrate on three of them as being particularly useful for understanding "dirty dairying", its consequences and subsequent responses. For Li, rendering technical means:

> extracting from the messiness of the social world, with all the processes that run th[r]ough [sic] it, a set of relations that can be formulated as a diagram in which problem (a) plus intervention (b) will produce (c), a beneficial result.
>
> (2007a, 265)

Practices of "rendering technical" not only work to simplify a complex reality but they also transform the "messy" aspects of a situation into a network of intelligible relations that are more governable. Rendering technical is similar to the problematization process, since "the identification of a problem is intimately linked to the availability of a solution" (Li 2007b, 7). Here we can usefully draw parallels from policy science: according to classical public policy analysis, a public problem is in the process of being solved when an authority acts on a target group that is considered to be the origin of the problem. This process follows the well-known "naming, blaming, claiming" argument (Felstiner, Abel and Sarat 1980–1981). The authors show how an unperceived injurious experience becomes a perceived one. This transformation implies recognizing a situation by *naming* the negative experience, *blaming* an actor or a group who is considered to be responsible, and finally *claiming* a solution. The designation of a target group is also the fruit of social construction. Naming certain actors as responsible for a problematic situation is a political activity that is embedded in problem-framing.

Furthermore, rendering technical is deeply connected with what Li calls anti-politics: "questions that are rendered technical are simultaneously rendered non-political" (Li 2007b, 7). In her terms, the practice of anti-politics refers to the act of stripping off the controversies, negotiations, arrangements (i.e. the politics) of a situation by redirecting contentious elements into the realm of technical expertise (Li 2007a, 265).

Finally, Li defines re-assembling as the practice of "grafting on new elements and reworking old ones; deploying existing discourses to new ends; transposing the meanings of key terms" (2007a, 265). As we will see, newly formed assemblages can be re-used by different actors and reworked to fit a specific goal.

The assemblage approach is useful in its compatibility with wider insights from actor–network theory – particularly about the wildness or vitality of non-human actors. Water is complex and uncertain in some key ways: it crosses boundaries in ways characteristic of "wicked problems" in the environment, the pollution of water is often from diffuse sources, the measurement of quality has its own metrological dynamics and politics, and there is no stable set of cultural or social points of view on the values and utilities of water. The world of water quality is unstable, complex, difficult to measure and, as a result, unknowable in an easily accessible way. This instability is fundamental to the character of the problem and its associated political practices. It both enabled the stark effectiveness of a campaign that dramatically simplified these dynamics, as well as having an essential role in shaping the re-assembling of a governance response by the key stakeholders after the crisis had emerged.

While the framing of "wicked problems" is familiar in discussions of environmental governance, our case study requires an acknowledgement of a problem that is wicked in multiple ways. A first mention of wicked problems comes from Rittel and Webber (1973) describing problems that are hard to solve, in contrast to "tame problems" (p. 160). For Head, the wickedness stems from the "complexity of elements, subsystems and interdependencies", "uncertainty in relation to risks, consequences of action, and changing patterns" and "divergence and fragmentation in viewpoints, values, strategic intentions" (2008, 103). Furthermore, water pollution can be understood as a wicked problem, because it is an issue that exceeds the limits of a single dimension of public policy. Water pollution in New Zealand brings in the legal use of natural resources (under the RMA 1991), the management of property rights and specific regional practices of land-use planning. The number of stakeholders linked to the issue is a parameter that also need to be considered. Water pollution issues concern farmers, fishermen, hunters or other water users, but also non-human actors that other groups speak in behalf of, such as living organisms affected by a material alteration of a waterway. In this way, water problems can be linked to the ontological flattening and "wilding" characteristic of actor–network theory and its turn to "vitality" (Bennett 2009; Carolan 2013). As the following section will show, the quality of water is complex, inconsistent, contingent on different values, and includes a lot of non-human actors and vitalities that make it challenging to "know" and to contain, let alone govern.

Water quality and the complexity of non-point pollution

What is water quality? The good or bad quality of a waterway depends on the value that is assigned to it, an assignment made by its use, among other criteria. Johnson, quoted by Davies-Colley (2013, 33), describes water quality as:

> A measure of the condition of water relative to the requirements of one or more species and/or to any human need or purpose ... [and] the suitability of water composition for supporting a range of water values, including habitat for aquatic life and human uses including recreation.

Water quality refers to the physical, biological and chemical components that constitute it. In this, it differentiates from water quantity (even though volume can be a relevant measure of the quality of water bodies). But, more importantly and fundamentally, water quality is related to values: a waterway is not only a waterway, but, for instance, a place dedicated to fishing for brown trout, a reservoir used for irrigation or drinking, a living space for a certain eel species or even a childhood memory. For example, within the framework of the River Values Assessment System, Hughey and Booth (2012) detail a list of six categories of values (here synonymous with use): recreation, character, ecological, cultural, developmental and other values. Each value or use attributed to a waterway brings in one or several measures of the quality of the water, which are: physical and chemical characteristics, nutriments rate, optical variables and microbiological indicators (Davies-Colley 2013). We can also add to this typology "less tangible" values that some associate with a waterway. The visual degradation of a particular space or the mere knowledge of its degradation can negatively impact the personal value associated with it. Economic values of water are part of the problematic. For example, tourism is an important economic sector for New Zealand (Bain and Dandachi 2015) and it relies notably on the "clean" and "green" image of the landscape, including waterways, which stands in stark contrast to other economic actors like dairying.

This high diversity of possible uses or values show that it is not possible to speak of water quality as being represented by a universal constant. The "will to protect" water must be contextualized and is bundled within wickedly complex relations of needs, values and uses.

Water quality problems in New Zealand are primarily the result of non-point source pollution (point source pollution having been already subjected to legal constraint in the 1970s). Within the context of our wider argument, the diffuse aspect of water pollution makes it difficult to point to a specific individual or group (with a few uncommon exceptions involving extreme infringements) thus making it difficult to pin down or strongly identify a single culprit. This plays its part in creating "invisibility" as a characteristic of water quality. By demonstrating the complexity of non-point discharge and by establishing a list of potential threats for water and the different natural factors that alter its quality, we want to show how unstable and unknowable water quality has been as a field of specific governance and political action.

The substantial complexity of water pollution in New Zealand can be illustrated through three approaches: the diversity of water bodies, pollutants and soils. First, water pollution impacts on water bodies differently whether they are rivers, streams, lakes, wetlands or in underground aquifers. For example, a river with a weak flow rate induces a higher tendency to be affected by pollutants (Davies-Colley 2013); as for lakes, by their stagnant nature, they are more vulnerable than rivers. Higher temperatures as well as a limited depth and size are factors that also increase their vulnerability (Parliamentary Commissioner for the Environment 2012). Second, pollutants are of a diverse nature: sediments, nutrients (mainly nitrogen- or phosphorus-based molecules) or pathogens constitute the main categories of pollutants that have an impact on water composition and result respectively (and approximately) in murky waters, eutrophication and toxicity (Parliamentary Commissioner for the Environment 2012, 2013). Third, the very nature of the soil is also a determining factor in the way contaminants move – whether the soil is, for example, alpine or gleyed. Other factors include the lag time between the pollutant discharge and its effects in water (Howard-Williams *et al.* 2010) or the high number of farmers involved in a catchment or around a river making it nearly impossible to target a single accountable farmer for a pollution issue.

A final element to this opacity and instability of water quality as an object of governance is that even among farmers there are varying points of view. In a study of farmers in Canterbury (one of the South Island dairying regions), Duncan (2013) shows that they offer reasons explaining why their contribution to water pollution is perceived to be minimal. Among the reasons are: spatial characteristics (the distance of their actions from the river, the absence of permeable soil on the farm), the nature of their soil (their clayey composition, the depth of the topsoil) or other reasons (the presence of filtering aquifers for nutrients, a low pluviometry in the region). These remarks seek to show the complexity of the movement of nutrients from the farm to the water:

> The fact is, little is known about what happens beyond the root zone beyond modelling and assumptions about attenuation. As far as farmers are concerned, this relationship is not direct – there are many factors that can impede the movement of nutrients from the farm to the river and, it would seem, moderate responsibility.
>
> (Duncan 2013, 7)

Consequently, she adds that "[f]armers (i.e. those who are expected to change their ways) see the problem as temporary and contingent upon a range of highly variable factors and its effects influenced and impeded by a number of equally unknowable circumstances" (Duncan 2013, 8). Duncan (2016) argues that farmers rely on knowledge practices that accommodate the variability of biophysical factors, as opposed to modelling science, which eschews variability and is based on variables which constitute authorities' conceptions of them as the water quality problem.

In summary, the "problem" of water quality lies well within the category of the "political" not because of any overt strategy or chicanery to hide it from the public gaze, but mainly due to a set of inherent complexities stemming from the underlying biologies, the complex interactions between farms and waterways and the difficulty for even directly involved land-users to know what their influence is. Water quality is therefore a wicked problem because it is a problem in which there was no immediate foothold for the established suite of scientific and regulatory mechanisms to step into. That ungraspable quality was erased in 2001 through a clever and direct ontological reframing of the problem.

"Dirty dairying": the creation of a new ontology

A search of the content of New Zealand media (national and regional) with the Newztext[3] tool shows the emergence of the expression "dirty dairying" in June 2001. This exactly aligns with the date when Fish and Game advertised their bitter critique of the dairy industry in several local newspapers. Since then, the combination of "dirty" and "dairying" has frequently been used to define water pollution problems from intensive agriculture. The conjunction of these two common words was simply non-existent in the media before this date.

The campaign mobilized a number of tactics identified in a previous section of this chapter as being effective in moving issues from being private issues to public problems. By specifically associating milk to water degradation, it created a new ontological juxtaposition, generating a peculiar assemblage around the water pollution problematic. Thus, within the frame of Felstiner, Abel and Sarat's problematization theory (1980–1981), the constitution of this problem named the problem as dirty waterways (naming), identified dairy farmers as the group of actors accountable for this issue (blaming), and offered a way to solve it (claiming) by asking for more regulation from the industry itself and regional councils. The problematization of "dirty dairying" aligns with the second step of Li's practices of assemblage – rendering technical – as we see a new set of relations between different elements being formulated in an unequivocal way.

Following the launch of the campaign, numerous articles constituted a written war between environmentalists and farmers that helped embed the "dirty dairying" concept (Dearnaley 2001; Stuff 2001a, 2001b). Since then, the combination of "dirty" and "dairying" are regularly used in the media (1370 occurrences in the media such as articles, press releases or radio information from June 2001 to December 2016 – see Table 10.1) and official reports. Examples are numerous: "Commissioner to investigate dirty dairying" (Radio New Zealand Newswire 2002), "Final warning for dirty dairying pair" (Neems 2009), "Cleaning up dirty dairying" (The Dominion Post 2017) and so on.

Clearly, quite quickly after 2001, "dirty dairying" as an ontological juxtaposition had become a thing. The next question is how this began to have effects and trigger specific reactions.

"Dirty dairying" as a discourse makes visible a specific part of the network constituted by water in collaboration with other heterogeneous elements (which affect its "quality"). It is here an alignment of specific assemblage thinking and wider ideas in actor–network theory, particularly the works of Michel Callon (1986). Indeed, some of the practices contributing to assembling are strikingly similar to "interessement", one of the four steps of Callon's sociology of translation: "Interessement is the group of actions by which an entity […] attempts to impose and stabilize the other actors it defines through its problematization" (1986, 62). In either an assemblage logic or an actor–network approach, elements linked together exceed the boundaries of the human world and connect objects like waterways to pollution (including cows' excretion and urination, or molecules of nitrates).

This crystallization is then perpetuated by the media and takes shape in governance instruments. The creation of a new ontological coupling, as a thinking category, echoes the creative capacity of discourse (Feindt and Oels 2005). In an uncertain world, the "dirty dairying" discourse proposes a certain web of (causal) relations as being the reality itself. The expression brought the two

Table 10.1 Number of occurrences of the expression "dirty dairying" in New Zealand media

Year	Occurrences	Year	Occurrences
2001	99	2009	129
2002	123	2010	128
2003	66	2011	125
2004	56	2012	132
2005	27	2013	131
2006	18	2014	110
2007	58	2015	72
2008	68	2016	28

Source: Newztext Search.

previously ontologically separated realms of farming and environmental issues together and therefore created a discursive coupling on which it was possible to exercise a form of power. The problem of water pollution was not new per se: the phenomenon known as water pollution was already addressed by media, scientific literature and legislation; but the expression "dirty dairying" amplified and reconfigured it. The key foothold was to create an association between a previously unknowable problem and a specific culprit – dairy farmers. Thus, the "dirty dairying" campaign defined a new potential target group to which policy intervention could be applied. The use of this expression highlighted the ecological pressure which the country was experiencing around the intensification of milk production and built from this association a problem, which, even if it was previously recognised, did not have such an easily knowable quality.

From a public perspective, the perception of New Zealanders about the main causes of water quality has evolved since 2000 in a way that compellingly bears out the power of this coupling. During 2001, farming as a cause of water quality degradation was considered to be just one factor like any other along with industrial activities, hazardous chemicals, sewage and storm water (Hughey, Cullen and Kerr 2010). It is now – in 2016 – the clear top concern with 60% of surveyed people perceiving farming as having the strongest negative impact on water quality in New Zealand (Hughey, Cullen and Kerr 2016). We do not argue that this dramatic trend is solely correlated with the "dirty dairying" campaign; but it seems nevertheless a very important contributor to this change.

Making water pollution governable

The "dirty dairying" campaign created a new field of political possibilities around water quality. A new ontology of water quality was now in operation and a regulatory and political response was urgently needed. This response would initially come from the major players in the dairy industry. Founded, coincidentally, in 2001, the dairy company Fonterra occupied a quasi-monopoly on the collection of milk in New Zealand and was compelled to act in response as one of its first actions as a new business entity. It quickly took over the problem of "dirty dairying" and proposed a solution embodied in the *Dairying and Clean Streams Accord* (hereafter the Accord), a policy created jointly between Fonterra and the Ministry of Primary Industries (formerly known as the Ministry for Agriculture and Forestry). The Accord's provisions started in 2003 and ran until 2012.

The Accord represents that next stage in the rolling out of practices within an assemblage framework. It can be seen as performing a concerted remodelling of the problem configuration. It was also an opportunity to take the lead in responding to the crisis, thus avoiding stronger state regulation of the industry (Jay 2006). The five objectives proposed by the document were: (1) the establishment of fences on the banks of rivers, streams and lakes, (2) the construction of culverts to protect small waterways at stock crossings, (3) compliance with the regional councils' rules on effluent discharges from dairy sheds, (4) the adoption of a nutrient budget system to manage nitrogen in farming systems, and (5) the protection of significant wetlands with fences (Ministry for Primary Industries 2013). In 2013, the *Sustainable Dairying: Water Accord*, proposed by dairy farmers' representative organisation Dairy NZ, succeeded the original Accord (Dairy NZ 2013).

The Accord's re-appropriation of "dirty dairying" was politically highly effective: it took up the key ontological juxtaposition created by the campaign, namely a link between dairy farming and watercourses, and replied to it with a new solution: keep the cows out of the water! Thus, the main strategy in the Accord was the protection of water by preventing cows from approaching small streams, rivers and lakes. This was discursively highly effective, even though: "[T]here is [...] room for debate about what is a 'stream' and about whether protection of surface water (as opposed to groundwater) is sufficient to offset the effects of dairy effluent on paddocks" (Jay 2006, 272). In Callon's terms, this separation was laid across materials, vitalities and actions that don't necessarily observe human boundaries and overflow outside networks.

Technically, practices implementing three of the five objectives of the Accord were almost achieved in 2012, the remaining two being the wetlands protection objectives and the 100% compliance with regional council rules (Ministry for Primary Industries 2013). The Accord was also criticized as deploying a partial vision of the problem with the means not corresponding to the objectives needing to be achieved (Deans and Hackwell 2008; Holland 2014). The *Sustainable Dairying: Water Accord* then extended the original Accord objectives to include more detailed riparian, water use and nutrient management as well as dairy conversions. It also included the small number of other dairy companies and cooperatives as well as Fonterra.

In the end, what we observe in the case of these new agreements and practices is the act of making problems governable (Callon 1986; Lascoumes 1996; Oels 2005). The (re)organization of a problem is carried out in such a way that it is possible to exercise a policy intervention against it. Whether they are industry-driven agreements or governmental regulatory practices, we observe a common quality – the technical re-appropriation of a complex situation. Rose, quoted in Li (2007a, 279), mentions "switch points where an opening turns into a closure". Here, the campaign launched by Fish and Game represented the opening and the policies stemming from Fonterra or the government worked towards creating a closure. The regulatory answer to a problem is stripped of its political aspects, namely the wicked complexity, material vitalities, and the multisectoral arrangement of diffuse water pollution, and transformed into something that can be managed through technical measures. In short, the choice of a policy and the instruments it incorporates translates a specific configuration of the problematization (Lascoumes and Simard 2011). In responding to the crisis of dairying and water, it is not hard to see a significant disjunction between extensive objectives (improving New Zealand freshwater) and very specific instruments.

Conclusion

In conclusion, the term dirty dairying has changed the agri-environmental debate in New Zealand. The concept, which emerged from a campaign led by an NGO, put dairy farming at the heart of the environmental issue of water pollution by associating it with dirty practices.

Water pollution is a wicked problem, especially because of non-point discharges. A multitude of factors indicate its complexity. The nature of the pollutants, the type of freshwater bodies and soils, meteorological indicators, sources of pollution and values or uses attributed to rivers reveal the inherently wicked nature of the problem. Moreover, it is a problem that crosses political sectors and engages a large number of actors.

It is striking to see how Fish and Game's dirty dairying campaign froze some of these relations by associating the problem of water pollution with the previously unobjectionable realm of agriculture. To use Li's terms, this association rendered technical this situation in a very specific way. This had powerful consequences, and since the campaign began, the media then frequently used this previously non-existent coupling, a transition that clearly demonstrates the relevance of discourse and its ability to bring problematic realities into existence. In this sense, one can speak of the construction of a problem but not, ultimately, its resolution.

This new ontological alignment provoked a re-appropriation, or re-assembling, by dairy industry stakeholders who proposed governance solutions that had the effect of translating one assemblage into another. The practice of re-assembling is therefore found in both the problematization of an issue and in the answer to this newly constructed problem. The politics of assembling and re-assembling, however, still took place in an unstable terrain, and while the simple juxtaposition of dairying and dirty has been unfrozen, the other, wilder, elements of the network of actors continue to flow through and beyond the boundaries of governance. The governance project of water quality will always be subject to vital materialities and unknowable totalities, resulting in many bounded, partial and temporary fixes. In this example, we have been able to see to what extent agri-environmental governance and the public problems it seeks to frame are not self-evident, but rather the result of the will of actors who assemble the elements according to particular and political interests. For all these reasons, by taking an assemblage approach to understanding agri-environmental governance, we are able to better grasp both the governance practices and limits of assembling and re-assembling water quality.

Notes

1 Iwi is the Maori word meaning tribe(s). It is commonly used in New Zealand English.
2 https://fishandgame.org.nz/about/f-and-g-position-statements/dairy-farming-and-the-environment/.
3 www.knowledge-basket.co.nz/.

References

Bain, Carmen and Tamera Dandachi. 2015. "'100% pure'? Private governance efforts to mitigate the effects of "dirty dairying" on New Zealand's environment" in *Handbook of the International Political Economy of Agriculture and Food*, edited by Alessandro Bonanno and Lawrence Busch, 40–58. Cheltenham: Edward Elgar Publishing.

Bennett, Jane. 2009. *Vibrant Matter: A Political Ecology of Things*. Durham: Duke University Press.

Blackett, Paula and Richard Le Heron. 2008. "Maintaining the 'clean green' image: Governance of on-farm environmental practices in the New Zealand dairy industry" in *Agri-Food Commodity Chains and Globalising Networks*, edited by Christina Stringer and Richard Le Heron, 76–87. Aldershot: Ashgate.

Callon, Michel. 1986. "Some elements of a sociology of translation: Domestication of the scallops and the fishermen of St Brieuc Bay" in *Power, Action and Belief: A New Sociology of Knowledge?*, edited by John Law, 196–223. London: Routledge.

Carolan, Michael S. 2013. "The wild side of agro-food studies: On co-experimentation, politics, change, and hope", *Sociologia Ruralis* 53 (4): 413–431.

Dairy NZ (2013), *Sustainable Dairying: Water Accord. A Commitment to New Zealand by the Dairy Sector*, July 2013. www.dairynz.co.nz/media/3286407/sustainable-dairying-water-accord-2015.pdf

Davies-Colley Robert J. 2013. "River water quality in New Zealand: An introduction and overview" in *Ecosystem Services in New Zealand – Conditions and Trends*, edited by John R. Dymond, 432–447. Lincoln: Manaaki Whenua Press.

Deans, Niels and Kevin Hackwell. 2008. Dairying and declining water quality. Why has the *Dairying and Clean Streams Accord* not delivered cleaner streams?. Wellington: Fish & Game New Zealand and Forest & Bird.

Dearnaley, Mathew. 2001. "Milk versus water: a clash of cultures". *New Zealand Herald*, 11 June 2001.

Duncan, Ronlyn. 2013. "A view from the Farm-gate: Farmers' perspectives on water quality", Conference paper presented to the New Zealand Agricultural & Resource Economics Annual Conference, Farm Impacts of Environmental Policy, 28–30 August. Christchurch: Lincoln University.

Duncan, Ronlyn. 2016. "Ways of knowing – out-of-sync or incompatible?: framing water quality and farmers' encounters with science in the regulation of non-point source pollution in the Canterbury region of New Zealand", *Environmental Science & Policy* 55: 151–157.

Feindt, Peter H. and Angela Oels. 2005. "Does discourse matter? Discourse analysis in environmental policy making", *Journal of Environmental Policy & Planning* 7 (3): 161–173.

Felstiner, William L. F., Richard L. Abel and Austin Sarat. 1980–1981. "The emergence and transformation of disputes: Naming, blaming, claiming ...", *Law & Society Review* 15 (3/4): 631–654.

Forney, Jérémie and Paul V. Stock. 2014. "Conversion of family farms and resilience in Southland, New Zealand", *International Journal of Sociology of Agriculture and Food* 21: 7–29.

Head, Brian W. 2008. "Wicked problems in public policy", *Public Policy* 3 (2): 101–118.

Holland, Phil S. 2014. "The dirty dairying campaign and the clean streams accord", *Lincoln Planning Review* 6 (1–2): 63–69.

Howard-Williams, Clive, Robert Davies-Colley, Kit Rutherford and Robert Wilcock. 2010. Diffuse pollution and freshwater degradation: New Zealand Perspectives,

Selected papers from the 14th International Conference of the IWA Diffuse Pollution Specialist Group, DIPCON 2010.

Hughey, Ken F. D. and Kay L. Booth. 2012. "Monitoring the state of New Zealand rivers: How the river values assessment system can help", *New Zealand Journal of Marine and Freshwater Research* 46 (4): 545–556.

Hughey, Ken F. D., Ross Cullen and Geoff N. Kerr. 2010. A decade of public perceptions of the New Zealand environment: A focus on water and its management. Lincoln University. www.researchgate.net/publication/265042430_A_DECADE_OF_PUBLIC_PERCEPTIONS_OF_THE_NEW_ZEALAND_ENVIRONMENT_A_FOCUS_ON_WATER_AND_ITS_MANAGEMENT

Hughey, Ken F. D., Ross Cullen and Geoff N. Kerr. 2016. *Public Perceptions of New Zealand's Environment: 2013*. Christchurch: EOS Ecology.

Jay, Mairi. 2006. "The political economy of a productivist agriculture: New Zealand dairy discourses", *Food Policy* 32 (2): 266–279.

Lascoumes, Pierre. 1996. "Rendre gouvernable: de la 'traduction' au 'transcodage': l'analyse des processus de changement dans les réseaux d'action publique". *La Gouvernabilité*, CURAPP, 325–338. Paris: Presses universitaires de France.

Lascoumes, Pierre and Louis Simard. 2011. "L'action publique au prisme de ses instruments. Introduction". *Revue française de science politique* 61: 5–22.

Li, Tania. 2007a. "Practices of assemblage and community forest management", *Economy and Society* 36 (2): 263–293.

Li, Tania. 2007b. *The Will to Improve: Governmentality, Development, and the Practice of Politics*. Durham: Duke University Press.

LIC (Livestock Improvement Corporation) and Dairy NZ. 2016. New Zealand Dairy Statistics 2015–16. Hamilton.

MacLeod, Catriona J. and Henrik Moller. 2006. "Intensification of New Zealand agriculture since 1960: An evaluation of current indicators of land use change", *Agriculture, Ecosystems and Environment* 115: 201–218.

Ministry for Primary Industries. 2013. The Dairying and Clean Streams Accord: Snapshot of progress 2011/2012, February 2013.

Muirhead, Bruce and Hugh Campbell. 2012. "The worlds of dairy: Comparing dairy frameworks in Canada and New Zealand in light of future shocks to food systems" in *Rethinking Agricultural Policy Regimes: Food Security, Climate Change and the Future Resilience of Global Agriculture* edited by Reidar Almas and Hugh Campbell, 147–168. United Kingdom: Emerald.

Neems, Jeff. 2009. "Final warning for dirty dairying pair". *Stuff*, News, 25 July 2009.

O'Brien, Thomas. 2013. "Fragmentation or evolution? Understanding change within the New Zealand environmental movement", *Journal of Civil Society* 9 (3): 287–299.

Oels, Angela. 2005. "Rendering climate change governable: From biopower to advanced liberal government?", *Journal of Environmental Policy & Planning* 7 (3): 185–207.

Parliamentary Commissioner for the Environment. 2012. *Water Quality in New Zealand: Understanding the Science*. Wellington.

Parliamentary Commissioner for the Environment. 2013. *Water Quality in New Zealand: Land Use and Nutrient Pollution*. Wellington.

Radio New Zealand Newswire. 2002. "Commissioner to investigate dirty dairying", 26 June 2002, Time 12:34.

Rittel, Horst. W. J. and Melvin M. Webber. 1973. "Dilemmas in a general theory of planning", *Policy Sciences* 4: 155–169.

Ryan, James. 2014. Farming in a fishbowl: Insights from environmental leaders. Kellogg Rural Leaders Programme 2014.

Statistics New Zealand. 2017. Agricultural Production Statistics: June 2016 (provisional), Wellington.

Stuff. 2001a. "Dairy: Farmers under fire over 'dirty dairying'", *Stuff*, Rural, 18 July 2001.

Stuff. 2001b. "Dairy: 'Dirty dairying' protest goes to industry heads", *Stuff*, Rural, 19 July 2001.

The Dominion Post. 2017. "Cleaning up dirty dairying", *The Dominion Post*, 11 January 2017.

11 Beyond soyisation

Donau Soja as assemblage

Dana Bentia and Jérémie Forney

Introduction

The assemblage approach allows us to adopt an oblique angle on a food standard introduced by *Donau Soja* (DS), an organisation concerned with the quality and origins of soybeans in Europe with the intention of redirecting the pathway of soybeans and related practices into specific sustainable avenues.[1] It is, however, an oblique perspective, because in this chapter we do not approach the new standard and label as an end product or as a technology of regulation but rather as a process with a history and which has developed in distinctive socio-material contexts. DS is a multi-stakeholder initiative that operates on multiple levels and from many centres. While it is focused around the creation of a new standard for soy grown in Europe, this instrument stands for a whole agenda concerned with scientific research, seed breeding, farming and retail practices. So, this new standard emerges at the conjunction of a variety of actors, places, policies, and events, in ways which continually add to and multiply the scope of the initiative. In this sense, the aim of this chapter is to foreground DS as a unique assemblage of policies, partnerships, and regulations in Europe that emerge around a single crop, and which is, by its constitution and creation *performative*: it bears the promise of sparking change in the European food regime and new forms of agri-environmental governance in Europe.

This chapter is based on an ongoing research exploring the DS transnational network in several of its locations across Europe. Applying a multi-sited ethnographic method, this research "follows the thing" (Marcus 1995) – European-grown soybeans – through this particular initiative in order to understand the specific logics of governance it relies on and the assemblage-building work that is taking place in the making of DS. The data on which this chapter is based comes from 20 interviews with actors in the DS network in Austria, Romania and Switzerland, document analysis, as well as participant observation at several conferences and events organised by DS.

We contend that DS particularly lends itself to be approached from an assemblage perspective in at least three ways. First, DS, as an initiative, is very heterogeneous and thus incorporates a series of relations that have an emergent character and which acquire different qualities as a consequence of being enrolled in the initiative. Second, soybeans, as a valued agricultural crop, circulate as a series of relations that make a difference to the development and outcomes of projects. As the assemblage perspective encourages including human and non-human actors in a more horizontally flattened ontology, we stress that the materialities of soy are multiple and closely bound not only to soy's notoriety but also to its ambiguity resulting from its ubiquity in different regimes of value and its role in the mobilisation of practices. And third, we believe assemblage, as an approach and a method, supports non-linear ways of thought and perception, and in this way, it resonates with complexity theory and its emphasis on open systems, process, and states far from equilibrium. In the particular case study we depict in this chapter, we emphasise certain temporal configurations around the history of soybeans in order to give a sense of the sheer difficulty involved in reterritorialising soybeans. In other words, the nature of assembled and dis-assembled soy relations over spacetimes is intimately tied to multiple temporal trajectories that contribute to its incorporation into the global food regime. In this way, we align ourselves with Pálsson and Rabinow's view on the role of assemblage in highlighting "a specific historical, political, and economic conjuncture in which an issue becomes a problem" (2005: 94). Furthermore, Allen underlines that assemblage "holds together, despite being made up of a co-existence of diverse logics and priorities often pulling in different directions" (2011: 155). DS is made up of a multiplicity of intentions and logics but still holds together and this not only produces internal tensions, but also very specific dynamics.

Moreover, our aim is to highlight some of the process dimensions involved in disassembling a series of soy regimes and reassembling certain capacities, possibilities, practices, and places. This chapter conceives of the process of reterritorialising soy as a move away from what we call 'Global Soy' towards 'Homegrown Soy'. In this way, our aim is to address the complexities involved in this attempted shift and specifically move the focus away from topographic dichotomies, and underline further that "an assemblage is the product of multiple determinations that are not reducible to a single logic" (Collier and Ong 2005: 12). As we focus on circumstances, events and socio-temporal configurations, we propose an entanglement between Global and Homegrown Soy, thus positing the impossibility of exploring the latter independently of the former.

Following on from this introduction we develop our chapter in three stages. We first describe how soy has become central in the food system, what problems this situation has generated and what have been the answers so far. Then we depict some of the distinctive traits of DS as revealed in the process of reassembling actors, places and knowledge. Finally, we highlight the prospects and possibilities opened up by DS in view of a set of dynamics that emerge in the articulation of re-territorialisation projects, desires, and forces.

Soy territorialities

Soy is the fourth largest agricultural commodity in the world following wheat, rice and corn. Europe is the third largest consumer of soy following the US and

China and relies for around 94% of total supply on imports from the US and countries in Latin America. While its roots in the US and Europe date to the second half of the nineteenth century, its global career started just about 70 years ago and has gone through exponential growth over the short span of the last 20 years. The strongest factor for its demand on the European market represents the livestock sector where it is fully embedded in the feed infrastructures and feed practices for conventionally reared chickens, pigs, and cows.

Apart from the utter scale of its use, there is further a striking ambiguity about soybeans. DS builds its initiative on a food product that a majority of consumers are largely unaware of. Consumer imaginaries around soy are mostly related to its Asian origins and its more recent spread within the vegetarian and vegan market. Historically, there are reports of consumers never really crossing the threshold of acceptance of soy (Daniel 2005). This is because its ubiquity is to be found in the processed food sector or in what the food industry calls 'embedded' consumption. Its consumption is, in other words, almost invisible. As feed and as a food additive soybeans as a visible component of food systems is reserved to the experts in the respective fields. Mintz et al. refer to how soybeans involve highly modernised, industrial processes in the extraction of oil, the manufacture of feed, the fabrication of soy proteins and its many derivatives (2008: 6). Moreover, the value chain of soybeans is exceptionally long.

In the following we sketch soy's notorious global career with milestone developments in the post-WWII era, and a further defining stage with the advent of biotechnology, in order to then highlight a bundle of events that expose its 'peaking' in light of the wicked problems of environmental destruction linked to failed human decisions and actions.

Measurabilities beyond calculation

By numbers alone, soybeans demonstrate a staggering growth trajectory. In terms of production volume, land use, and international trade, soy is among the most important crops in the world today. Over the past 60 years soybean production has increased by almost 1,000% (Oliveira and Schneider, TNI 2014; WWF 2014), while the land area under soy cultivation has more than quadrupled (FAOSTAT n.d.; USDA 2014). Globally, soy farms now cover one million square kilometres – equivalent to the total area of France, Germany, Belgium and the Netherlands combined (WWF 2016). In 2013, the world harvest amounted to 284 million tons from 113 million ha (Profundo 2015). The EU-28 countries consumed 31.6 million tons in 2013.

But the impacts and implications of such stunning growth turned strikingly dark and came to be recurrently denounced especially over the last decade, resulting in increased visibility and political contestation of the virtues of soy. Some of the most vocal reports and analyses come from several NGOs who took it upon themselves to critique soy. Organisations such as Friends of the Earth, the World Wildlife Fund, and the Transnational Institute trace some of the relations that came to be enacted through soy to demonstrate the unparalleled scale of political, economic, and environmental problems around this one crop. The unintended consequences of the soy revolution include: biodiversity loss, deforestation, land grabs, environmental pollution, intensive industrial-scale agriculture, and more generally, several high carbon practices derived from using soy. The reports relate soy's notoriety to factors such as national and supra-national policies and trade laws in the aftermath of WWII. The Friends of the Earth report from 2010 links the expansion of soy cultivation to EU's post-WWII CAP policies and explains how these created an opportunity for soy through the lack of import tariffs compared to other major crops. Paradoxically, coupled payments per output did not lead to more soy cultivation in Europe but to the growth of what were conceived of as the more profitable crops of wheat and maize. Soy was to be outsourced and later also offshored (see GRAIN 2016). Lack of import tariffs for legumes made importing lucrative, embedding large economies of scale. An infrastructure of traders, oil processors and feed manufactures developed to feed cheap soy from abroad to the livestock industry in Europe.

Eventually, concerns with the security of vegetal protein supply in the European Union began to emerge, with a study from the European Parliament from 2013 stating that protein crops (grain legume species such as fava beans, peas, chickpeas, lupins and soybeans) are now grown on less than 2% of arable land in the European Union. The protein crop area as a proportion of all arable land had declined from 4.7% in 1961 to 1.8% in 2013. Over the same period, the actual use of protein-rich grain in animal feed had increased dramatically. Clearly, imported soybeans have become a central and strategic element of the whole European meat industry. This state of affairs is not a simple product of inappropriate natural and agronomic conditions in Europe for soybean production. On the contrary, soybeans are not new to Europe. Some sources trace the history of its cultivation to well before that which has taken place in the Americas. European regions, especially those along the Danube, are reported to be particularly suited to soy production. Soy has been cultivated, for instance, in the Danube region since 1875.

Temporal configurations

The way that Global Soy was assembled and territorialised over little more than half a century is related to some of the major drivers to path-dependent patterns in the food system. These are intimately tied to dominant linear approaches in agriculture alongside anthropocentric rationales around food economy and food security which together have contributed to the consolidation of a productivist paradigm. But such consolidation, i.e. territorialisation, emerged from the intersection of processes which each have their own timescales.

The exponential growth of soy is undoubtedly related to the development of biotechnologies and their upsurge in the market since the "roaring nineties" (Stiglitz 2003). In 1994, the Roundup Ready soybean, the first genetically modified plant, was introduced to the market in the U.S. Benefiting from the coexistence policy of the European Union (see Reynolds and Szerszynski 2014) GM soybeans rapidly sneaked through the backdoors of market regulation as an 'embedded' food ingredient and feed compound. Today 90% of soybeans imported in Europe are genetically modified. The advent of GM soybeans can be regarded as a tipping point that experienced path dependency and created a lock-in situation from which it is very hard to break out. The techno-fix of biotechnology also largely contributed to further path-dependent patterns between soy, meat, and fossil fuels. These, in turn, led to a situation where total per capita protein consumption (including meat and vegetable-derived protein) is about 70% higher than recommended (Westhoek et al. 2011: 13). Moreover, the path-dependent character of the development of GM soy has triggered a further pattern where seeds and seed breeding are more and more inflexibly aligned to the infrastructure of biotechnology industries.

The moments in history that significantly propagated the enrolment of soya in industrial scale agriculture reflect nothing short of a fascination for its versatility along with its immense promise for catapulting post-WWII societies out of poverty. Yet, the imaginaries tied to its protein content as a gold standard for stock feed, its oil content as a magic refiner for processed foods, and its genetic modification as the ultimate source of unbounded growth, have 'tipped' it into cultures of excess (see Urry 2010) as well as made it an accomplice in death and destruction.

Environmental politics and call for soy de-/reterritorialisation

But what was once a silver bullet solution for a huge commodity sector, now has turned towards potentials for soy also to act in a new role as a silver lining. The DS organisation was founded in 2012 to confront some of the lock-ins created by Global Soy in Europe. Pressures to enhance sustainability – especially in relation to climate change – have created the space and impetus for changing the rules of the game in which governments and markets act and count. A study conducted by the Sustainable Europe Research Institute, an independent research group from Austria, concluded that 77% of all CO_2 in Austrian pork emissions were coming from soy. It claimed that around 50% of carbon emissions from Austrian pork meat (or 1.1 M tons of CO_2 per year) could be reduced if (regional) home grown soy was used instead of overseas soy (see Hinterberger et al. 2011). In this way, the study drew attention to the fact that the decoupling of livestock production from feed production had created a heavy burden for the environment while disguising the total amount of external cost of meat production.

The intensification of the livestock sector went hand in hand with an upsurge in meat consumption: from 1960 to 2007 pork production increased by 294%, eggs by 353% and poultry by 711% (WWF 2014). Yet cheapness and unbounded expansion came at a cost. When tropical forests and grasslands are lost to soy plantations, CO_2 is released and deforestation is a major contributor to global CO_2 emissions. Moreover, the production of one kilogramme of intensively reared beef requires ten kilogrammes of animal feed (including soybeans) and 15,000 litres of water (Friends of the Earth 2010).

The extent of the ubiquity of soy in the food system is captured in a report by the WWF which calculates the 'soyfootprint' of European consumers (2016). This amounts to a staggering 60 kilogrammes a year and is primarily associated with the consumption of conventional meat, dairy and processed foods of the most diverse kinds. Soy has been transmogrified into both a building block of the industrial processed food regime and an engine for its growth. In this way, it liaises with other ubiquitous ingredients such as salt, sugar or fat. The path-dependent pattern observable here in the industrial processed-food sector is similar to the pattern already observed in the meat sector.

In this section, we used these statistics not only to give a sense of the 'spatial fixes' (Harvey 2001) used in the governance of soy but also a sense for the far-reaching interdependent processes and trajectories over time that piled-up to create a clarion call for change. As such, accounts of the pernicious influence and effects of soy created momentum for alternatives, with concerned groups such as the European-based DS and the global-level Roundtable for Sustainable Soy initiating action.

The creation of DS was substantially influenced by the fact that Europe is almost totally dependent on imports of protein crops for feeding livestock. Whereas Europe is mostly self-sufficient regarding the three other major crops of wheat, corn, and rice, in terms of soy, it imports 94% of soy supplies from the Americas – a large proportion of it being genetically modified. The degree to which soy consumption has increased over the past decades is seen to further add not only to European dependency on other continents but also to the unsustainability of intensive livestock practices across Europe. The consequences are both an accentuation of reliance on cheap protein from afar being fed to European livestock – which further disconnects feed from livestock production – as well as the creation of an excess of phosphates beyond the carrying capacity of soils. Thus, the tensions behind the creation of DS bring into focus a double lock-in whereby European markets almost totally depend on GM soy on the one hand, and, on the other hand, most supplies come from overseas. DS sought to respond to these tensions by creating a certification programme to guarantee GM-free and origin-controlled quality for soybeans.

Relations of exteriority and first steps to soy reterritorialisation

The DS scheme was not created in a vacuum. To the contrary, DS arrived with good timing. It benefited from the convergence of at least three main distinct developments. First, at the supranational level, the "Greening" of the Common Agricultural Policy created payments for ecosystem services that were intended to strengthen the ecological dimensions of agriculture. In this respect, soybeans are particularly well suited to act as a cover crop and thus improve soil fertility. Moreover, they do not need fertilizers due to their nitrogen fixing capacity. Second, at the national level in countries like Germany, strategies were being

Figure 11.1 Map of the Danube River Basin as pictured on DS brochure.

developed to address the sustainability of protein supplies by facilitating research, shorter supply chains based on increased regional cultivation of legumes, and, last but not least, specific agricultural policy interventions. Third, European consumers' resistance to GMOs (see, for instance, Konefal and Busch 2010), and the associated proliferation of GMO-free labelling at national levels, created further momentum for initiatives like DS.

The DS initiative needs also to be regarded against the background of an emerging array of programmatic agreements and declarations relating to soy. These include: the Brussels Soy Declaration, whereby European soy industries and retailers support the cultivation and even expansion of non-GM soy from Brazil; the Basler Criteria for Responsible Soy, where deforestation and land conversions are rejected; and similarly, the Roundtable for Responsible Soy and the 2015 Berlin Declaration for a GMO-free Europe. Some of these agreements resulted in the creation of certification systems, audits, labels and standards. Currently, there are about 50 different standards for soybeans globally. This begs the question of how DS has emerged and become something different to other standards and how it is related to co-existing initiatives.

Soy reterritorialisation

The DS project is a unique endeavour because of its focus on the traceability, quality assurance, and certification of a single crop grown in Europe. It has gathered a multitude of actors around two main projects: the certification of GM-free soy and the certification of 'place of origin' provenance for soy grown in the Danube region. DS is a multi-stakeholder initiative with its headquarters in Vienna and further offices in Serbia, Romania, Ukraine and Germany (and also has representatives in Italy, Moldova and Poland). The organisation has a board of 12 members, a steering committee with 14 members, an advisory board of ten members and a scientific advisory board of ten members. Members are individuals from a variety of sectors – from the private to the public – including businesses along the soy chain, breeders, farmers, governments, NGOs, and civil society. Apart from the two main projects there are at least a dozen more objectives that the DS initiative follows. The multiplicity of objectives illustrates the complexity of the initiative. As stated on the DS website:[2]

> The project's most important objectives are the promotion and expedition of regional soya bean cultivation according to clearly defined quality criteria, as well as the expansion of infrastructure in order to attain these objectives. In the forefront are:
>
> - promoting both cultivation and processing of GM-free soya within the Danube region for Europe – using the Donau Soja trademark;
> - establishing reliable supply and value-added chains via member businesses, contributing to the independent European supply of protein;
> - directing a funded breeding, research and monitoring programme for GMO-free soya seeds and soya plant protection concepts for the Danube region.

These core objectives already point to the fact that DS calls for a substantial overhaul over policies, farming practices, cultivated areas, retail chains, and seed breeding research. This rhizomatic incorporation of heterogeneous food domains suggests the promise of bringing about change in multiple relationships in the governance of soy. Yet, these objectives did not emerge in a linear manner, nor were they all present from the very start of the initiative. A handful of farmers and businesses, who used soy on a daily basis, came together to facilitate the sourcing of soy from Europe of non-GM quality in an effort to reduce dependency from other continents. In this process – similar to the opening of Pandora's Box – a whole set of troubles came to be disclosed, such that the need emerged to address the web of relations created by soybeans as they permeated a multitude of elements of the food industry. Soy was not simply a technical problem, it was a network of relations. Not only did global soy cause problems in the Global South but was also complicit in the intensification of the animal production sector, the related uncoupling of animal sector from the feed sector, the excess of phosphates in the ground, the abuse of herbicides, the concentration of seed breeding, the shrinking of the number of seed varieties, monocropping, and the halving of legumes grown in Europe. DS brought hope and launched a "process of qualification" (see Allaire 2004) of soybeans not just to counter 'GM soy from nowhere' but to boost and transform a wider assemblage of European practices in agriculture, trade, and seed breeding, as well as agricultural policies. Thus, non-GM European soy started to multiply its qualities.

Re-forming soy networks

DS, as an assemblage, does not act alone. Within few years it developed into a transnational poly-centred 'network' of like-minded agricultural experts where each regional or national chapter is steered by consultants, researchers or business persons from 20 countries. Currently, DS has 257 members including civil society bodies, businesses and entrepreneurs, governmental and non-governmental organisations, and members from most of the sectors of the value chain, such as seed breeding companies, soy producers, traders, soybean processors, feed and food industries, and many of the largest retail companies in Europe.

DS has created differentiated financing to support the formation of networks of heterogenous parts. Extraordinary members such as non-profit organisations and associations are exempt from membership fees. Ordinary members such as producer associations or retailers pay fees that are differentiated according to their annual turnover. For example, a business with a turnover of less than €100,000 per year pays €50, while a business with a turnover of €50 to €150 million pays €4,500. Additionally, DS charges licence fees for first processors of soybeans amounting to €2 per ton of soybeans. Financial support also comes from public partners such as the Austrian Development Agency (ADA) and the Deutsche Gesellschaft für Internationale Zusammenarbeit (GIZ). The aim of DS over the next couple of years is to become self-financed.

The DS project entails a huge array of interventions across the supply chain (ranging from production methods, storage facilities, traders, transport and logistics, first processors, feed manufacturers, and retail companies) as well as actors adjacent to the supply chain, like seed breeders, various scientific consultants, and political bodies. Finally, DS aims to raise acceptance of soy among consumers. Interventions entail various degrees of complexity, change, and control in the food system and add up to a substantial re-ordering of infrastructural relationships.

Some of the initiatives build on pre-existing work by other initiatives, and this provides the opportunity to further consolidate trajectories that have already been traced into existence, or to focus on other areas that were left behind. In Austria, for instance, where a non-GMO certification system was already established, work at the local level focused on areas that were more neglected than others, such as support for mountain farmers. Switzerland presents an interesting case in several respects. Switzerland does not use GM soy either for food or for feed. However, sustainability initiatives for responsible soy sourcing by the dominant retail chains in the country – Coop and Migros – exist and they emerged few years prior to the conception of DS.

One valued activity that acts to boost DS goals is the creation of a sense of belonging and of enthusiasm through the organisation of frequent 'speed-networking events' in Vienna, annual conferences in Austria, Germany or

Hungary, as well as demonstrative 'field days' where interested participants exchange knowledge. Such events are intended to create the kind of horizon of expectation and hope that is necessary for a business endeavour to take off and prosper.

Geographical reterritorialisation: re-localisation in the Danube basin

The DS project aims then at reconnecting diverse actors and places and, in this process, the Danube itself is poised to act as the main connector. The Danube region needs significant development, such as improved shipment, logistics and infrastructure. Alongside this infrastructure, there are about 1.8 million ha of fallow land that could be used for soy without the need to produce less of anything else and without replacing other crops. This last point made the choice of the Danube region even more attractive as it theoretically would allow avoiding competition between soy (for feed) and other crops (for food). Furthermore, some scenarios posit Eastern Europe as having a high potential to increase food production. In countries transitioning to free trade economies, agricultural outputs are expected to increase by 2.5% every year over the next 15 years. In this respect, DS proposes that rather than increasing cereal exports from Europe, it would be better to reassemble some of the existing elements and future potentials for homegrown protein and legume production (Krön and Bittner 2015: 3).

These objectives point towards a re-localisation of soy along with a structural re-ordering of the power relations that steer the cultivation and circulation of soy. This endeavour marks a shift away from the 'Global Soy' system and the path-dependencies of its global value chains and instead steer towards 'Homegrown Soy'. The Danube region is set to act as both the symbol and agent of this transformation. A second stage that is currently being pursued is the development of regional processing facilities and short value chains with the aim of creating added value for the countries and regions that produce it.

Preliminary research shows us that Homegrown Soy does not mean the replacement of Global Soy nor the invention of a new system. In 2012, European soy production amounted to 3.8 million tons and almost doubled within three years to 6.6 million tons in 2015. The targeted growth for 2025 is 17 million tons of soybeans along with an increase of other grains and legumes. Thus, DS envisions that by 2025 half of soy demand will be covered by non-GM European production. The other half is to be covered with sustainable imports.

The re-localisation and re-ordering of soy relations is centred on a powerful attractor – the Danube river basin – that is invested with both material and symbolic value. The 'process of qualification', referred to earlier, becomes one where soy is no longer ubiquitous and invisible, but is conferred an identity cloak. This identity cloak steers all efforts and intentions on Homegrown Soy in a way that is concerned with a harmonized European standard as much as with working through uneven developments in various regions.

Reassembling knowledge

Thus DS takes a different direction from the more orthodox (and limited) linear visions of technologically-leveraged agricultural change as well as from backward looking trade protectionism. Moreover, differentiated foci depending on the specificities of each site, region or country, further support the situated and 'site-sensitive' features of the projects. This general positioning results from a conjunction of diverse types of knowledge and their circulation within the DS network. In other words, knowledge is central in DS as a project of re-assemblage around soy.

The distinctive features envisioned for each region and country originate from a profoundly relational understanding of place by the founder of the initiative, Matthias Krön. Having previous knowledge of soy processing and trade through a non-dairy drinks business he co-owned for some years in Austria, Krön developed a sense of the structures, agents, and socio-political geographies that drive soy. He got to know Eastern European landscapes and the roots and routes of soy in Romania's Danube River basin. He became aware of the uneven nature of agricultural developments as much as the uneven geographies of power that still persist (almost three decades after the fall of the Iron Curtain) between Eastern and Western Europe. Indeed, at the core of the DS project, there is a feeling that Eastern European farmers are excluded from more fully participating in the European agricultural market.

The technical figures and measures of soy in the Danube area and future action plans rely and build upon research from Vienna's Institute for Soil Sciences and the Working Community of the Danube Regions. This research envisions possible scenarios based on the analysis of two parameters that are brought into interdependence: the yield gap and the diet gap (see Foley *et al.* 2011 and Rittler 2016). The concept of yield gap recalls notions of under- and over-productivity when environmental conditions are similar. In this way, Eastern Europe/Romania counts as being 50% underproductive while Western European countries count as being over-productive. The diet gap refers to consumption patterns that 'overshoot'. The Institute's research concludes that halving the production of meat, eggs and dairy production in Europe could lead to: 40% reduction in nitrogen emissions, 25–40% reduction in greenhouse gas emissions, 23% per capita decrease in cropland use for food production, enhanced human health (40% reduction of intake of saturated fat), soymeal use reduced by 75%, and nitrogen-use efficiency in the food system would increase from 18% to 41–47%. So DS is not only a certification programme but also a science-based platform of measures and metrics that co-constitute knowledge through the promotion of different collaborations at scientific, business, and practical farm/cultivation level. It has a scientific board that readily and regularly contributes to the decisions and communications of the organisation's steering committee.

In Romania, for instance, the work of the past two years focused on the creation of several demonstration fields where regular meetings with farmers and agronomists could facilitate the dissemination of knowledge about the most varied aspects of soy cultivation and thus encourage farmers to take up a practice that has been largely discontinued especially over the last decade. Furthermore, it also served to get the new generation of farmers accustomed to soy. Last but not least, the goal is to do away with the notion that GM soy produces higher yields.

DS projects presuppose various degrees of coordination across sites and this, in turn, entails consolidation of its main programmes. As a hub for scientific research and seed improvement companies, DS pushes the idea that seed breeding is important in upscaling seeds adapted to European conditions and stresses further that this is even more important in a context where seed breeding largely serves big corporations dedicated to transgenic research. So, what DS does, is to provide a meeting ground for research from various countries and institutions to be shared in order to first create a database of genotypes and then to mega-zone and harmonize the different maturity groups of various seeds for Europe.

Many farmers and agricultural experts believe that soybeans are very demanding agricultural crops and require in-depth knowledge and expertise on cultivation. This is one reason why DS believes that many farmers need to be informed about its versatility and benefits on the European market and also gives so much importance to knowledge creation and exchange. The soybean assemblage is the realm of experts. Mutual learning between farmers, soy processors, and breeders is one key element for the development of a long-term understanding of the sort of changes and practices to be undertaken. These intersections of different knowledges emerge as hubs where the many materialities and qualities of soy are made visible, talked about, debated, and weighed and measured.

Soy reassembled: dynamics, tensions, prospects

Through the formation of new networks, the process of re-localisation, and the constitution of new flows of knowledge, the assemblage that is consolidating around DS produces strong dynamics of harmonisation and development as a European standard. DS is reclaiming soy for Europe. Soy is set to be uncoupled from its global trajectories and placed on a transition pathway to sustainability. The move from Global to Homegrown Soy is, however, much more than a spatial reclamation. As with other environmentally oriented standards, DS is a process that entails sanctioning a series of agricultural practices such as banning the use of desiccants prior to harvest as, for instance, glyphosate or diquat. This is a strategy born not only out of reaction to the current contestations around the use and abuse of a series of herbicides but also a statement against monoculture crops and in support of crop rotation along with other best practices included in the manual and guidelines published by DS. Possible measures of success are located by DS in the harmonisation of standards at a European level. At the moment, DS aligns with efforts from non-GMO campaigners to have a unitary GMO-free labelling system rather than one for each country or region. The shared view is that a single label is beneficial to trade and ultimately also would aid the take-off of DS programmes.

However, DS is not mere resistance to GM and Global Soy. It is a dynamic project focusing on future possibilities for soy production in Europe. This points to another set of dynamics resulting from this assemblage, which are more counterintuitive because they work towards reducing the need for soybeans wherever possible, by changing the protein provision in feed strategies. This entails the enrolment of other practices such as crop rotation, animal husbandry, plant protection, all of which require improvement and adjustment, and further, a stronger, more sustainable, protein strategy. Indeed, while DS aims to boost soybean cultivation in the Danube region and its status among farmers, it is at the same time attempting to decentre it. This is strategised, on the one hand, by reducing its use and centrality in the food system (see Westhoek et al. 2014) and, on the other hand, by aligning the role of soybeans with those of other legumes and sources of vegetal proteins and in this way strengthening the protein transition strategy for Europe. The articulation of these two sets of dynamics – consolidating the standard and decentring soy – generates, on the one hand, a series of tensions, and, on the other hand, a stimulating context open to possibilities and innovations.

As an example, one central measure of territorialising the above mentioned practices and aims went into advocating for the Danube basin as an appropriate region for developing the aims of the initiative. The instrument of stabilisation of this process is the DS standard. But setting these boundaries does not lead to an immutable, exclusive, or homogeneous entity. In order to include those European suppliers which are not from the Danube basin, DS has created Europe Soya, an additional trademark following the same certification procedures as DS. This shows that the initially created boundaries are actually porous. Moreover, DS is co-constituted by dynamic spatialities. These emerge not only from within DS, but also from its partnerships with other organisations that have already built up certain networks in specific regions, as for instance the five-year-long collaboration with the *Deutsche Gesellschaft für Internationale Zusammenarbeit* (GIZ), which runs activities in Serbia and Bosnia-Herzegovina. Other partnerships and collaborations keep emerging as DS organises networking events, conferences or field demonstrations with farmers' organisations which are themselves already implicated in lobbying or advocacy activities for sustainable farming.

A further dynamic element of the strategies enacted by DS is the targeting of food retailers. DS assigns the food retail chains a role as key players in shaking up the multiple ways in which soy is used, sourced, and translated. A bundle of soy-related practices have the potential to be enrolled in a mix of push and pull strategies. DS calls for and actively engages in the initiation of varied programmes by the retail industry. Currently, the Swiss companies Coop and Migros and the British supermarket chain Waitrose are taking the lead in this kind of experimentation. Waitrose has become the first UK retailer to introduce responsibly sourced non-GM soy for animal feed from Europe. In October 2016, the supermarket chain landed its first shipment of soy grown in the Danube Region for use as a source of protein in pig feed used by the retailer's dedicated pork supplier – Dalehead Foods. The two Swiss retailers have also initiated similar programmes in respect to dairy, chicken meat and eggs, using a variety of labels, such as Donausoja Poulet or Coop-Naturafarm eggs.

These possibilities and experiments developing in the open space created by the articulation of the two major dynamics characterising DS have not emerged from nowhere. They are held in a productive tension by the processes involved in upscaling soy and its materialities. We understand upscaling as an intricate and meticulous process that is shaped substantially by monitoring, measuring, and controlling the different qualities and standards of soy along and beyond the value chain. It is a process that results from a close and deep understanding of the materialities of soy, such as: where it can grow, its relation to soil as a plant, its nature as a source of protein in order to generate more sustainable diets which also require lowering of environmentally costly meat consumption.

Conclusion

In this chapter we have set out to show how soybeans catalysed the mobilisation of a diversity of processes that are partially steered by a group of actors interested in boosting the versatility and significance of soy in European agriculture. Leveraging off soybeans as a controversial contested global crop, their re-rooting and re-localisation in the European soil and market as an alternative to Global Soy has been implemented in ways that have not imitated what are imagined to be orthodox agricultural development pathways. Rather, it is an intricate work of reassembling the many spaces it inhabits in its "career" including scientific, regulatory, political and economic relationships. Therefore, we found it important to refer to some key temporal dimensions that framed its biography not just for the sake of contextualising but also as a way to re-centre analysis on the tangled range of issues that have directly and indirectly shaped the inception and direction of the DS initiative. In this way, we started off by first highlighting the centrality of soy in the current globalised food system. DS emerged in the context of a growing contestation over soy as a silver bullet for commodity production of plant protein, resulting in massive international trade, deforestation and monoculture in producing countries, and utter dependency of a whole food system in importing countries. DS developed as a complex assemblage of actors, places and knowledge, working to re-localise soy production within the European boundaries and build new relations between places of production and consumption.

This reterritorialisation of soy as Homegrown Soy as an alternative and countermotion to Global Soy has developed through efforts of harmonisation and coordination, and encouragement of production through: the formation of an organisation, the creation of a standard and a certification programme, and the designation of a label, all of which are held together by a sense of belonging and enthusiasm shared among its participants. The resulting spark has animated the subsequent dynamics of upscaling. But these dynamics are aligned with another, somewhat counterintuitive, set of dynamics that works to de-centre soy by reducing overall uses in globalised food systems. This line of creative tension between the two dynamics, far from blocking the processes, creates a fertile space for innovative development and an openness toward new possibilities. Furthermore, soy reterritorialization in the DS network is definitely still an ongoing process. Applying an assemblage perspective here certainly allowed us to emphasise both the performativity of the assemblage and the dynamics and motions resulting from perpetual processes of de- and reterritorialisation.

Notes

1 This chapter is part of the on-going research project "New directions in agri-environmental governance: Re-assembling food, knowledge and autonomy" funded by the Swiss National Science Foundation (No: 157414).
2 www.donausoja.org, accessed 20.03.2017.

References

Allaire, Gilles. (2014) Quality in Economic: A Cognitive Perspective. In: *Qualities of Food*, ed. by Mark Harvey, Andrew McMeekin and Alan Warde. Manchester: Manchester University Press.
Allen, John. (2011) Powerful assemblages? *Area* 43(2): 154–157.
Collier, Stephen J. and Aihwa Ong (2005) Global Assemblages, Anthropological Problems. In: *Global Assemblages. Technology, Politics, and Ethics as Anthropological Problems*, ed. by A. Ong and S. Collier, Oxford: Blackwell Publishing.
Daniel, T. Kaayla (2005) *The Whole Soy Story. The Dark Side of America's Favorite Health Food*, Washington, DC: New Trends Publishing, Inc.
European Parliament (2013) The Environmental Role of Protein Crops in the New Common Agricultural Policy. Directorate General for Internal Policies, Policy Department B: Structural and Cohesion Policies, Agriculture and Rural Development.
FAOSTAT (Food and Agriculture Organization Statistics Division) (n.d.) *Crop Production STAT Calculators*. Rome: FAO, www.fao.org/faostat/en/#data/QC, accessed 12.02.2017.
Foley, Jonathan A., Navin Ramankutty, Kate A. Brauman, Emily S. Cassidy, James S. Gerber, Matt Johnston, Nathaniel D. Mueller, Christine O'Connell, Deepak K. Ray, Paul C. West, Christian Balzer, Elena M. Bennett, Stephen R. Carpenter, Jason Hill, Chad Monfreda, Stephen Polasky, Johan Rockström, John Sheehan, Stefan Siebert, David Tilman, and David P. M. Zaks (2011) Solutions for a cultivated planet. *Nature* 478: 337–342.
Friends of the Earth Europe (2010) How the CAP is causing soy expansion and deforestation in South America, www.foeeurope.org/Soy, accessed 20.05.2017.
GRAIN (2016) The global farmland grab in 2016. How big, how bad?, www.grain.org/article/entries/5492-the-global-farmland-grab-in-2016-how-big-how-bad, accessed 04.04.2017.
Harvey, David (2001) *Spaces of Capital: Towards a Critical Geography*. New York: Routedge.
Hinterberger, Fritz, Eva Burger and Gregor Sellner (2011) Schweinefleischproduktion in Österreich – Klimaauswirkungen und Ressourceneffizienz. Sustainable Europe Research Institute (SERI) Nachhaltigkeitsforschung und–kommunikation GmbH.
Konefal, Jason and Larry Busch (2010) Markets and multitudes: How biotechnologies are standardising and differentiating corn and soybeans. *Sociologia Ruralis* 50/4: 409–427.

Krön, Matthias and Ursula Bittner (2015) Danube soya – Improving European GM-free soya supply for food and feed. *Oilseeds & fats Crops and Lipids* 22(5): 1–10.

Marcus, George E. (1995). Ethnography in/of the world system: The emergence of multi-sited ethnography. *Annual Review of Anthropology* 24(1): 95–117.

Mintz, Sidney, Chee-Beng Tan, and Christine M. Du Bois (2008) Introduction: The Significance of Soy. In: *The World of Soy*, ed. by M. DuBois, C. Tan and S. Mintz, Urbana and Chicago: University of Illinois Press.

Oliveira, Gustavo de L. T. and Mindi Schneider (2014) The Politics of Flexing Soybeans in China and Brazil, report published by the Transnational Institute.

Pálsson, Gísli and Paul Rabinow (2005) The Iceland Controversy: Reflections on the Transnational Market of Civic Virtue. In: *Global Assemblages. Technology, Politics, and Ethics as Anthropological Problems*, ed. by A. Ong and S. Collier, Oxford: Blackwell Publishing.

Profundo (2015) Mapping the soy supply chain in Europe. A research paper prepared for WNF, www.profundo.nl/page/show/themes/p718#__2015__p-718, accessed 09.07.2017.

Reynolds, Larry and Bronislaw Szerszynski (2014) The Post-Political and the End of Nature: The Genetically Modified Organism. In: *The Post-Political and Its Discontents. Spaces of Depoliticisation and Spectres of Radical Politics.*, ed. by J. Wilson and E. Swyngedouw. Edinburgh: Edinburgh University Press.

Rittler, Leo (2016) Potentials of intensification and diet choices to enhance soil use efficiency in the Danube region. (Unpublished Master's thesis, BOKU Wien).

Stiglitz, Joseph (2003) *The Roaring Nineties*. New York: W. W. Norton & Company.

USDA (United States Department of Agriculture – Foreign Agricultural Service) (2014, July) Oilseeds: World markets and trade. http://usda.mannlib.cornell.edu/usda/fas/oilseed-trade//2010s/2014/oilseed-trade-07-11-2014.pdf, accessed 01.06.2016.

Urry, John (2010) Consuming the planet to excess. *Theory, Culture and Society* 27(2–3): 191–212.

Westhoek, Henk, Trudy Rood, Maurits van de Berg, Jan Janse, Durk Nijdan, Melchert Reudink and Elke Stehfest (2011) *The Protein Puzzle. The Consumption and Production of Meat, Dairy and Fish in the European Union*. The Hague: PBL Netherlands Environmental Assessment Agency.

Westhoek, Henk, Jan Peter Lesschen, Trudy Rood, Susanne Wagner, Alessandra De Marco, Donal Murphy-Bokern, Adrian Leip, Hans van Grinsven, Mark A.Sutton and Oene Oenema (2014) Food choices, health and environment: Effects of cutting Europe's meat and dairy intake. *Global Environmental Change* 26: 196–205.

World Wildlife Fund. (2014). *The Growth of Soybeans. Impacts and Solutions*. Gland, Switzerland: WWF International.

WWF (World Wildlife Fund) (2016) Soy Scorecard. Assessing the use of responsible soy for animal feed, http://wwf.panda.org/what_we_do/footprint/agriculture/soy/soy_scorecards/soy_scorecard_2016/, accessed 15.01.2017.

Part III

Assemblage for building new AEG practices

12 The politics of big data
Corporate agri-food governance meets "weak" resistance

Michael Carolan

Big data tools are frequently referred to as the next "big thing" in conventional agricultural circles (Dawson 2016). This is in no small part due to the expanding amount of information collected relating to farm-level crop production (big soil data) combined with extensive weather data (big climate data), which together form the backbone of precision agriculture technology. According to the United States Department of Agriculture's (USDA) Agricultural Resource Management Survey (ARMS), in 1997, only 17 per cent of corn acres were cultivated using precision agriculture equipment. In 2010, the most recent year available for corn production practices, 72 per cent of corn acres were planted with this technology (USDA 2015). The global precision farming market reached US$2.3 billion in 2014, with an estimated annual growth rate of 12 per cent through 2020 (Michalopoulos 2015). In a recent report, the Joint Research Centre of the European Commission wrote that "precision agriculture can play a substantial role in the European Union in meeting the increasing demand for food, feed, and raw materials while ensuring sustainable use of natural resources and the environment" (Zarco-Tejada et al. 2014: 9). In the case of the Netherlands, precision techniques are now used to manage 65 per cent of the country's arable farmland, a figure that was only 15 per cent in 2007 (Michalopoulos 2015). Such trends indicate that agri-food firms are taking notice of these applications. Monsanto, for example, has acquired numerous farm data analytic companies since 2012, most notably Climate Corporation for US$930 million. Climate Corporation produces two popular software platforms: Climate Basic and Climate Pro. Monsanto has stated that its Climate Pro sensors on harvesting equipment generate roughly seven gigabytes of data per acre (Bobkoff 2015). With roughly one million acres of farmland in the U.S. alone, we are talking about a lot of data.

This "big thing", however, is not without its critics. One source of concern lies in what is called the data divide (Andrejevic 2014: 1673), which speaks to the asymmetries between the data *haves* and *have-nots*; though, admittedly, some of these "have-nots" are big data *don't wants*, as you will see shortly. This asymmetry is largely a function of farm scale, geography (not all regions of the world are like, say, the U.S. Corn Belt, where there is a John Deere dealer 20 miles in any direction), capital, credit, and position within value chains – e.g. the highly concentrated farm equipment sector gives firms like John Deere tremendous market power (Carolan 2018).

Not surprisingly, then, farmers express unease about who precisely owns "their" data. To quote from a report based on a survey conducted by the American Farm Bureau (2015),

> Fully 77.5 percent of farmers surveyed said they feared regulators and other government officials might gain access to their private information without their knowledge or permission. Nearly 76 percent of respondents said they were concerned others could use their information for commodity market speculation without their consent.

Moreover, while 81 per cent believed they retain ownership of their farm data, 82 per cent said they had no idea what companies were doing with it.

The editors of this collection make reference in their introductory chapter to how diverse actors are being enrolled in a multifaceted process known as neoliberalization. A critical examination of this coming-together, including better understanding its association with how goods and bads are distributed and the imaginaries they afford, is often classified under the category of agri-environmental governance (AEG). In this chapter, I examine less traditional actors in AEG, including code, intellectual property regimes, motherboards, iPhones, and the like. In doing this, I not only hope to transcend pre-existing categories; for example, the very concept of "big data" is critically unpacked. But also, I ask agri-food scholars to avoid making universal value judgements about artefacts tied to code and cloud-based technological forms. To be clear, I do not think big data ought to be unequivocally celebrated. Yet equally, for reasons detailed later, we would do well to avoid the assumption that at its face it is an artefact of broader neoliberalizing forces. We can and should make value judgments. In the end, however, those verdicts need to hinge on what code-assemblages in question *afford*.

Now to address the question of, where does this chapter situate itself within the social science and in particular agri-food literatures?

There is a nascent but growing body of scholarship emerging out of critical food studies that looks at the subject of big data (see e.g. Bronson and Knezevic 2016; Carolan 2017a, 2017b; Zoomers, Gekker, and Schäfer 2016). Big data is also inherently *anticipatory*; after all, the whole point of information gathering in this context is to make accurate (and thus profitable) predictions about the future. This brings us to another emerging field within the critical social science literature, specifically, on how anticipatory action does not just prepare us for worlds but *creates* them (see e.g. Anderson 2010; de Goede, Simon, and Hoijtink 2014). This chapter brings these lines of scholarship together by interrogating the world-making potentials that reside in practices tied to big data in agriculture.

I hope to do this, however, *weakly*.

Clifford Geertz (1973: 23) wrote about how "small facts speak to large issues, winks to epistemology, or sheep raids to revolution, because they are made to".

Geertz was critiquing strong theory – what Foucault (2003: 30) likened to "fascisms in our heads" (see also Carolan forthcoming). Geertz's worry was that once we start letting theory overtly guide our investigations and name events we risk missing grainy details that can help us grasp what is really going on, which is necessary if we are to avoid mistaking the abstract for the concrete. As opposed to employing strong theory, with its, in the words of Gibson-Graham (2006: 4), "embracing reach" and "reduced, clarified field of meaning", I hope to engage playfully in a weaker approach. That is to say, I engage in a style of scholarship that does not elaborate and confirm what we already know but instead "observes, interprets, and yields to emerging knowledge" (Gibson-Graham 2014: S149). My aim is thus to be attentive to both specificity and difference, which means resisting any urge to cleanly sum up epochs, such as by declaring ours a digital age (see e.g. Schmidt and Cohen 2013). Instead, this chapter offers a series of concrete examples that, when combined with and overlaid alongside other observations, reveal dimensions of political life that operate in the "cracks" (Massumi 2002: 133) of convention. Weak scholarship, at least as I understand it, is thus by its very nature critical *and* hopeful.[1]

I do all this by looking at three case studies. These data come from (1) 25 large-scale commodity farmers in Iowa and Illinois who use big data and precision agriculture to make management decisions, (2) 20 employees (technicians, sale reps, and engineers) from various big data companies located from around North America and the U.K., and (3) 18 farmers from around the U.S. engaged to various degrees with the loosely organized group called "Farm Hack". First, I briefly introduce each empirical case. Next, I present the findings from an instrument used to generate word clouds for each of the three populations based on the "keywords" *food security* and *precision agriculture* (more on what I mean by "keywords" in a moment). The chapter concludes discussing what it means to be a weak assemblage theorist.[2] Out of this conversation comes the realization that the antonym of *big* data is not small but *weak* data.

Setting the empirical stage

This section provides an overview, in no particular order, of three projects that will be read through each other to say something event-*full* (Deleuze and Guattari 1987) about the world. While each represents a separate study, the methods used and questions asked overlapped in places, which allows for some interesting comparisons and observations to be made.

Conventional farmers

These data come from in-depth person interviews with 25 Iowa and Illinois farmers. Interviews occurred from May 2014 through to September 2015. Respondents were obtained through a random snowball sampling technique, where individuals known to myself were approached for an interview and then asked to supply the names of additional possible participants. All of the farmers interviewed managed at least 1,200 acres, which reflects a combination of both land owned and leased. When farm households were first contacted, the researcher asked to "speak to an individual of the household that would be comfortable talking about their operation's use of big data, cloud technology, and precision technology". The purpose of this question was to allow households to self-select for who ultimately gave the interview. This query in each instance directed me to the male figure of the household, which is to say that all 25 interviews are with men. The primary crop commodities raised on these farms were corn and soybeans. Interview questions elicited a discussion about technologies used on the farm, when they adopted them (and why), and the perceived benefits and potential risks of the technologies used. Beyond this, farmers were engaged in conversations about what the future of agriculture looks like: e.g. what will be raised, who will be doing it, and the management practices involved. Interviews lasted between 70 and 120 minutes and were tape recorded and later transcribed. All respondents were promised anonymity and pseudonyms are used below with that promise in mind. Lastly, I averaged an additional 1.5 hours – range: 30 minutes to 3.5 hours – with each respondent. This time was spent engaging with their farm-specific big data applications. Extensive field notes were taken during this period, as these conversations were not recorded.

Big data industry

The sample interviewed from big data industry consisted of 20 individuals; a group composed of engineers, sales personnel, and tech specialists – those who develop, sell, and fix the software and hardware, respectively. Specifically, nine worked for implement firms, nine worked for firms that produce and sell predictive analytic software, and two worked as technology/big data consultants. Interview guides were designed to elicit a conversation about the technologies respondents produced, sold, and repaired – e.g. views toward them, their perceived benefits and potential risks, their role in future foodscapes. Interviews lasted between 60 and 120 minutes and were tape recorded and later transcribed. All respondents were promised anonymity and pseudonyms are therefore used to ensure that end. In addition to formal interviews, I spent an hour (approximately) with each participant being shown the big data applications that they were most familiar with. While this time was not tape-recorded copious fieldnotes were taken.

Farm hack

Research for this case study began on June 2014 and continued until January 2016. I grew the sample population by first reaching out to respondents whom I knew. I then further grew the sample by utilizing a snowball sampling technique. My intent was not to study Farm Hack as an organization per se but to examine how digital and legal "locks" were used and understood within this community. Those interviewed included individuals with different levels of

Farm Hack involvement, from the deeply committed to others who, in the words of one, "participate from a distance" – monitoring the website, attending an occasional meeting, etc. A total of 18 producers from around the U.S. were interviewed who reported varied degrees of involvement with Farm Hack. Six managed less than 100 acres; five managed between 101 and 500 acres; four managed between 501 and 1,000 acres; and three managed more than 1,000 acres. Interviews lasted between 50 and 70 minutes and were tape-recorded and transcribed. Pseudonyms are used to protect the identity of respondents. Finally, I logged more than 50 hours of participant observations with this group. Most of that time was spent being shown around each individual farm, though I did attend two Farm Hack events. Extensive field notes were taken when no formal interviews were being conducted.

According to the group's website, Farm Hack is "a worldwide community of farmers that build and modify our own tools. We share our hacks online and at meet ups because we become better farmers when we work together" (http://farm-hack.org/310app/). There is no official membership list. The community is intentionally porous. As I was told by one respondent, the "hacking ethos is resistant to solidifying a group with membership lists, because that explicitly makes people 'not one of us', which is a step away from people thinking if-you-not-with-us-you're-against-us." My principal interest in looking at this community involved better understanding how these farmers respond to firms' utilization of digital and legal locks. As such, Farm Hack came to be understood as a call and response to a highly proprietary style of socio-techno-agri-food governance.

Keywords: introducing word clouds

The book *Keywords*, written by the iconoclastic, tweed-wearing Welsh academic and literary critic Raymond Williams (1985), offers a unique inquiry that I have taken methodological inspiration from when engaging with the subject of how we *make* worlds and not just *reproduce* them.

Like eyes are to the soul, words, according to Williams, are a portal into the very assumptions that underlie our ideas about the world. When we adopt meanings to a term we, often unknowingly, adopt ideas about how the world ought to be, which makes this inquiry into our shared vocabulary of immense practical consequence. As mentioned above, one of the aims in each case study was to understand how respondents imagined their respective foodscapes, and the futures made thinkable through those outlooks. In addition to using conventional qualitative interviews, I hoped to representationally grasp these ontological questions, which are by their very nature more-than-representational, by interrogating certain keywords. The specific methodological technique employed to accomplish this was the word cloud. (A word cloud is an image constructed of words in which the size of each indicates its frequency or importance.) It could be argued that word clouds deal in the currency of ontic measurements. For respondents, these keyword descriptions had a matter-of-fact quality to them. (Ontic refers to aspects of reality taken as unproblematic and objectively given, which is generally how respondents treated their views of food security and precision agriculture.) Yet combining these data with that from other methodological sources – interview, observational, and practice-based – allows for *ontological* conclusions to be made, thus giving insight into *why* respondents grasped the world(s) they did.

Using word clouds, I show how respondents from each of the case studies held radically different understandings of the keywords "food security" and "precision agriculture", which suggests different (anticipated) agri-food imaginaries. I argue that these different imaginaries can be linked, at least in part, to the practices and encounters – a.k.a. *assemblages* – engendered by these spaces.

Word clouds were created using data gathered from the following questions: "Select three terms describing what *food security* means to you?" and "Select three terms describing what *precision agriculture* means to you?" Before answering, participants were shown a list of roughly 50 terms for each keyword. The terms on this list were defined, to ensure all participants were operating from a shared understanding of the concepts. Terms were generated from extensive past research looking at how farmers, eaters, and others think about food-related phenomena (see e.g. Carolan 2011, 2015). The words elicited from this instrument were then plugged into word cloud generating software. Words yielding two or fewer response were not included to improve the "cloud's" readability.

I will now present the findings of the word cloud instruments, for both keywords. This initial presentation is ontic. This will be immediately followed by an ontological analysis, looking at *why* these groups viewed and enacted the world(s) they did.

Keyword: "food security"

The world clouds generated for the keyword "food security" can be found in Figures 12.1, 12.2, and 12.3. To start this analysis, note the difference in the top six concepts for each group. Among conventional farmers, those terms are as follows: high yields, precision agriculture, free markets, big data, intensification, and mechanization. The top six for those working for big data agricultural firms: big data, precision agriculture, internet-of-things (the inter-networking of everyday devices creating opportunities for direct integration of the physical world into computer-based systems, resulting in greater efficiency, accuracy and economic benefit), high yields, innovation, and globalization. Finally, the top six for Farm Hack respondents: open source, internet-of-things, social capital, innovation, sharing economy, food access.

Individuals from all three groups expressed some degree of technological optimism. For instance, while conventional growers did not name "Internet of Things" (often called, simply, IoT) at a level sufficient for inclusion in the word cloud, their grasp of "big data" had clear IoT qualities. (All three populations were admittedly primed to think about big data and cloud-based computing, knowing my research was looking into those subjects. The clouds were therefore

Figure 12.1 "Food Security" word cloud, conventional farmers.

Figure 12.2 "Food Security" word cloud, big data agricultural firms.

Figure 12.3 "Food Security" word cloud, Farm Hack.

likely skewed to include related concepts. Nevertheless, this priming effect was equal across groups. The differences across world clouds are thus real and significant.) In the words of one Iowa grower, "[Big data] gives me a connectivity that my dad wouldn't have dreamed of, where I can look at multiple data points – soil type, historical yield averages, weather forecasts – from my phone and make a management decision." Yet while everyone interviews expressed some positive sentiments toward technology, the *level* and *kind* of optimism varied across groups.

Among Farm Hack participants, this becomes clear looking at their most frequently mentioned terms. For this group, the Internet of Thing is something best built from the ground up, where users' needs and values are prioritized as opposed to privileging the needs and values of shareholders, venture investors, and global capital. A farmer from Vermont gave me the following representative (albeit somewhat philosophical) quote where these sentiments are clearly expressed:

> Monsanto's big data, or John Deere's or even the government's, isn't value-free. Those platforms presuppose, and thus tacitly promote, large-scale capital-intensive farms, and thus tacitly disincentivize smaller- and medium-sized labour-intensive farms. Look at the micro-data feeds that give predictive data analytics their power. They're all fed in from sensors installed on large, heavy, state of the art tractors; equipment someone farming 1,000 acres really only needs.
>
> (Jeff)

In an article titled "Do Artifacts Have Politics?", Winner (1980: 122–7) tells the story of the famous early twentieth-century political entrepreneur Robert Moses and the low-hanging overpasses leading into the beaches of Long Island. According to Winner, Moses had these overpasses built to a specific height, under which only automobiles could pass. Buses stood too high and could not pass through these overpasses and therefore could not service the beaches. This was done intentionally, Winner claims, because the typical bus-user at the time was African American. In doing this, these overpasses served political ends: they helped keep the beaches of Long Inland a space for the wealthy automobile-owning (read: white) residents of the area. In discussing this example, Winner's point is this: material – and digital – artefacts affect and are in effect a type of politics. Technology must be understood not simply as "tools we use" but as "forms of life". In this spirit, this movement to optimize some forms of valued life over others, or what Foucault (2003: 241) referred to as "the power to 'make' live and 'let' die", also ties to issues of governance. That was Jeff's point about how certain forms of big data "promote" – or *make live* – large-scale capital-intensive farms, and thus tacitly disincentivize – or *let die* – "smaller- and medium-sized labour-intensive farms".

Conventional growers, conversely, expressed distinctly productivist orientations when asked to explain "food security", as evidenced by their emphasis on such phenomena as technology and profits and by their faith in free markets and trade, though as we will see in the "precision agriculture" word cloud their feelings toward technology are clearly mixed. Those employed by data firms held even narrower understandings of food security, limited almost entirely to technological intensifications.

Keyword: "precision agriculture"

The world clouds generated for the keyword "precision agriculture" can be found in Figures 12.4, 12.5, and 12.6. As before, note the difference in the top six concepts for each sample population. Among conventional farmers, those terms are as follows: high yields, profit maximization, resource-use efficiency, labour-use efficiency, anxiety, and sustainable intensification. The top six for those working for big data agricultural firms: capital intensification, labour-use efficiency, profit

Figure 12.4 "Precision Agriculture" word cloud, conventional farmers.

Figure 12.5 "Precision agriculture" word cloud, big data agricultural firms.

Figure 12.6 "Precision agriculture" word cloud, Farm Hack.

maximization, farmer independence, high yields, and nitrogen-use efficiency. Finally, the top terms listed among Farm Hack respondents include data sharing, food sovereignty, environmental sustainability, high yields, sustainable intensification, and farmer independence.

Building on a point made earlier, to say understandings of "precision agriculture" were mixed does not do justice to the data, as that would imply simple dichotomous – for/against – attitudes. Beyond attitudes, respondents across the three cases reported wildly divergent understandings of the keyword *itself*. As might be expected, those employed by big data firms were rather bullish toward the technology. The technology in this case meaning something, to quote one engineer (Lyle), "that allows farmers managing a couple thousand acres to farm them better than their grandparents would have with a couple hundred [acres] to contend with" – recall what I said earlier about how these techniques, from the standpoint of governance, *make live* and *let die* certain agri-food futures.

Conventional farmers were the most ambivalent of the three groups toward the keyword "precision agriculture", in the sense of having strong positive and negative attitudes. Note, for example, the term "anxiety" prominently displayed along with "high yields" and "profit maximization" in their world cloud. That anxiety centred principally on not knowing how the (big) data would be used, and not being clear on who owned it. To quote Neal from this group:

> It's a mixed bag. I do think having all that data at my fingertips helps the bottom line. And others know that too, so there is an aspect to this where I don't really have a choice but to use this technology if I want to remain competitive.

This quote also provides context for the appearance of "dependency" in this group's word cloud. He continued: "But what really worries me is that I don't know who else has access to my crop and field information, assuming it's even *my* information. I've heard it's not technically mine; that I signed it over to Climate Corp." As mentioned earlier, the Climate Corporation – owned by Monsanto – is a big data company that advertises its services and platforms as tools for farmers to help maximize yields by combining weather, soil and field data.

As with their previous word cloud, Farm Hack respondents held understandings that tended to vary in kind from those expressed by the other groups, as evidenced by the appearance of such terms as "data sharing", "food sovereignty", "experimentation", and "collaboration". Jill offered the following introspective quote, which sums up how the understanding of this population differs from the others on matters relating to *precision agriculture*:

> Technology can be your best friend when raised with the same values that you hold. [...] That's just a rather longwinded way of saying when platforms are designed to solve problems at the community level, which of course assumes there's a community in place to share ideas and experiment; if you have that these conditions in place these platforms can be freeing.

The assemblages we live (and die) by

The aim for the remainder of this chapter is to sketch out some of the processes whereby rules, resources and routinized behaviours give way to agri-food imaginaries among these three groups. To start this discussion let us look at how *farmer independence* was identified by respondents. Note also that the term made an appearance in the "precision agriculture" word clouds for both big data employees and Farm Hack participants, though conventional farmers were keen to bring the concept up during face-to-face interviews.

Those working for big data firms who used this term spoke of how their hardware and algorithms made them "less reliant on guesswork and the opinion of others", as one sales rep explained (Stan). Adding: "Now they [farmers] can look at their iPad or iPhone and just know; they're basically told. No need for guesswork or opinions anymore." (Ironically, this being *told* what to do is what made some conventional growers nervous about these platforms, out of concern they reduce independence and increase their dependency on firms.) Later in the interview Stan made this revealing comment: "With today's analytics farmers don't have to rely on anyone anymore, really. No more need for a fertilizer or seed guy – just you, your tractor, and our program". Note his subtle insertion about farmers *needing our program*, without a hint of irony, when talking about how these platforms allegedly enhance farmer independence. Conversely, those associated with Farm Hack, when talking about the concept, made guesswork and the opinion of others a central component of what it means to be independent. As Kevin explained, talking about the "freeing" nature of working and learning alongside others:

Can you tell me one thing you do that isn't because you learned about it from someone else? Of course not! As I see it, the more you listen to the ideas of others, the more you find ways to get together, the more independent you are.

One way to begin unpacking these findings is with the concept of "affordance". While originating from the field of ecological psychology (Gibson 1977), the idea has been adopted elsewhere to push for a more "relational" (Carolan 2013) view of the world (see e.g. Carolan 2011). In its most general form, affordances describe possibilities, which I understand to include action, thought, and the world itself, that become enacted through practice. Affordances can also, however, be *de-*generative, by limiting what is thinkable and do-able.

What big data, conventionally understood, are said to afford – high yields, labour use efficiency, capital intensification, etc. – presumes an actor embedded within a very specific socio-material web. In these worlds, credit is assumed to be readily available, along with implement dealers and their IT specialists, and those affording infrastructures (cheap oil, dear labour, grain elevators, reliable transportation networks, subsidies, etc.) that make large-scale operations possible. And yet, as I was reminded of by one Farm Hack respondent (Joe), "precision agriculture at a smaller scale can be accomplished with a little sweat equity, some open source code, a twenty dollar microprocessor, and a soldering iron." His point: there are different ways to *do* cloud-afforded foodscapes.

Big data, at least as practised by firms and conventional growers, also affords *individualism*, which is not the same as independence. Recall Stan's (big data employee) earlier comments about how "today's analytics" allow farmers to not "rely on anyone anymore", while later adding how big data affords a type of freedom where it is "just you, your tractor, and *our* program".

This speaks to a thread running through interviews with big data employees and conventional growers. That connective ligament animating conventional big data: the idea that independence can be *bought*. Just as pesticides allow farmers to buy individualism – after all, integrated pest management requires an *integrated* farm management plan that spans multiple operations – proprietary platforms like Climate Pro free farmers from their "fertilizer or seed guy", though, again, what Stan failed to mention (though he implied it) is that this strategy merely substitutes one dependency for another.

Another quote from a conventional grower expressing similar sentiments went like this: "My dad had to have two fulltime hired hands. I have twice as much land and I can get everything accomplished with the help of my son, my John Deeres, and the Mobile Farm Manager app" – the app is part of the MyJohnDeere.com platform. Again, independence that is *dependent* upon a farmer's John Deere equipment and the company's Mobile Farm Manager app does not sound much like independence to me.

Especially problematic about outlooks like this is that they lead farmers to see their neighbours as natural competitors: as those from whom which independence must be sought. "This," as Emery (2015: 48) argues, "has the effect of masking the structural dependencies which farmers face [...] and limits the alternatives available to them to realize a view of independence that is maintained, rather than opposed, by interdependent collective action." Those interviewed in the big data industry and conventional farmer groups were clear that social change resided within the actions of farmers, as *sovereign* individuals – as sovereign *consumers* no less, given the emphasis on buying their way to independence. Never was there mention of a need for collective action with other producers and stakeholders (e.g. eaters).

Farm Hack respondents, meanwhile, spoke as though they were living in a different world; one where, looking at the word clouds, phenomena like "experimentation", "food sovereignty" – yes, food *sovereignty* – "collaboration", "sharing", and "social capital" where privileged. These keywords gave rise to anticipated futures that looked noticeably different from those expressed by the other two groups.

When discussing precision agriculture and food security, those associated with Farm Hack were quick to talk about the distributive agency of their assemblage. What I mean is that a premium was repeatedly placed on making sure their respective worlds, as far as possible, were held together with social capital, empathy, and a respect for difference and change. This latter point is where the idea of "experimentation" (from the world cloud) entered the picture, noting that it is hard to be socially, culturally, and materially innovative if you are expected, for example, to have your fields, rows, and fence lines looking a certain way (Burton 2004).

These agri-food imaginaries came about *because of* code and precision agriculture platforms and not *in spite* of them. To illustrate this point, I will reproduce an exchange I had with Brad, a smaller-scale farmer from Pennsylvania and occasional attendee of Farm Hack events. In his words,

> We should embrace the types of technologies available to us. [...] Just because my grandpa didn't use it shouldn't automatically exclude a technology. He ran all his equipment using leaded gasoline. Should we still be using that just because he did?

A few sentences later he continued, "What's important is that we need to build our technologies *together*. Those are the technologies we ought to get behind."

Intrigued, I asked what he meant by this. Brad went on to tell me, and show me, an open source "bot" – his word – that he created "with the help of friends". The gadget's brain is an Arduino board (an inexpensive microcontroller board common in open source applications) that is connected to various sensors in one of his greenhouses. The sensors measure air and soil temperature, humidity, and soil moisture levels for each of the structure's rooms. The microprocessor is also connected to numerous other elements (drip hoses, windows, etc.) that collectively regulate the interior environment. The computer is programmed to maintain an environment within very narrow parameters.

"Mind you", Brad again, "farmers are not typically trained in hardware design or software programming. But we are part of a culture that values the idea of DIY" – Do It Yourself. Adding,

This is where the hacking *community* comes into the picture. We're a group of self-taught, community-taught actually, techies who apply this high-tech craft to something that has been around for millennia: growing food. Precision agriculture doesn't have to be only about large-scale monocultures and dependence upon the Monsantos of the world.

Conclusion: a call for weak data

Big data tends to be conventionally understood to mean *a lot* of data assembled to make some predictions about the world. (Recall from earlier Monsanto's claim about how their Climate Pro sensors generate roughly seven gigabytes of data per acre.) One big data engineer put it to me this way, when asked what the "big" in big data means: "It stands for more data than we could humanly make sense of without the use of sophisticated algorithms – a lot of data, I guess you could say" (Martha).

Those associated with Farm Hack did not speak regularly of big data, even though many were using algorithms, code, microprocessors, and sensors to manage their operations – remember Brad's "bot". When asked about this apparent discrepancy, their responses typically mentioned something about how the adjective (big) did not accurately capture where the value of these technologies and techniques reside. The following quote comes from Robert, a 500-acre corn, soybean, wheat, pig, and dairy farmer from Indiana: "We have nothing against using sensors and amassing as much as data as necessary to manage our farm. But for us" – *us* being the Farm Hack community – "the big data we're interested in looks nothing like the terabytes that require proprietary technology from Monsanto to make sense of." With that he took a deep breath, which he then expelled between clenched teeth, making a hissing sound. His expression told me he was thinking about what (or how much) to say.

> The value of these systems lies in the fact that they're amendable to our needs and values, big and small, versus exclusively catering to the needs and values of investors who don't know the first thing about issues like rural vitality or food sovereignty and who think the only way the world can be fed is through ever-increasing capital and energy intensification.

According to the aforementioned word clouds, Robert's comment about the "values" of conventional big data is not that far off.

I heard this a lot from those with Farm Hack, about how big data, in the words of Nicole, "isn't anything to be afraid of when it's free" – *free*, in this context, meaning being open to interpretations about how, to paraphrase Robert's prior words, the world ought to be fed. In many ways, this parallels what was said earlier about weak theory. Recall from the beginning of the chapter Clifford Geertz's (1973) and Gibson-Graham's (2014) concern about letting theory overtly guide investigations and name events. Instead, their desire is to advocate for investigations open to emerging knowledge and the "cracks"

(Massumi 2002: 133) of difference. This brings me to the concept of *weak data*: data that are responsible-able.

Haraway (2003) argues that response-ability is constituted through the ability to respond – relationalities that enable more-than-representational engagements "through which entities, subjects and objects, come into being" (p, 71). As such, response-ability is more than about reacting through a purely reasoned response (reason-ability) or universal principles. Speaking of universal principles: think about the one-sized-fits-all values embodied in, say, the Green Revolution. The same can be said about big data, at least as it is conventionally understood: the lives made to live in these capital-intensive, highly proprietary assemblages look, feel, know, and taste much the same – a monoculture-of-governance when what we ought to be embracing is diversity.

Big data, as conventionally practised, is concerned principally with ontic measurements, where objects are compared with other objects that are exterior to it (Crease 2011). This tendency is not unique to big data but a defining quality of conventional foodscapes more generally, as evidenced by their obsession with audits and evaluations (see e.g. Campbell, Murcott, and MacKenzie 2011; Hatanaka, Bain, and Busch 2005). One risk in doing this is that the measurement ends up substituting for the goal (Busch 2016). Note in word clouds the reduction of food security and precision agriculture to, for example, resource use efficiency, high yields, and biofortification. Meanwhile, ontological considerations are black boxed. Questions about the good, just and beautiful become defined through (ontic) measures: e.g. 200 bushels per acre become good, just and beautiful, especially when compared with 175 bushels per acre. Foucault (1980) referred to this black boxing of imaginaries as the *dispositive* (or assemblage): an outlook made "natural" by the strategic arrangement of experts, capital, and historical inertia.

Weak data, meanwhile, affords ontological questions, which make "it" amendable to multiple worlds while also helping to ensure measurements are not confused for ends. In Robert's words, from Farm Hack, "My farm is data-driven only in the sense that they help me achieve my farm management goals. The data never determine those goals for me."

Weak data are also open to questions about the good, just, and beautiful, which in turn open up debates about what imaginaries live and die. My interview with Clark, a self-described "Farm Hack enthusiast", captured this point well. He went into detail describing how it is not only difficult to alter commercial software and hardware, as most farmers lack those skills in addition to the necessary communities of practice to acquire them. In most cases, such hacking acts are also illegal. The (U.S.) Digital Millennium Copyright Act, passed in 1998 to prevent digital piracy, declares it a breach of copyright to break a technological protection – to break into, in other words, a tractor's engine control unit (tECU), essentially the brains of any "smart" piece of farming equipment.

In Clark's words, "The Act makes you a criminal for trying to help other farmers by making their John Deere work for them and their views." His comment was in reference to his desire to create easy-to-follow "hacks" that would allow farmers to fix their own equipment without needing the rely on, in his words, a "John Deere approved technician". That *need* to turn to John Deere for any and all repairs within conventional foodscapes is, again, evidence of Foucault's (1980) *dispositive* – a resilient assemblage of experts, capital, and ideological inertia. To ensure that this dependency does not unintentionally harm firms, companies like John Deere have even written into their contracts that they cannot be sued in the event that a repair delay harms the farmer by slowing their ability to tend to their crops. Farming, after all, is a profession based heavily on timing – e.g. getting seeds planted and crops harvested during optimal windows.

Meanwhile, groups like "Farm Hack take that hacker identity to heart", Clark explained. Later adding that the group wants "to give farmers the know-how to crack those codes, when legal, or to make their own 'smart' pieces of equipment". "We" – *we* being Farm Hack – "still need people", Clark explained. This stance implies holding a position that recognizes that mutual need is not the same as dependency; in fact, it is just the opposite of it.

In sum, scholars need to interrogate the food futures made possible with the help of code, microprocessors, sensors, and "smart" pieces of farming equipment. When doing this, attention should also be paid to the potential of these platforms for creating cracks of difference, which in turn leads to questions about what these assemblages might *afford*. This will help scholars avoid certain traps that come with critiquing big data, such as those that arise when scholarship comes across as too *strong* – as in, big data = serfdom (or dependency, corporate control, neoliberalization, etc.). Such a position is too essentialist. It assumes we know definitively what big data *is* while believing that being to be fixed. Taking too "strong" a stance toward what colloquially might be called big data also makes it difficult to delineate between those code-assemblages that add to the world and those that subtract from it.

The stakes are huge. As we organize foodscapes around data and the anticipated futures they make thinkable, we are dealing with questions that go beyond what we will be eating in the future. As evidenced by six word clouds, these assemblages will help define what the future itself looks like, from who is farming in it to who is allowed to live, who is allowed to get by, and who is allowed to thrive. The lives we hope to live and die by are at stake.

Notes

1 I am not questioning the value of critical scholarship. Allowing oneself *only* a critical stance not only closes off opportunities to witness and call forth generative acts of resistance and (hopefully) change. Perhaps most dangerously, such a stance risks perpetuating the very foodscapes being riled against by making them look and feel inevitable while casting resistance as futile.
2 Before moving forward, it is worth mentioning that I will not be bringing the assemblage concept into the foreground at every opportunity. This is to maximize the space available to draw theoretical connections across the case studies, recognizing too that the editors have provided an excellent overview and theoretical positioning of assemblage thinking at the book's beginning.

References

Anderson, Ben 2010. Preemption, precaution, preparedness: anticipatory action and future geographies. *Progress in Human Geography* 34: 777–798.

American Farm Bureau 2015. The Voice of Agriculture, American Farm Bureau, from www.fb.org/newsroom/news_article/178/, last accessed 16 March 2017.

Andrejevic, Mark 2014. Big data, big questions: The big data divide. *International Journal of Communication*, 8: 17.

Bobkoff, Dan 2015. Seed by seed, acre by acre, big data is taking over the farm. *Business Insider* 15 September Available online at www.businessinsider.com/big-data-and-farming-2015-8, last accessed 9 March 2017.

Bronson, Kelly and Irena Knezevic 2016. Big data in food and agriculture, *Big Data & Society*, 3(1), http://journals.sagepub.com/doi/abs/10.1177/2053951716648174, last accessed 12 March 2017.

Burton, Rob 2004. Seeing through the 'good farmer's' eyes: towards developing an understanding of the social symbolic value of 'productivist' behaviour. *Sociologia Ruralis* 44(2): 195–215.

Busch, Lawrence 2016. Looking in the wrong (la) place? The promise and perils of becoming big data. *Science, Technology & Human Values* 42(4): 657–678.

Campbell, Hugh, Anne Murcott and Angela MacKenzie 2011. Kosher in New York City, halal in Aquitaine: challenging the relationship between neoliberalism and food auditing, *Agriculture and Human Values*, 28(1): 67–79.

Carolan, Michael forthcoming. Weak theory, stronger communities, and vibrant agro-ecosystems. *Journal of Rural Studies*.

Carolan, Michael 2011. *Embodied Food Politics*. Burlington, VT: Ashgate.

Carolan, Michael 2013. The wild side of agro-food studies: On co-experimentation, politics, change, and hope. *Sociologia Ruralis* 53(4): 413–431.

Carolan, Michael 2015. Affective sustainable landscapes and care ecologies: getting a real feel for alternative food communities. *Sustainability Science* 10(2): 317–329.

Carolan, Michael 2017a. Publicising food: Big data, precision agriculture, and co-experimental techniques of addition. *Sociologia Ruralis*. DOI: 10.1111/soru.12120.

Carolan, Michael 2017b. Agro-digital governance and life itself: Food politics at the intersection of code and affect. *Sociologia Ruralis*. DOI: 10.1111/soru.12153.

Carolan, Michael 2018. *The Real Cost of Cheap Food*, 2nd edition. New York: Routledge.

Crease, Robert P. 2011. *World in the Balance: The Historic Quest for an Absolute System of Measurement*. New York: W.W. Norton.

Dawson, Allan 2016. Digital agriculture the next big thing, says Monsanto official, *Manitoba Cooperator* 3 May, www.manitobacooperator.ca/crops/digital-agriculture-the-next-big-thing-says-monsanto-official/, last accessed 26 March 2017.

de Goede, Marieke, Stephanie Simon, and Marjin Hoijtink 2014. Performing pre-emption. *Security Dialogue* 45(5): 411–422.

Deleuze, Gilles and Felix Guattari 1987. *A Thousand Plateaus: Capitalism and Schizophrenia*, Minneapolis, MN: University of Minnesota Press.

Emery, Steven 2015. Independence and individualism: conflated values in farmer cooperation? *Agriculture and Human Values* 32(1): 47–61.

Foucault, Michel 1980. The Confession of the Flesh. In: *Power/Knowledge: Selected Interviews and Other Writings*, edited by C. Gordon, 194–228. New York: Pantheon Books.

Foucault, Michel 2003. *Society Must Be Defended: Lecture at the College de France, 1975–1976*, Mauro Bertani ed., David Macey trans., New York: Picador.

Geertz, Clifford 1973. Thick Description: Toward an Interpretative Theory of Culture. In: *The Interpretation of Cultures: Selected Essays*, edited by C. Geertz, 3–30. New York, NY: Basic Books.
Gibson, James 1977. A Theory of Affordances. In: *Perceiving, Acting and Knowing: Toward an Ecological Psychology*, edited by R. Shaw and J. Bransford, 67–82. Hillsdale: Lawrence Erlbaum Associates.
Gibson-Graham, J.K. 2006. *A Postcapitalist Politics*. Minneapolis, MN: University of Minnesota Press.
Gibson-Graham, J.K. 2014. Rethinking the economy with thick description and weak theory. *Current Anthropology* 55 (S9): S147–S153.
Haraway, Donna 2003. *The Companion Species Manifesto: Dogs, People, and Significant Otherness*. Chicago, IL: Prickly Paradigm Press.
Hatanaka, Maki, Carmen Bain, and Lawrence Busch, L. 2005. Third-party certification in the global agri-food system. *Food policy* 30(3), pp. 354–369.
Massumi, Brian 2002. *Parables for the Virtual: Movement, Affect, Sensation*. Durham, NC: Duke University Press.
Michalopoulos, Sarantis 2015. Europe entering the era of 'precision agriculture.' EurActiv.com 23 October Available online at www.euractiv.com/sections/innovation-feeding-world/europe-entering-era-precision-agriculture-318794, last accessed 20 November 2015.
Schmidt, Eric and Jared Cohen 2013. *The New Digital Age: Reshaping the Future of People, Nations and Business*. New York: Alfred A. Knopf.
USDA 2015. Crop production practices for corn, United States Department of Agriculture, Washington, DC, https://data.ers.usda.gov/reports.aspx?ID=46941, last accessed 29 March 2017.
Williams, Raymond 1985. *Keywords: A Vocabulary of Culture and Society*. Oxford: Oxford University Press.
Winner, Langdon 1980. Do artifacts have politics?. *Daedalus* 109(1): 121–36.
Zarco-Tejada, P., N. Hubbard and P. Loudjani 2014. Precision agriculture: an opportunity for EU farmers – potential support with the CAP, 2014–2020, Joint Research Centre (JRC) of the European Commission; Monitoring Agriculture ResourceS (MARS) Unit H04. Available online at www.europarl.europa.eu/RegData/etudes/note/join/2014/529049/IPOL-AGRI_NT%282014%29529049_EN.pdf, last accessed 20 March 2017.
Zoomers, Annelies, Alex Gekker, and Mirko Schäfer 2016. Between two hypes: will "big data" help unravel blind spots in understanding the "global land rush"? *Geoforum* 69: 147–159.

13 Assemblage and the epistemology of practice
Imagining situated water governance

Ruth Beilin

This chapter examines water governance and locates it within three social-ecological assemblages, in order to shift key elements that form the dominant structures of water management history and current policy in Australia. The intention is to create spaces that allow us, as Latour (2016) suggests, *to assemble the public in different ways*. Water governance emerges as comprised of entwined properties and relationships and giving rise to different narratives. The purpose in exploring particular assemblages is twofold: to challenge the current, normative attempts to silo water and land management decisions as separate, and even static, social and/or ecological formations; and to describe a methodology for undertaking this examination that empowers action. I argue that using assemblage as a conceptual framing *and* pairing it with an epistemology of practice creates an analytical methodology, that facilitates exploration of what is happening within the assemblage, exposing potential and emergent possibilities that focus attention on the meaning of local and the idea of situated water governance.

This chapter begins with a background introduction to the complexity of issues that collide when considering the tangible physical and social water narratives; and to also emphasise the arbitrary, contested, imaginative and intangible realities of locating and managing water in the Australian landscape. The second section focuses on two assemblages that the Australian Government created with the Water Act of 2007 (CGoA 2007). These are environmental, and consumptive flows; and considers the mooted formation of a third assemblage, that of cultural flows. In providing a description of each of the legislated flows as an assemblage, the scene is set to explore how they un-situate water despite being intended to very specifically create certainty about location and use. In considering cultural flows, the evidence suggests that it continues the subjugation of Indigenous rights. In section III, I briefly draw out the key criteria in DeLanda's (2006) social theory of assemblage. I do this principally by example, deconstructing the environmental flow assemblage from section two. In section IV, I pair the epistemology of practice with assemblage thinking to provide a methodology for creating action on the ground. This discussion of practice is based in the writing of Cook and Wagenaar (2012) and in the on-ground application and thinking of West (2016). Section V brings these components together in an imaginary, counter narrative of situated water governance. Section VI discusses the counter narrative and the contemporary Australian narratives in the context of the overall utilization of assemblage theory and this practice orientation for empowerment and action. The conclusion returns to the present, reflecting on the American West experience, and the historical parallels in Australia, including the persistence of the many contradictions that the combined methodology of assemblage and practice lays bare.

Section I Background

It is critical to understand the complexity of 'situated water' in Australia. There is a fundamental relationship between people and water and land. This is an Indigenous story as well as a post-1778, colonial one. But Indigenous and colonial narratives originate in starkly different and incommensurable ontologies. Indigenous knowing respects the multiplicity of dynamic connections and fluidity inherent in land-water-people (Stewart-Harawira 2012). These are actively performed in Indigenous relationships with government and in response to various water governance issues. By contrast, the colonial–settler narrative that dominates governance, separates people, the land and water as individual elements within assemblages.

There is a tangible physical relationship associated with seeking water in the landscape. For humans, this is frequently about establishing its geographic and topographic location. This is the scientific meaning of situated water. A river, for example, in other parts of the world, can be expected to have a visible ecological location in a place and in connection to water. Indeed, if the assemblage under discussion involves a river, its relationships to place(s) and geological formations are usually of interest. But in the Australian context, this is ambiguous because for many places, the river is only sometimes a place of water – only sometimes wet, and otherwise, visible only as a dusty bed or dry floodplain. Locating the physical presence of water is a challenge, and a survival issue, for many humans and non-humans and for would-be regulators.

Frequently even less visible than the water itself, is the watershed or catchment. A catchment implies some kind of land formation, and though government has used catchment management as an administrative way of marking jurisdictions and flows, for those living on the interior side of eastern Australia's Great Dividing Range there is often no physical reality to the idea of catching, or containment, and instead, vast plains to negate such expectations. An assemblage here might depend on the interaction of the elements involved in relationships to contain, or boundary, water in some way. These elements include representations of power within the catchment authorities, municipalities and settler-colonial property laws. These interactions shift the conception of that spatial containment, influencing government and local governance institutions or their organisations. These governance mechanisms are therefore, the articulation of settler–colonial approaches to human and non-human relationships to, and the subsequent capacities associated with a physical and social expression of water in a catchment. Almost immediately, the tension between actual and situated, and imagined and un-situated water becomes apparent.

The scale of a catchment in the Australian continent (often being tens of thousands of square kilometres) overwhelms the possibility of finding one description to evoke its presence (or apparent physical absence). The catchment is also problematic as it does not correspond with how colonial settlement occurred and few administrative lines, such as districts or municipalities, follow its topographical demarcation (Beilin 2001). Management is also ambiguous as different regimes, complimenting or contrasting different land uses, converge within catchment boundaries. The agricultural management at the recharge on the 'top' of the catchment hillside, is generally significantly different from its discharge area kilometres away in the plains or undulating flats. The Australian catchment then, is unlikely to be effective as a management or governance unit, and yet, in many landscapes, this is the situation (Cohen and Davidson 2011).

Section II Extracting three water assemblages from settler–colonial ontology

Two of the assemblages described here are the result of the Water Act 2007.[1] The third, that of cultural flows, is part of Indigenous attempts to establish their right to manage water in their landscapes.

Assemblage 1 *The environmental flow*

The Water Recovery Strategy for the Murray–Darling Basin (DoE 2014, 9) says that 'to return the river system to health, the Basin Plan requires recovery of 2,750 gigalitres of surface water for the environment as opposed to agriculture and other commercial uses'. The concept of a legislated **environmental flow** is historically a creation of The Water Act 2007 (CGoA 2007) when water was set aside from consumptive use for the environment. Jackson (2017, 122) notes how water has been 'reformed to reframe the environment as a water 'user' legally entitled to water allocations with other users'. The political imperative for environmental water was the Millennium Drought (1997–2009) in south-eastern Australia (CSIRO 2014). During that time, many species were reduced to small watered pools. Subsequent floods also caused disruption and death through the heightened movement of water-borne contaminants. The key element in this overall environmental flow assemblage is a vision of a continuous river (the imagined pre-1788 and white settlement river) and an ideal nature without people. The environmental flow is intended to provide biodiversity security as directed by science and effected by engineering. The flow objectives are differentiated into six categories: zero flows – ponds; low flows – cover the bottom of the channel but no depth; freshes – flows that are short term but can fill the channel as when there is rainfall; high flows – when there is a persistent increase in base-flow and these are contained within the channel; bankfull flows – completely fill the channel; and overbank flows – that spill out on to the floodplain (MDBA 2016, 42). Each of these flow criteria creates a different nature that is relatively unpredictable, depending on uncertain variables, for example, the outcomes of current and future seasons. Each creates multiple interactions within the affected habitats and with their wider landscapes. Within these overall assemblages, the flows represent varying incarnations of a nature that is intended to be more predictable, and as a consequence of that envisaged certainty, can be more readily commodified for national and international markets.

Assemblage 2 The consumptive flow

The **consumptive flow** allocation represents the dominant, historical use of the water. It is largely insensitive to the notion of a catchment, arbitrarily commodifying the flow as isolates or objects rather than elements in a system. It focuses on the extractive rights associated with provisioning towns and providing water for irrigation. Its access and allocation tends to reflect the white settler history of the Murray–Darling Basin (MDB) region. The Water Recovery Strategy for the MDB (DoE 2014, 2) says:

> A key priority for the Australian Government is to ensure the Murray-Darling Basin remains Australia's primary food bowl. The Government is committed to ensuring that Australian farmers produce as much food and fibre as is sustainably achievable for the Australian people, and for export to the world.

Water recovery is a phrase that represents buying back water from irrigators and improving the technical delivery of water to irrigators by modernising the channel delivery systems. This assemblage depends on socio-technical alignment, water recovery and water rights, generally manifest through licensing. Weirs and dams capture water, and then measure it out as directed by technical administrators, administration of water licences (rights) and on site, on demand channels. The technology draws on various capacities that are centrally managed by operators and through equipment to deliver as a unified and purposeful convergence that ultimately is meant to ensure production values. This alignment makes the management and delivery of the water seem certain and tends to hide the extensive history of over allocation of water licences, the governance issues associated with the allocated flows and the dependency on the mechanical system. It also makes it seem that the water can be more easily quantified and commodified. Water trading based on water rights, has significant economic benefits in Australia, with this mostly irrigator-run market estimated to be worth $2.4 billion annually in turnover of trade in 2011 (Nikolakis and Grafton 2014).

Assemblage 3 Cultural flows

The **cultural flows** are 'water entitlements that are legally and beneficially owned by Indigenous nations of a sufficient and adequate quantity and quality, to improve the spiritual, cultural, environmental, social and economic conditions of those Indigenous Nations' (MLDRIN 2007/10). While the environmental and irrigator water is legally understood as a right, and a need, there is no such surety for cultural flows, though Indigenous cooperation, as manifest in framing their rights as 'cultural flows' suggests that to align with Indigenous ways of being, systemic ways of understanding flows are being invoked. This assemblage is not recognised in Commonwealth law. Indigenous people can only have 'expectations' rather than rights and needs, as despite having ownership of 20% of the land they have less than 0.01% of the established water rights. Cultural flows are understood to encompass water from 'the environmental reserve and consumptive water pool' (Environmental Justice Australia 2014, 38) but in fact Indigenous people get physical control of virtually nothing. The cultural flows assemblage reflects the economic and cultural needs of Indigenous people, and so acknowledges the immutability of land-water-people. But the emphasis on culture in the framing of 'cultural flows' continues what Ayre and Mackenzie (2013, 754–755) experienced in Western Australian water planning negotiations. There, the diminishing of Indigenous ontology (ways of knowing and doing) by suggesting it is just about culture, continuously isolated Indigenous people from discussions that were not deemed cultural. Significantly, while Indigenous land-water-people is in multiple relationships with government in contemporary management assemblages, Indigenous disempowerment around water is rarely named or when named, rarely acted upon by the dominant structures. The reinforcing of Indigenous disempowerment by entrenching cultural associations with water but providing no rights to it, points to where power rests within this assemblage and how important it is to interrogate this formation specifically to understand how the power of the state continues to subjugate Indigenous life. In the absence of an official recognition of Indigenous rights as part of the legislated flows, this assemblage is a place-marker, making overt the historical power that continues to obscure Indigenous rights.

These three assemblages represent different narratives of water governance practices. Each of these three is a version of the same settler–colonial narrative which transcends various scales of space and time and creates various possible 'other' water assemblages that echo the same ontology. In general, these narratives attempt to stabilise and maintain the internal relationships between their described elements; noting their representation is predominantly as if these properties are temporally and spacially static. But in their everyday evocation, the interaction of the elements that constitute each narrative unsettle the narrative of stasis that underpins their normative governance, shifting power and creating emergent properties. For example, the environmental flows depend on managers enabling water in these semi to highly regulated systems that can be diverted to identified habitats in response to climate conditions. This control depends on monitoring, auditing, disciplining the water, the technology and the users. However, the scale of the landscape, the market trading that also underpins Australian water governance and the complexity of these interactions across scales (local to regional and season to season) create a thousand emergent properties within the idea of the flow and/or its manifestation within the river or basin system. Importantly, even if environmental water is designated to a habitat, the effect is not certain. The designation does not ensure that unscrupulous irrigators will not attempt to divert it to their irrigation channels; or that expected fauna or avian species will be able to respond and sustain their lives at that location, especially if the subsequent flows are not assured (Kingsford, Bino, and Porter 2017).

Situated water governance emerges, then, as a central concern in these assemblages of siloed water, its use and place, where place may only be conceived as a (sometime) original access point (where the river is really a floodplain, for example, with no clearly marked channels); or as the location of water withdrawal (for example, where consumptive users usurp environmental flows); or when, as in Indigenous understanding, water is integral to land-water-people as a dynamic composite and governance and administration are other properties interacting with this composite, in attempting or creating relationships.

In the next section, I draw out the key theoretical criteria that clarify the usefulness of an assemblage lens.

Section III Assemblage and confluence

From the above three larger assemblage narratives (consumptive, environmental and cultural flows) we can elicit the core criteria for an assemblage as suggested by Deleuze and Guattari in *A Thousand Plateaus* (1987), and elucidated by DeLanda (2006).

Assemblage is a way of making sense of the interaction of elements and the relationships they form with each other and that define the assemblage. In the example of water governance, there are many elements that interact as in the three flows indicate. Deleuze and Guattari argued that the focus of our attention on particular elements (and the exclusion of others that are also in relationships with our elements of interest) leads to a heightened amplification of the assemblage so it is understood as a whole (not reducible to its parts). As in these narratives, the elements include relationships with non-material aspects of the assemblage like institutions and emergent properties may include overtly 'seeing' the manifestation of power or disempowerment.

DeLanda provides three criteria for assemblage to be more than just a collection of elements. They are irreducibility, amplification and decomposability. Irreducibility refers to the assemblage overall. As an example, the environmental flow is more than the sum of its parts: it is comprised of a set of calculations about the total amount of water available in that season, deducting the amount required for consumptive water licences, and then allocated to particular places and habitats along the river. Each of these elements can be separated out and they can exist outside this environmental flow assemblage. But their interaction creates the official environmental flow and there are emergent properties that are the consequence of their interaction.

This points to the second criteria, that of *amplification*. The articulation of an environmental flow has social, economic, cultural and ecological consequences.

Framing the environmental flow as an ecological good allows urban taxpayers (who are 92% of the population, though all taxpayers fund this allocation) to contribute to the idea of maintaining healthy river and wetland systems in regional Australia. The environmental flow is amplified into images of healthy rivers and the sustenance of Australia's 'natural world'. This amplification is a consequence of the interaction of the environmental flow with place and time creating emergent properties that depend on that amplification. If there is no environmental flow, we know that these habitats and species are endangered and will likely disappear.

The third criteria is *decomposition*. The elements in the environmental flow are not fused. They are not a totality. Therefore, they can continue to exist outside the formation of the environmental flow assemblage. They interact to form the environmental flow but they may also exist in different combinations or actions in other assemblages at the same time. In this way, the machinery and calculations that are used to create the environmental flow as a movement of water in a landscape, may also be used to deliver or clarify the consumptive flow, for example.

Finally, what is crucial according to DeLanda (2006), is that each element exercises its capacities in order to fully emerge. The interaction of the elements in the environmental flow creates the possibilities for habitat and healthy rivers but if they stop interacting, their relationships end, emergence ends and so does the assemblage as described. Decomposition is critical to the concept of assemblage. It emphasises the importance of interaction and the specific characteristics of that interaction, even though the element or property is not itself defined by the interaction. Environmental flow depends on the interaction of climate, society and water being governed by policies and rules that are adhered to through local governance structures.

Governance becomes the trigger for re-imagining these assemblages and their relationships. But having identified the trigger, the interaction between the elements assembled requires examining too. It is here that the pairing of a practice focused epistemology assists in re-thinking the assemblage. The practices that construct water governance narratives variously hide or make visible the histories and rules of use, the user rights or expectations, and the social and ecological consequences of this management. Examining these practices (what people do, how these actions create other elements) provides other possible ways of seeing and understanding these interactions and the reasons for the relationships: creating the possibility of other assemblages.

In summing up this section of the chapter, note how action pervades the assemblage. The assemblage is dynamic, emphasising emergent outcomes as a consequence of the relationships between the elements or properties that are its focus. But to examine these interactions requires acknowledging the 'doing' that goes into relationships, and the importance of noting context and acknowledging the contingencies that arise from action and within actions. This focus on interaction, relationships, and dynamic change that allows for emergence has many synergies with practice theory.

Section IV The epistemology of practice

The epistemology of practice as inspired by the writing of Cook and Wagenaar (2012) and Wagenaar's *Meaning in Action* (2011) was field tested in a natural resource management context in 2014. It was a situated examination of a social-ecological study of an adaptive management project in a national park in Australia (see West, Beilin and Wagenaar [forthcoming]). In stepping through this process, I am indebted to the detailed methods and analysis in West's (2016) *Interpreting complexity: exploring social-ecological relations from the inside-out*.

Cook and Wagenaar (2012) emphasise the practices that emerge as part of 'doing', and I argue here that this begins when we engage with assemblage as a concept, in the field. The assemblage amplification draws attention to the interactions between relationships and the consequent emergent properties. These open the spaces for the possibilities or potential for action. Cook and Wagenaar (2012) describe 'the doing' as *actionable understanding, ongoing business* and the *eternally unfolding present*. These are always different, contingent and they do not attempt to reduce complexity. This approach emphasises the potential of small acts and very local responses as significant and notable. It similarly counters the meta-narratives that globalised forces easily impose on local sites or that governments represent as neo-liberal policies, such as those that regulate the river for the water markets, in effect organising the supply and demand of all nature as inputs in the global market system.

Actionable understanding

This first step in the epistemology of practice is one of *negotiation* between the actors who are engaged and their antecedents who are part of the social and ecological memories of the site. The beginning is actually a taking up of the thread of each narrative to engage the participants in *constructing a mutual purpose*. Each must conceptualise the situation they encounter and the memories and experiences they bring in a way that allows others to understand their position and the importance of their ways of knowing in the context of the place. Some of the participants will speak in an effort to represent the non-human species. These may be environmentalists or farmer conservationists or Indigenous people or government agencies or scientists or other stakeholders. These voices are critical to the rest of the project, because this step generates the ideas and the identification of the kinds of practices that will allow an *actionable set of practices* to emerge. This generation of practices is not immutable, but a beginning in deriving mutually acceptable ways of acting and to construct the boundaries and framework for subsequent practices.

Those that have been arguing for the dominance of the consumptive extraction of water within this site (a localised site along the river), must let this go; as must those arguing for environmental flows. The cultural flows emerge here as an adhering quality that enables the negotiation of meaning and importance. Here is the expectation of a different view that acknowledges the wellbeing of the river *as the wellbeing of the land and the people* as one property, in an integrated way. The interface that is required for this to occur is negotiated here.

Ongoing business

The ongoing business evolves from this site experience and is woven into the negotiations and mutual derivation of purpose described here. In order to identify likely practices and their actors (because different participants may undertake actions that are not part of their usual way of operating), we begin with listing self-identified skills that are associated with particular tasks, and add those that others recognise from past experiences. Each participant comes with a 'bag of tools', some of which may be based on formal ways of ordering and knowing like scientists evoke when calling on their disciplinary learning, and some of which belong to custom, culture, place, and world views. These provide the operational impetus for understanding how the negotiated practices will be undertaken. This step also provides the recognition of how operational cultures dictate or assume some rules and requirements. In recognising the multiplicity of views, there is an opening for their conditions to be examined by the individual and the collective, so that the reassembly may be, will be different, *emerging* with adjustments that reflect the participants' engagement with 'the business' at hand.

Routine actions are not exactly the same, even if we think of them as routine. Within the context of different participants, different expectations and negotiations about 'the business', routine actions become part of the wider discussion and generate their own project procedures. In this process, and as this creates mutual recognition of skills, experience, understanding, knowing and capacity, the actors' roles emerge.

Ongoing business is also where disruptions to everyday practice are first recognised. The disturbance to 'business' creates a pause in the activities that once again focuses attention on what has been negotiated and also on how it can be achieved. The capacity to undertake ideas or specific tasks may be re-imagined, re-examined, re-tasked.

Eternally unfolding present

In order to achieve an outcome such as the reimagining of what 'situated water governance' entails, we now have a collection, an assembly of immediate actions immersed in a setting and part of actors' 'doing'. These become the immediate practices of the eternally unfolding present. Each reflects not just the determinations that brought the practices from and to the field, but the current context of that doing. In this way the daily realities of weather, health, politics, social interaction construct a particular version of that practice. The inability to exactly replicate actions is a recognition of the uncertainties with which we live and the importance of acknowledging this uncertainty, empowers us to make overt the interpretations that occur *in situ* in most environmental encounters

(West, 2016). West (2016) notes that in the eternally unfolding present, the imperative of time is excluded from the immediate discourse because of the immersion in the situated doing and knowing. In the immediate emergent assembly of these practices there is enough time.

Situated water governance could, unpacked in this way, offer different logics based on different histories and with different actors who create different assemblages through their daily practices. The socio-ecological approach is to begin in place, on the ground or in the water, not on the banks of the river or on the bridge that we may construct as philosophers or academics above the river (see Latour 2005/8) but em-barked and re-situated in the river itself. From here, different ways of seeing allow different ways of doing and knowing to emerge and reinforce the centrality of relational action and interaction in rethinking approaches to water. This is not to suggest that it is simple to overcome the dominant paradigm of un-situated water and its powerful actors, but rather that in combining approaches that conceptualise water governance differently, the dominant paradigm does not appear so invincible or the only way of understanding the situations we confront.

Section V Epistemology of practice and a counter narrative assemblage

In this section I pair the epistemology of practice with assemblage theory. The intention is to take the concept of assemblage from its theoretical constructs to the field, where thinking through a practice lens and articulating different, situated water governance assemblages, could assist us to act differently with regard to water management.

Water as an element of water governance or a system such as a river, operates as a particular object-subject in the world. As we manage our engagement, there is a subjective interaction with it, in which it is both object and subject – as, for example, an element of policy or an extractive task. If we think of it as an object alone, water is ostensibly de-cultured – counted as a resource or commodity that has to be valued external to its place of origin or collection. This is one way water becomes un-situated. (An exception to this is for example, the marketing of bottled water in which the water comes from an Indigenous cooperative and is marketed as being a spiritually enhancing beverage (see http://yaruwater.com/).)

In the main, however, water as an object denatures it, transforming its powerful importance in culture and nature, translating these into a product and commodity and metered allocation. Perpetuating the dominance of one-use-one-meaning paradigm in the wider landscape and tying it to a scale of agricultural and animal production has made the process and the disappearance of local water rights seem inevitable and even socio-economically progressive. It underpins the assumption that this scale and use is the more 'efficient' use of a precious liquid in a drying landscape. The removal of this assumption and the opening of an invitation to reconstruct the management of water *in situ* requires a bigger discussion than just this chapter can provide. The conditions for achieving such discussions will include specific incentives for local people and landscapes. Such discussions will depend on processes that acknowledge human and non-human needs and expectations and reflect social and environmental justice (see Environmental Justice Australia 2014).

Assemblage assists the reader to re-assemble Australian water history through a different description of water claims than those currently confining us. As well, through re-positioning water within, for example, a river basin-water-governance assemblage, there is the possibility of re-conceptualising the agency of local (which currently includes international actors in many cases – such as on water boards) and situated governance and detailing this through a critique of what otherwise exists. Further, in re-imagining what might be, in terms of water governance, we re-assemble a different imaginary; it is one that has practical and political outcomes and one that allows us to re-formulate the processes of engagement as we experience and reflect on that experience of change. As Vogler (2002, 627) notes "… the new shapes that reimagined lives take on under the pressure of shifts in the social imaginary are often only available to individuals retrospectively and find their first articulations in shifting social relations and points of practice." The assemblage-practice methodology assists in focusing on this shift.

In considering the spatio-temporal processes around such a reconstruction of purpose in the twenty-first century, and how these collide at particular sites, Cathcart (2010) argues that European settlers first claimed waterholes rather than landscapes. He writes that these watering places were sites of Indigenous gathering and known locations of importance. Powerful colonial forces incorporated the waterholes as part of land claims or selections and in doing so realigned the value of the water as a tool (an object), to make the waterhole just part of the reason for settling there (good fields, pasture-like conditions *and* water). Ironic that in just over 200 years, that assemblage, stabilised in white settler histories (as something that is just part of the landscape rather than the dominant force) and the colonial project, is now destabilised and dislocated by a different formation of market purposes, as a recent review of the northern basin indicates a significant waterhole mapping project is to be undertaken (MDBA 2016, 39). Undoubtedly, the practices required to consolidate the right to water by the invading settlers, effectively hid the practices that had secured that same water for use in Indigenous land management and socio-cultural ways of living. These Indigenous histories were not allowed to co-exist or overlap as they do in the European context where Roman springs and spas became the bedrock of English towns and villages; but rather, Indigenous histories were disappeared and practices annulled to ensure a dominant narrative and no equity claims within the European settler formations. Their re-instatement demands active scrutiny.

These significant histories of previous situated water governance – for example, that of Lake Condah and the eel farming (https://theconversation.com/the-detective-work-behind-the-budj-bim-eel-traps-world-heritage-bid-71800; McNiven and Bell 2010) – remind us that in the contemporary light, other ways of assembling and encountering can be part of daily practices within these spaces and territories. Other connections can be made to the land and to water. The methodology described here offers different ways of imagining and generating these possibilities.

Assembling land tenure, new populations and agro-ecological processes

This assemblage is an imagined form of resistance to the normative narrative that constructs production and conservation as alien to each other, and nature and culture as oppositional forces that must be regulated to counter the deterministic tendencies of each. Here the counter-assembly aims to synergistically engage with nature-culture and the potential for the creation of different pathways as situated water governance. Again, DeLanda's (2006) description of the three characteristics of assemblage that elucidate the importance or clarify the relationships between its elements are: irreducibility (more than a collection), amplification (enhanced so more than the sum of the parts and this leads to emergence) and decomposition (some parts may be part of other assemblages, they can be detached from one and put into another). These assist us to counter reductionism and essentialism – two historic characteristics of water resource management. If water has been historically harnessed as a technical resource management function rather than understood or valued as a socio-cultural element, the first practice in 'actionable understanding' is to negotiate a different purpose – the recognition of the water in place, as part of a social and physical being: one that integrates needs, expectations and an understanding of limits and potential changes.

The elements then are, at the meta level, land and water and within it at varying scales, people and non-human species (including livestock and crops). But in order to make it feasible to provide an example of this situated water governance, it is, as Latour has said, important to deliberately seek alternative voices. In this story, the voices are young people from the city, who want to live in the countryside, be small-scale producers on small holdings of land and create regional food networks for supply and distribution. In Victoria, Australia, the river becomes the Goulburn Broken Catchment and there is a regional catchment management authority (GBCMA). Parts of it are very productive lands for industrial agriculture that are grazed and farmed by family farmers and corporate farmers that are families or non-familial businesses. Family farmers are predominantly aging individuals who must sell their farms to realise superannuation, and who carry very high levels of debt associated with restructuring of markets, modernisation of irrigation schemes, previous years of drought and unseasonable variations in climate over the last 15 years (Sysak 2013). Reconstituting the land tenure to allow 'closer settlement blocks' of say 3–5 hectares could be activated as part of this changed scenario.

Financing the entry of these young people could be supported through resettlement schemes. Historically government had a closer settlement scheme approach for returned soldiers, after WW I and II. This made it possible for those who had no employment in the urban centres, no inheritance claim and little money to take up land. The proviso this time would be around agro-ecological processes (see IPES-Food 2016). The intention in taking up these blocks is for there to be a commitment to regional food supply and to agro-ecological practices to create landscape scale management.

As part of 'ongoing business', relations are established between the incomers and those who continue to manage land and water in other ways. Governance structures here are about negotiating changes to individual conceptions of their 'bag of tools' that is the application of known skills and the encouraging of information flow across these communities. In returning to small holder landscapes, there is the need to adapt equipment, and ways of doing to these scales. GBCMA has been very active in promoting resilience thinking as a way to make residents aware of the ecological limitations of the region (GBCMA 2013). Ecological changes at small scales, aggregated where possible by uptake across the landscape, could be expected to improve surface and ground water quality, as well as indigenous and introduced species biodiversity – as for example, increased areas for habitat. Ongoing business can also be about sourcing labour for associated cottage industries (e.g. farm forestry, seedbanks, horticultural seed certification farms, and farm gate value adding). Increasing regional employment would assist with keeping youth and good ideas in the region. This is not about farm labour and land tenure per se but about building new industries around sustainable living, technology and small-scale enterprises.

In 'the eternally unfolding present' we remember that early white settlers had a particular understanding of farming, driven by land agents and the possibilities of a new world (to them). Current land managers have proved their resilience across many disastrous changes driven by floods and drought; and by markets and scales of production that eviscerate the ecological realities of their places, but it has also led to maladaptation (Beilin, Syzak, and Hill 2012). In situated water governance, played out at a smaller scale, there is as Crossley (2003) describes, the opportunity to recreate habitus – radical habitus. This means ways of operating within *now*-identified niches that have been neglected because the common view of how this landscape functions or is socially or ecologically structured makes other possibilities virtually invisible. For example, clarifying or testing what can be done in areas that are newly created through the intersection of land tenure, people and agro-ecological processes. In the daily processes of articulating what it is to live in a region with a conscientious attempt to provide alternative, practical ways of sourcing and having food flow as a part of situated water governance; new ways of operating and managing will emerge from new ideas that are generated as a consequence of this assembly.

This is the political work of assembly. In the case of situated water governance, we can conceptualise it at multiple levels within multiple landscape views. Activities at one site will be experienced tangibly or otherwise, because of their physical and/or cultural connectedness. Water, as an emergent property of the immediate and place-based landscape, is a commons; at other sites, with their manifestations of its commonality, there will be related (but different) emergent properties in their relational assemblages. The collective properties exist in the sense that it is the interaction of material and non-material elements aggregating to the disposal and governance of the water. If we think about this in the context of the current management of the river, a series of complicated weirs and dams ensure a particular delivery system. However, these constructions cannot ensure water. The lack of water does not inhibit the governance of the current system. The rules and regulations allow for the adjustment of the flows. These decisions constantly demand the re-interrogation of the meaning of environmental water and irrigation water and the values it represents. Making these decision practices transparent and their eternal negotiation of contingencies or refusal to negotiate contingencies overt, means that substituting a different model like the small-holder agro-ecological assembly described above, presents another possibility. This one, focused on small scale and *in-situ* management may also help us respond to the continuously emerging and unresolved Indigenous rights to water (Environmental Justice Australia 2014).

Section VI Discussion

Swyngedouw (1999) argues that Australia's adoption of river basin management – a scalar leap from managing a river to managing as a catchment or regional water supply – was the central platform in moving governance from the realm of those engaged in the local use of water, to those who develop or administer technical and mechanical decisions based on controlling access. The translation of a local water source into a regional resource requires ways of conceptualising and managing that seem independent of localism and accepting of the non-material component of water. This affirmation of the invisible as a part of the commodification of land-and-water slips insidiously into our application of water management as auditable 'facts'. While, in the nineteenth and twentieth century we have experienced how the need to redistribute, compartmentalise, reallocate and transport water sets a path for increasing structural improvements like dams and irrigation schemes (Worster 1985; Reisner 1986; Cathcart 2010), in the twenty-first century we now recognise that the flows and weirs maintain water in the 'wrong' season; and provide water flows that channelled through landscapes they can no longer be diverted to because of water trading.

Managing and creating flows requires a framework at state levels and ever more sophisticated expertise that tends to remove local jurisdictions as distance is extended and ownership becomes global. Preliminary governance decisions are vested with scientists, engineers and administrators as the mediators of this transformation – not those who live locally now or in the past (Barber and Jackson, 2016) and who experienced the social and ecological realities of their places. More recently, this distance-based decision framework also reflects private property development (see the example of Cubbie Dam, Strang 2013; Head 1999) and responds to private corporate markets. Issues of access and availability are scrutinised, not for impact on the local landscape, but as part of the national export effort and ideas about efficient use (for productive purposes) that drive policy. (See the Commonwealth of Australia 2015, Agricultural Competitiveness White Paper; Beilin 2015).

In considering two of the water flows as assemblages produced by The Water Act of 2007, and the third as a recognition of Indigenous rights, we can use DeLanda's criteria to assess their validity as structures. In pairing these assemblages with an epistemology of practice we can focus on the action (changing conceptions, changing practices) that the relationships create in their interaction. This provides a methodology that allows the distancing from historical influence, a re-situating of governance at the local, and, in the resistance to reifying three water assemblage narratives, exposes their underlying weakness. They are constructed to focus on the mechanics of delivery rather than the social and ecological consequences; and in the case of cultural flows, reinforce legal disempowerment, even as they suggest a limited access might occur.

The imagined assemblage of small-holder agro-ecological settling (one that actively involves Indigenous co-imagining), allows a re-examination of the national policy agenda of endlessly increasing production rather than one that encourages a recognition of the limitations of soil and water in production narratives. An agro-ecological overlay locates people-land-water within their situated practices, and in a dynamic recognition of temporal and spatial scales, locates these practices in the eternally unfolding present. In the imagined assemblage, actionable understanding will reinforce resistance to the administrative need to command and control (see Holling and Meffe 1996) the catchment, river, and all flows.

Consequently, ensuring a broadly inclusive deliberative participation is core to achieving the kind of background and intentions that will generate water narratives that were previously submerged and multiple histories that speak of other voices than the current three. It is here that the governance of the assemblage becomes so crucial. Recognising that as water enters different spaces, new assemblages are necessarily formed, with some of the same but also some new aspects of engagement – creating appropriate adaptive governance networks becomes critical to responding to the awakening assemblages. As each assemblage is complex and not reducible to the change in one or other particular element, it is important to approach each formation prepared to re-map rather than to expect a template.

Conclusion

Worster (1985, 329) writes about the management of water and the consequent desertification of the American West, asking whether people can be pried from their history and walk free – saying that "… History is always easier to understand than it is to change or escape". Arguably, the catchment management models in America and instigated in Australia in the 1990s reposition water management within the ecological limitations of their physical locations. Situating water management in the Australian context, meant creating situated water governance through, initially, in the Victorian context, Catchment and Land Protection Act (1994), and the Catchment Management Authorities (CMA). These governance mechanisms would involve the expertise of local communities and ideally act in the interests of local water management. As an advocate of locally based CMA governance, I had not foreseen the appropriation of the local by corporate global interests – despite Latour's (1993) long established argument for the intimate attachment between the global–local; nor had I understood the exacerbated decline in communities across the regional and rural landscapes, and that their local landscapes would become homogenised within local-global markets. The now legislated trading of water has further un-situated flows. Despite local social-ecological management governance through the CMAs being intended to very specifically create certainty about location and use, decisions are frequently made up stream or through trading that can be counter to the maintenance of local social-ecological outcomes. As Habermas (2015) has argued in the context of nation-states and the EU, I similarly argue that technocracies rather than governance are empowered in the current Australian water governance management of the legislated flows and these shape discussion of any cultural flow. In the main, they are able to create un-situated and out of place flows that are rarely informed by public discourses before they occur. Habermas, concerned with the fate of the collective over that of the nation-state, argued for transparent rationality as a way to ensure basic rights. The assemblage approach provides the possibility of transformative re-imagining in which not just people but their engagement, and co-construction of water and landscapes are part of informed, inclusive public discourses. This is a fundamentally political and transformational and challenging task that citizens can undertake in an effort to change the consequences of our historical water governance. The alternative is that water scarcity will close down regions and water markets will continue to remove water from them until local places are no longer habitable.

Assemblage and the 'doing' of practices associated with maintaining or deconstructing these assemblages allows us to think about all these contradictions. The tensions inherent in water governance are particularly transparent when we do. Immediately as we focus on governance at any one point in time, the paradox of management is clear and the power relationships emerge. Water is managed as if it is stable and fixed, while the opposite is necessarily true: water is mobile and the previously described mechanics of moving it around in our highly altered systems is designed to enhance or impede that mobility. And more recently in the context of Australian water trading, water is moving through markets and landscapes that never experience its moisture or taste its origins.

Note

1 Examples are drawn from the Murray–Darling Basin rivers and include the Northern Rivers feeding into the Darling.

References

Ayre, Margaret, and John Mackenzie. 2013. "'Unwritten, unsaid, just known'; the role of Indigenous knowledge(s) in water planning in Australia". *Local Environment* 18: 753–768.

Barber, M., and Sue Jackson. 2016. "Remembering 'the blackfellows' dam': Australian Aboriginal water management and settler colonial riparian law in the upper Roper River, Northern Territory". In *Other People's Country: Law, Water and Entitlement in Settler Colonial Sites*, edited by Timothy Neale and Stephen Turner, 6–25. London: Routledge Press.

Beilin, Ruth. 2001. "The brave new order: Power, visibility and the everyday landscapes of Australian farmers". In *Environment, Society and Natural Resource Management: Theoretical Perspectives*, edited by Vaughan Higgins, Stewart Lockie, and Geoffrey Lawrence, 185–197. London: Edward Elgar.

Beilin, Ruth. 2015. "Agriculture, water and nationhood: reboot or rewrite?" *Georgetown J of International Affairs: Culture and Society.* Summer/Fall: 77–90.

Beilin, Ruth, Tamara Sysak, and Serenity Hill. 2012. "Farmers and perverse outcomes: the quest for food and energy security, emissions reduction and climate adaptation". *Global Environmental Change* 22: 463–471.

Cathcart, Michael. 2010. *The Water Dreamers.* Melbourne: Text Publishing.

CGoA (Commonwealth Government of Australia). 2007. The Water Act. www.legislation.gov.au/Details/C2016C00469.

Cohen, Alice and Seanna Davidson. 2011. "The watershed approach: challenges, antecedents, and the transition from technical tool to governance unit". *Water Alternatives* 4(1): 1–14.

Commonwealth of Australia. 2015. Agricultural Competitiveness White Paper, Canberra. Accessed December 2015. http://agwhitepaper.agriculture.gov.au/SiteCollectionDocuments/ag-competitiveness-white-paper.pdf.

Cook, S. D. Noam and Hendrik Wagenaar. 2012. "Navigating the eternally unfolding present: towards an epistemology of practice". *The American Review of Public Administration.* 42(1): 3–38.

Crossley, Nick. 2003. "From reproduction to transformation: Social movement fields and the radical habitus". *Theory Culture and Society* 20(6): 43–68.

CSIRO (Commonwealth Scientific and Industrial Research Organisation). 2014. The Millenium Drought Fact Sheet. Accessed 24 March 2017. www.seaci.org/publications/documents/SEACI2Reports/SEACI2_Factsheet2of4_WEB_110714.pdf.

DeLanda, Manuel. 2006. *A New Philosophy of Society: Assemblage Theory and Social Complexity.* London: Continuum Press.

Deleuze, Gilles and Félix Guattari. 1987. *A Thousand Plateaus.* Minneapolis, MN: University of Minnesota Press.

DoE (Department of Environment). 2014. Water Recovery Strategy for the Murray Darling Basin. Commonwealth of Australia. Accessed 25 March 2017. www.environment.gov.au/system/files/resources/4ccb1c76-655b-4380-8e94-419185d5c777/files/water-recovery-strategy-mdb2.pdf.

Environmental Justice Australia. 2014. Water Citizenship: Advancing community involvement in water governance. Accessed 16 November 2016. https://envirojustice.org.au/sites/default/files/files/Submissions%20and%20reports/envirojustice_water_citizenship_report.pdf.

GBCMA (Goulburn Broken Catchment Management Authority). 2013. Goulburn Broken Regional Catchment Strategy 2013–2019. State of Victoria. Accessed March 2015.

www.gbcma.vic.gov.au/downloads/RegionalCatchmentStrategy/GBCMA_RCS_2013-19.pdf.

Habermas, Jürgen. 2015. *The Lure of Technocracy*. Cambridge: Polity Press.

Head, Lesley. 1999. "The northern myth revisited? Aborigines, environment and agriculture in the Ord River irrigation scheme, stages one and two". *Australian Geographer*. 30(2): 141–158.

Holling, C. S., and Gary, K. Meffe. 1996. "Command and control and the pathology of natural resource management". *Conservation Biology* 10(2): 328–337.

IPES-Food. 2016. *From uniformity to diversity: a paradigm shift from industrial agriculture to diversified agro-ecological systems*. International Panel of Experts on Sustainable Food Systems. www.ipes-food.org Accessed 20 January 2017. www.ipesfood.org/images/Reports/UniformityToDiversity_FullReport.pdf.

Jackson, Sue. 2017. "Enduring injustices in Australian water governance". In *Resources, Environment and Justice: The Australian Experience*, edited by Lukasiewicz Anna, Stephen Dovers, Robin Libby, Jennifer McKay, Stephen Schilizzi, and Sonia Graham, 121–132. Melbourne: CSIRO Publishing.

Kingsford, Richard T., Gilad Bino and John L. Porter. 2017. "Continental impacts of water development on waterbirds, contrasting two Australian river basins: Global implications for sustainable water use". *Glob Change Biol*. 1–12. Accessed 24 July 2017. https://doi.org/10.1111/gcb.13743.

Latour, Bruno. 1993. *We Have Never Been Modern*. Cambridge, Mass: Harvard University Press.

Latour, Bruno. 2005/8. "What is the Style of Matters of Concern? The Spinoza Lectures". The Department of Philosophy of the University of Amsterdam. April and May 2005. Published 2008 van Gorcum.

Latour, Bruno. 2016. Plenary Address. Presented at PSi #22: Performance Climates, Melbourne, July 5–9.

McNiven, Ian, and Damein Bell. 2010. "Fishers and farmers: Historicising the Gunditjmara freshwater fishery, western Victoria". *The LaTrobe Journal* 85: 83–97. Accessed 4 August 2017. http://latrobejournal.slv.vic.gov.au/latrobejournal/issue/latrobe-85/t1-g-t8.html.

MDBA (Murray Darling Basin Authority) 2016. The Northern Basin Review. Understanding the economic, social and environmental outcomes from water recovery in the northern Basin. Accessed 7 August 2017. www.mdba.gov.au/sites/default/files/pubs/Northern-basin-review-report-FINAL.pdf.

MLDRIN (Murray & Lower Darling Rivers Indigenous Nations) 2007/10. "The Echuca Declaration". Department of Environment Water Natural Resources, South Australia. Accessed 24 March 2017. www.mldrin.org.au/wp-content/uploads/2013/06/FN_Water_Statement_2016.pdf.

Nikolakis, William, and R. Quentin Grafton. 2014. "Fairness and justice in Indigenous water allocations: Insights from Northern Australia". *Water Policy* 16 (S2):19–35.

Reisner, Mark. 1986. *Cadillac Desert: The American West and Its Disappearing Water*. New York: Penguin Books.

Stewart-Harawira, Makere. 2012. "Returning the sacred: Indigenous ontologies in perilous times". In *Radical Human Ecology: Intercultural and Indigenous Approaches*, edited by Williams Lewis, Rose Roberts, and Alastair McIntosh. Chapter 4. UK: Ashgate Publishing.

Strang, Veronica. 2013. "Cubbie Station and the waters of the Darling". In *The Social Life of Water*, edited by John R. Wagner, 36–60. New York: Berghan Books.

Swyngedouw, Erik. 1999. "Modernity and hybridity: Nature, regeneracionismo, and the production of the Spanish waterscape, 1890–1930". *Annals of the Association of American Geographers* 89(3): 443–465.
Sysak, Tamara. 2013. "Drought, power and change: Using Bourdieu to explore resilience and networks in two northern Victoria farming communities". PhD diss. University of Melbourne.
Vogler, Candace. 2002. "Social imaginaries, ethics and methodological individualism". *Public Culture* 14(3): 625–627.
Wagenaar, Hendrik. 2011. *Meaning in Action*. Armonk, NY: M. E. Sharpe.
West, Simon. 2016. "Embracing the primacy of experience: How a practice perspective can bring accounts of adaptive management to life". *Interpreting Cmplexity: Exploring Social-ecological Relations from the Inside-out*. PhD diss. Stockholm University.
West, Simon, Ruth Beilin and Hendrik Wagenaar. (forthcoming). "Introducing a practice perspective on adaptive management".
Worster, Donald. 1985. *Rivers of Empire*. Oxford: Oxford University Press.

Index

Page numbers in **bold** denote figures, those in *italics* denote tables.

access rights 9
actants *see* Actor Network Theory (ANT)
Actor Network Theory (ANT) 3, 11–12, 61, 166–167, 170; human actors 2, 11–13, 132, 214; non-human actors/actants 2–4, 7–8, 11–13, 39, 41, 54, 61, 65, 85, 130, 132, 166–167, 178, 220, 223
actors *see* Actor Network Theory (ANT)
adaptation 147–148, 225; climate change adaptation 41, 83
Africa 6, 116, 123–125, 202
agency, theoretical usage 2–4, 7–8, 10–15, 79, 98, 116, 129, 131–132, 147–148, 185, 207, 223
Agrawal, Arun 3
Agri-Environmental Governance (AEG) 2–8, 10–11, 13, 38–39, 41, 43, 45, 47, 49, 51–55, 57, 59–62, 73, 93, 95, 97, 99, 101, 103, 193, 196
agri-environmental payments *see* Payments for Ecosystem Services (PES)
Agricultural Multifunctionality Payment (AMFP), Japan 59–60, 63–65, 67–69, 71, 73–74
America *see* United States of America
animals 2, 41, 82–83, 85, 87, 130, 164
anthropocene 107
anthropology of policy 78–79
Asia 86, 91, 95, 99, 103–104, 179
assemblage theory 1–15, 19–23, 28–29, 33–45, 47, 49, 51–52, 54–56, 59, 60–63, 65–66, 73–75, 78–79, 84–87, 91–95, 98, 101–104, 107–110, 114, 118–119, 121–125, 130–133, 136, 139–140, 145, 147–153, 155, 157–162, 165–166, 169–171, 173, 177–178, 185, 187–189, 191–193, 196–197, 200, 205, 207, 209–210, 213–229
Australia 6, 10, 15, 22, 80, 213–217, 219, 223–224, 226–228
Austria 177, 181, 185, 187
autonomy 25, 28, 33, 51, 119

beef farming 45, 49–50, 182
Benabou, Sarah 4
Bennett, Jane 12, 108
Big Data 195–198, 200–210
biodiversity 4, 67, 76, 83, 99, 107, 116, 118, 122, 180, 215, 225

Callon, Michel 2, 110, 116, 129, 131–133
capitalism 2–3, 84, 93–94, 100, 107; capitalist agriculture 1
carbon 32, 107; carbon emissions trading 6, 9, 28, 38, 107–122, 180; carbon forestry 107–122; carbon sequestration 28, 113, 115, 120, 181
Carolan, Michael 10, 13, 41
certification 2, 5, 76–77, 82, 86, 100–101, 116, 182–185, 187, 189–190, 225; *see also* private sector governance, *private certifiers*
cheese *see* halloumi cheese
civil society 21, 33, 35, 91–92, 97, 99, 101, 113, 117, 123, 146, 155–156, 184–185
climate change 9, 41, 83–84, 107, 114, 120–121, 145, 147, 149, 181, 224; climate change adaptation 41, 83; climate governance 25, 112, 114, 118, 121; Intergovernmental Panel on Climate Change (IPCC) 112
class, social 5, 85, 97, 99

Collier, Stephen J. 4, 79, 178
Common Agricultural Policy (CAP) 24–26, 76, 83, 86, 180, 182
Community Farming Enterprises (CFE), Japan 62–63, 66, 69
conservation tillage 39, 43, 45, 47–49, 51, 55
corporate social responsibility 29, 113
Cultivation System *see culturstelsel*
culturstelsel 96–97
Cyprus 8, 76, 78, 80–89

dairy industry 9, 29, 44–45, 76, 80–81, 83, 85, 87, 161–165, 168–173, 187, 190
decision-making 1, 5, 7, 13, 20, 61, 132–135, 137, 139–140, 147–149, 226, 228; farmer decision-making 7, 38–45, 49–55
deforestation 9, 109, 111–113, 115, 117–118, 180–181, 183
degradation: environmental 1, 2, 32, 107; forest 109, 111, 112, 115; water 9, 164, 165, 167, 169, 171
DeLanda, Manuel 12, 22, 213, 218–219, 224, 227
Deleuze, Gilles and Guatarri, Félix 3–4, 8, 11, 13, 22, 61, 79, 92–94, 99–103, 122, 197, 218
democratisation 59, 92, 127, 132
desire (Deleuzian usage) 11, 112, 178
deterritorialisation *see* territorialisation/ deterritorialisation/reterritorialisation
DG Agri (General Directorate of Agriculture and Rural Development, European Commission) 81–82
Direct Payment to Mountainous Areas (DPMA) 63
dispositif 92, 98, 100–101, 209–210
disruptive power 6–7, 110, 129, 131, 139, 155
dividual 94, 100–101
Donau Soya 177–191, **183**
Dutch colonialism 92–93, 95–98, 102; Dutch Ethical Policy 97
Dwr Cymru (Welsh Water) 29–30

economic power 1, 6, 15, 32, 37, 78, 87, 95, 99, 103–104, 116, 123–124, 129, 133, 152, 158, 191, 217–218, 222
Ecosystem Enterprise Partnership-Ecobank project, Wales 23, 29–31
ecosystem services *see* Payments for Ecosystem Services (PES)
enactive (theoretical usage) 5, 6, 10–11, 13, 60, 73, 91–92, 102, 116, 127, 132, 140, 165, 189, 200, 206
environmental impacts 1, 114, 123, 145, 161, 168, 179
environmental lobby groups *see* NGOs
epistemology 196; epistemology of practice 213, 219–220, 222, 227
Europe 9, 16, 25–26, 31, 35, 37, 57, 63, 76–78, 84–89, 93, 95–97, 100, 103, 163, 177–192, 195, 223
European Commission 26, 76–78, 80–82, 86, 195
European Union (EU) 25, 63, 76–77, 80, 82–87, 180–181, 195
exclusion fencing 39, 45, 47, 49–51, 55
experimentation 10, 12–13, 22, 189, 205

Farm Hack 10, 197–202, 204–210
farmers 1–2, 6–7, 10, 19, 25–28, 30, 32–33, 35, 37, 48–58, 62, 64–66, 68, 71–73, 78, 83–85, 87–88, 96–103, 130, 153, 162–163, 167–172, 184–185, 187–189, 196–201, 203–207, 209–210, 216, 224; family farms 62, 76, 80, 224; identities 41–43, 210; unions 25, 33, 98, 102
First Milk, Wales 29–31
food safety 80, 82, 127–130, 133–140
food security 91, 180, 197, 200–203, **201**, 207, 209
Foucault, Michel 8, 11, 22, 61, 79, 92–93, 96–97, 197, 202, 209–210; discipline 8, 61, 92–93, 101; governmentality 3, 91, 93
Fukushima nuclear accident 9, 127, 130

Geertz, Clifford 196–197, 208
Genetically Modified Organisms (GMOs) 9, 183–185, 188
geo-labels 76–79, 81, 84–85
Geographical Indicators (GI) 77; *see also* Protected Geographical Indication (PGI); Protected Designation of Origin (PDO)
Geographic Information Systems (GIS) 25
Gibson-Graham, J.K. 197, 208
Gilles, Zsuzsa 84
Glastir scheme, Wales 25, 27–29, 32, 34
goats 83–85, 87; goat milk 80–83, 85, 87
governance, theories of 2–3, 6–9, 11, 91–96, 102–103, 109–110, 112, 121–122, 161, 202, 204, 209, 213–215, 217–218; governance instruments 7–9, 40, 78, 113, 131, 162, 170, 172, 177,

governance, theories of *continued*
189; *see also* Agri-Environmental Governance (AEG)
government: role of 3, 19,–20, 34, 62–63, 78, 86, 91–93, 102–103, 110–112, 119–121, 181, 184–185, 220; Australia, Government of 213–217, 224–226; farmer perceptions of 50–51, 196, 202; Indonesia, Government of 91, 95–96, 98–100; Japan, Government of 60–63, 67, 73, 127–129, 131–133, 135–137, 139–140; local 27, 61, 63, 67, 73, 114; New Zealand, Government of 162–163, 172; Republic of Cyprus, Government of 80–83; Uganda, Government of 9; United Kingdom, Government of the 31; Uruguay, Government of 145, 147–148, 150–152, 154–158; Welsh Government 25–32
Green Revolution 91, 98, 209
Guattari, Félix *see* Deleuze, Gilles and Guatarri, Félix

halloumi cheese 8, 76, 78–88
High Yielding Varieties (HYV) 98
human actors *see* Actor Network Theory (ANT)
Hungary 84, 186
hybridity 20, 22, 54, 61; hybrid neoliberalism 7, 19–20, 63

identity *see* farmer, farmer identities
imaginaries 21, 108, 179, 181, 196, 200, 207, 209
indigenous knowledge 10, 213–214, 217–218, 220
indigenous rights 113, 213–215, 217, 223, 226–227
Indonesia 3, 8, 91–93, 95–103; BRI (Bank Rakyat Indonesia) 98; Bulog (Badan Ursan Logistik) 98; KUD (Koperasi Unit Desa) 98
industrial production 3, 9, 76, 80–83, 85, 87, 93–94, 96–97, 99, 101, 113, 115, 179–182
intellectual property rights 87, 196, 214

Japan 6, 9, 59–60, 62–67, 69, 127–128, 130–136, 139, 140; Agricultural Multifunctionality Payment (AMFP) 59–60, 63–65, 67–69, 71, 73–74; Community Farming Enterprises (CFE) 62, 63, 66, 69; Government of 60–63, 67, 73, 127–129, 131–133, 135–137, 139–140; Japan Agricultural Cooperatives (JAs) 66; Japanese Ministry of Agriculture, Forestry, and Fishery (MAFF) 59, 62–65, 136, 139
Jordan Lake, North Carolina 41, **42**, 44, 46, 52–55

Law, John 2
Latour, Bruno 2, 22, 61, 213, 222, 224, 228
Li, Tanya Murray 4, 22, 91–92, 161
linearity and non-linearity 7, 20, 23, 78–79, 85, 94, 135, 178, 180, 184, 187

market-based approaches 2–4, 38, 52, 59, 64–65, 78, 92, 95, 109, 115, 122, 137, 187, 196, 216; Voluntary Carbon Markets (VCM) 115; *see also* water, water trading schemes
Marxist, Neo-Marxist 2
methodology 4, 115, 122, 213–214, 223–224, 227
metrology, metrics 4, 9, 28, 31, 33, 79, 115, 128, 133, 136–138, 140, 166–167, 187, 199, 209
milk 80–85, 87, 128, 141n2, 169, 171
monoculture 9, 190, 208–209
Montgomeryshire Wildlife Trust (MWT) 27–29
morality: farmer 38–39, 42, 92; moral logics 52, 54
multifunctional 40; payments 59–60, 63–65, 73; policy 8
multiplicity 7–8, 10, 12–13, 61, 73, 85, 92, 95, 102, 184, 214, 221

National Forestry Authority (NFA), Uganda 111
Natural Resources Wales (NRW) 29–30
Nature Fund, Wales 26–27, 30
neoliberal governance 2–7, 19–22, 34, 54, 59–63, 65, 73–75, 84, 92, 102, 107, 109, 110, 113, 117, 120–121, 123–125, 162–163, 196, 210–211; hybrid neoliberalism 7, 19–22, 52, 54, 59–63, 65–66, 73; neoliberal subjectivities 3
New Zealand 4, 6, 9, 161–165, 167–173
NGOs 2, 9, 19, 21–23, 25–27, 31, 33–34, 54, 63, 79, 86, 102, 111, 113–114, 116–117, 119, 120, 123–124, 134, 150, 161, 163–164, 173, 177, 179, 184, 191, 220–221, 225
no-till *see* conservation tillage

non-human actors *see* Actor Network Theory (ANT)
North Carolina 7, **42**, **44**, 45, 47, 49, 51–52

Ong, Aihwa 4, 79, 178
ontology 3–7, 9–12, 21, 41, 162–165, 167, 169–173, 178, 199–200, 209, 214–215, 217
overflows 7, 9, 108–111, 117, 119, 121–122, 129, 131, 133–135, 139–140, 172; *see also* Callon, Michel

participative approaches 2, 5, 8, 13, 29–30, 33, 38–40, 51, 59–60, 63–66, 68–69, 73, 100, 117, 120, 129, 140, 147, 151, 153, 157–158, 227
Payments for Ecosystem Services (PES) 4, 7, 19, 24–26, 28–34, 83, 112, 115, 182
peasants 2, 93, 97–99
performativity 5–6, 86, 107, 110, 115–117, 122, 171, 191, 214
policy, theories of 2–4, 10, 20–22, 61, 63, 78–80, 84–86, 91, 140, 166–167, 171–172; economic policy 78; policy instruments 8, 15, 38, 76–81, 162, 181; policy makers 2, 33, 152, 154; *see also* Common Agricultural Policy (CAP); European Union (EU); European Commission; Geographical Indicators (GI); neoliberal governance
power relations 1, 2, 9, 13, 111, 116, 121, 133, 186, 228
practice, theorisation of 3–4, 6, 10–13, 21–23, 41, 59–60, 79, 91–93, 107, 109–110, 119–121, 129, 132, 165–167, 169–170, 173, 206, 213–214, 219–224, 227–228
precision agriculture 94, 195, 197–198, 200, 203–205, **204–205**, 207, 209
private sector governance 2, 26–30, 61–62, 77, 92, 99, 101, 103, 113, 118–120, 146, 184, 196; private certifiers 2, 77
property rights 12, 157
Protected Designation of Origin (PDO) 77–78, 80–82, 86–87, 88n9
Protected Geographical Indication (PGI) 77, 86
Pumlumon project, Wales 23, **24**, 27–29

Rabinow, Paul 79
radionuclides 9, 127–136, 138–140, 141n20

REDD+ (Reducing the Effects of Deforestation, Degradation) 107, 111–117, 119–121
regulation: environmental 1, 26, 50–51, 53–54, 77–78, 112, 163, 169, 171, 177, 181; food 80, 85, 127–128
retailing 2, 100, 137, 177, 183–185, 189, 190
risk 25, 38, 40–41, 43–44, 49, 52, 127, 129, 133, 135, 139–140, 146–147, 154–155, 157, 166, 198
Romania 177, 184, 187
Rose, Nicholas 20–21, 172
rural development 27–28, 32, 76, 78, 83–84, 86

science: role of 31, 34, 79, 109–110, 112, 115, 127, 130–135, 138–140, 148, 151, 158, 164–165, 169, 177, 187–188, 190, 214–215; scientists 109, 128, 135, 154–156, 185, 220–221, 226
sheep 80, 83–85, 87, 88n3, 88n5, 162, 196; milk 80–83, 85, 87
Shore, Cris 78
small-scale producers 2, 62, 76, 78, 80–81, 86–87, 96, 98–99, 118, 148, 202, 207, 224–227
soil 2–3, 41, 45, 47–50, 53, 55–58, 77, 83–84, 87, 98, 100, 130, 138, 156, 168, 173, 182, 187, 190, 195, 202, 205, 207, 227
soybeans (soya) 9–10, 137, 145, 151, 177–191
stewardship, environmental 39, 44, 50, 52
supermarkets 2, 80, 136, 189
supply chains 6, 183, 185
sustainability 1, 3–4, 10, 13, 15, 29, 38, 78, 84–87, 99, 116, 181–182, 185, 188, 204
sustainable development 76, 84, 112, 156
Switzerland 177, 185
Swyngedouw, Eric 119

territorialisation/deterritorialisation/reterritorialisation 3, 7–9, 11–13, 108–109, 110, 180–182, 190–191
terroir 77
trading programmes, environmental goods *see* market-based approaches
Tsing, Anna 109

Uganda 9, 107–123; Uganda Wildlife Authority (UWA) 118, 120

United States of America 1, 9–10, 16, 47–48, 57, 66, 99, 114, 138, 154–155, 157, 169–170, 189, 201, 205, 207, 221, 224, 237, 239–240
Uruguay 9, 145–158

Wales 6–7, 19, 20–21, 23–24, **24**, 27–28, 30; *see also* Dwr Cymru (Welsh Water)
water 9, 29, 38, 41, **44**, 47, 83–84, 87; water governance 10, 12, 25, 29, 49, 150–158, 171–173, 213–228; water quality 9, 27, 29, 38–39, 44–45, 49–52, 84, 128, 134, 145–158, 161–173; water trading schemes 7, 29, 38–39, 50–51, 54–55, 107
Welsh Water *see* Dwr Cymru (Welsh Water)
Wildlife Conservation Society (WCS) 113
World Bank's Afforestation/Reforestation Clean Development Mechanism (A/R CDM) 113–115, 118, 120
Wright, Susan 78